D0425878

Zora *and* Langston

OTHER BOOKS BY YUVAL TAYLOR

Darkest America:
Black Minstrelsy from Slavery to Hip-Hop
(with Jake Austen)

Faking It:
The Quest for Authenticity in Popular Music
(with Hugh Barker)

Growing Up in Slavery:
Stories of Young Slaves as Told by Themselves
(editor)

I Was Born a Slave:
An Anthology of Classic Slave Narratives
(editor)

Zora *and* Langston

A STORY OF FRIENDSHIP AND BETRAYAL

YUVAL TAYLOR

W. W. NORTON & COMPANY

Independent Publishers Since 1923

New York | London

For information about permission to reproduce selections from this book,
write to Permissions, W. W. Norton & Company, Inc.,
500 Fifth Avenue, New York, NY 10110

For information about special discounts for bulk purchases, please contact
W. W. Norton Special Sales at specialsales@wwnorton.com or 800-233-4830

Manufacturing by LSC Communications, Harrisonburg
Book design by Chris Welch
Production manager: Beth Steidle

Library of Congress Cataloging-in-Publication Data

Names: Taylor, Yuval, author.
Title: Zora and Langston : a story of friendship and betrayal / Yuval Taylor.
Description: First edition. | New York : W.W. Norton & Company, [2019]
Identifiers: LCCN 2018050513 | ISBN 9780393243918 (hardcover)
Subjects: LCSH: Hurston, Zora Neale. | Hughes, Langston, 1902–1967. | African
American authors—20th century—Biography.
Classification: LCC PS3515.U789 Z93 2019 | DDC 813/.52 [B]—dc23
LC record available at https://lccn.loc.gov/2018050513

W. W. Norton & Company, Inc., 500 Fifth Avenue, New York, N.Y. 10110
www.wwnorton.com

W. W. Norton & Company Ltd., 15 Carlisle Street, London W1D 3BS

1 2 3 4 5 6 7 8 9 0

To my wife, editor, and best friend,

Karen

I think of Zora Neale Hurston and Langston Hughes as literary parents, or guardians. I am always amazed when I read of their arguments and fallings out, and the eternal blame for their difficulties that is heaped on one of them or the other.

When I consider the ending of their friendship I am filled with sadness for them. It is so easy to see how and why they would love each other. Each was to the other an affirming example of what black people could be like: wild, crazy, creative, spontaneous, at ease with who they are, and funny. A lot of attention has been given to their breakup . . . but very little to the pleasure Zora and Langston must have felt in each other's company. I like to think of them wandering about together in the early days, Zora showing Langston the close-up beauty of people in the deep South, and Langston returning the kindness, thoughtfulness and generosity that came easily to him with people he liked. I like to think of them telling each other jokes, eating fried chicken and watermelon, zooming about in Zora's little car, laughing. Which I figure was one of the main things they did.

In any event, I have drawn on these guardian spirits over the years, as I have drawn on my biological parents—who were also known to have a few fights and a royal falling-out or two—and I have never felt that they were fundamentally at odds. Or that their characters were particularly flawed. If anything, again like one's parents, I feel that, spiritually, Langston and Zora resembled each other. And certainly . . . I have felt nurtured and nourished by both of them.

ALICE WALKER,
"Turning Into Love: Some Thoughts on Surviving
and Meeting Langston Hughes" (1989)

CONTENTS

Zora *and* Langston

Lovingly Yours

Collaborators, social and literary gadflies, and very close companions, Zora Neale Hurston and Langston Hughes enjoyed a fascinating friendship. They worked together on a magazine called *Fire!!* and a comedy called *Mule Bone*, wrote scores of letters to each other, and traveled together through the South. Yet they had a terribly bitter falling out; Langston would later describe Zora as "a perfect 'darkie,'" while Zora would leave the friendship out of her autobiography altogether.

Zora and Langston were not, as far as we know, sexually involved, but their relationship was loving. Zora signed her letters to Langston "love" or "lovingly yours"; she told him quite honestly that he was not only her "best friend" but "the nearest person to me on earth." Their long and frank letters are suffused with warmth and feeling. This book explores their friendship from their first meeting in Harlem in 1925 to their final breakup in Cleveland in 1931—and beyond.

▼▼▼

Zora's 1937 *Their Eyes Were Watching God* remains the single most widely read book ever written by an African American (it outsells even *Invisible Man, I Know Why the Caged Bird Sings, The Color Purple, A Raisin in the Sun, Narrative of the Life of Frederick Douglass,* and *The Autobiography of Malcolm X*). Scholar Charles H. Nichols rightly called Langston "the most prolific and influential Afro-American writer in our history." Together Zora and Langston invigorated the Harlem Renaissance, promulgating ideas about African American expression that fundamentally changed the course of American letters.

Their friendship—by turns warm, engaging, inspiring, intellectual, adoring, jealous, inflamed, and doomed—informed practically everything they wrote during those years, and to a great extent thereafter. They jointly brought to life a new conception of African American literature quite unlike any that had come before. Controversially, they celebrated Negroes as almost elemental beings, in touch with instincts that white culture had lost sight of. But this shared vision greatly enriched their work.

Langston rarely engaged in physical relationships with people he knew well. Zora never admitted to having any sexual desire for him. Yet their relationship had all the hallmarks of a ménage à trois—or, more accurately, a ménage à cinq. For they shared the munificence of their wealthy white patron Charlotte Osgood Mason, who insisted on being called "Godmother," but who in her caprice and impatience was more like the Godfather. Paying them lavishly and trying to control their output, she enlisted each of them in her pet cause: to advance the idea of the American Negro as the archetypal primitive, a bridge to an uncorrupted world. Besides Mason, whose relationship with

Langston was the most passionate of his young life, two others were entangled with them: Louise Thompson, a lovely young black woman (for a short time married to the homosexual writer and editor Wallace Thurman) who helped them with *Mule Bone* and of whom Zora became wildly jealous; and Alain Locke, a black philosophy professor whose thwarted desire was likely one reason he turned against Langston in the end.

Mason's and Zora's almost simultaneous betrayal of Langston absolutely devastated him. He reacted with claims of plagiarism and a threatened lawsuit. But it devastated Zora too. Eight years after their breakup, she asked Langston's friend Arna Bontemps to tell him that "the cross of her life is the fact that there has been a gulf between you and her. She said she wakes up at night crying about it yet."

In the aftermath, Langston abandoned the primitivist ideology that had fed much of his most enduring work and turned instead to Communism. Zora, on the other hand, added more nuance to her primitivism and shaped it into a novel whose Shakespearean power remains unabated over eighty years after its creation. Yet Langston, whose capacity for adaptation seemed limitless, remained at the center of the African American literary scene, while Zora was pushed to its margins. The entire literary establishment, black and white, abandoned her, and she died forgotten, even by the man who was once her closest friend.

Despite a wealth of literature about the Harlem Renaissance, including excellent biographies of both Langston and Zora, until now their relationship has never been explored at length and in depth. Both distorted the facts in their autobiographies, and neither admitted therein how valuable their friendship had been. The truly religious devotion of Mason's disciples has been given short shrift, as has Zora's deep commitment to playwriting. Zora's rewrite of *Mule Bone* has never received the plaudits it deserves. The memoirs of Louise Thompson Patterson, the extensive interviews Hurston biographer Robert E. Hemenway did with many of the people who knew Zora best, and Langston's own notebooks and journals all remain unpublished. And *The Book of Negro Folklore*, edited by Langston and Bontemps, which was, at the time of Zora's death, one of the only books in print that included her work, has been almost completely forgotten.

In writing this book I have drawn on these and other unpublished papers and interviews (especially those in the James Weldon Johnson papers at Yale, the Alain Locke papers at Howard, the Louise Thompson Patterson papers at Emory, and the Robert E. Hemenway Collection at the University of Kansas). I have followed Zora and Langston's Southern road trip step by step, gone to the places they lived in and visited, and dug deep for the dramatic details. I have also, of course, consulted scores of previously published works.

Zora and Langston's position in American literary history is by now firmly established. But by going back to a time when it wasn't, a time when they were just forming their ideas, sharing them with each other and with their friends and benefactors, I hope to illuminate how deeply they shaped American literature and culture—and each other.

1

SPRING 1925

Opportunity

May 1, 1925, was a stormy day.

That afternoon, lightning struck the copper ball on top of the conservatory in the New York Botanical Gardens in the Bronx, shattering the ninety-foot-high glass dome that protected the plants inside; the thunderclap was so loud it broke hundreds of windows, leading local residents to wonder if there had been an earthquake.

That evening, in the convivial confines of one of the city's most elegant establishments, Zora Neale Hurston and Langston Hughes met for the first time, embarking on an epochal friendship that would produce a few thunderclaps of its own.

▼▼▼

Not many restaurants in Manhattan were as big or as magnificent as the Fifth Avenue. It took up much of the first floor of the Fifth Avenue Building, 200 Fifth Avenue, on the corner of 23rd Street, which was built in 1909 and still stands. Fronted by a huge Romanesque arch and covering over 60,000 square feet, it stretches to fourteen stories in height; in front stands an ornate cast-iron sidewalk clock, also dating from 1909, judged by some to be the most splendid such clock in the world. Remnants of the restaurant's interior can still be seen—marble semidomes and arches with recessed lighting, notched lintels, plaster ornaments on the ceilings, bronze ornaments on the doorframes, mosaic floors. The restaurant had opened in 1918 and was advertised as one of the largest and most scientifically equipped catering establishments in America, hosting, at night, "banquets, after-lodge suppers, business gatherings, dinner dances, smokers and beefsteak dinners," with a seating capacity of one thousand. The atmosphere was semiformal, with long tables and high-backed chairs; the walls were mirrored, and painted white and gold. No alcohol was served, of course—it was Prohibition—but, as the Harlem writer Bruce Nugent said, "if you had a pocket flask, that was your to-do."

The occasion that evening was the presentation of prizes by *Opportunity* magazine, the voice of the National Urban League, founded in 1910 to help black migrants in the North. Subheaded *A Journal of Negro Life*, and edited by Charles Spurgeon Johnson, *Opportunity* showcased African American arts to a greater extent than its competitors, *The Crisis*, the NAACP's more political publication, helmed by W. E. B. Du Bois, and *The Messenger*, a socialist journal launched by A. Philip Randolph. *Opportunity* was by no means apolitical, but it emphasized diplomacy rather than fiery rhetoric—it was the kind of magazine in which white critics reviewed black authors and vice versa. Its goal was the improvement of race relations, and nothing could have been more conducive to that goal than the Opportunity Awards Dinner of 1925.

Except for the judges (most of them white men), attendees paid

$2.75 for their dinner, a rather exorbitant price at the time. But, as Nugent explained, since most of the contributors couldn't pay, "something was always arranged in a pleasant fashion so that you wouldn't feel like you were a charity patient to get there." I have not found the menu for that night, but the third annual *Opportunity* awards dinner two years later began with soup and hard rolls followed by a plate of broiled spring chicken, mashed potatoes, and peas and concluded with dessert and coffee—rather plain fare for the Fifth Avenue, which usually served dishes like vermicelli croquettes, chiffonade salad, or potage à la reine. The awards presentation followed the dinner, and didn't conclude until eleven o'clock.

It's impossible to overestimate Charles Johnson's role in the Harlem Renaissance. Zora would call his work "the root of the so-called Negro Renaissance" and Langston would write that he "did more to encourage and develop Negro writers during the 1920's than anyone else in America." Johnson's goal in organizing the contest and dinner was to form a partnership between the leading lights of the white and black communities; the opinion of the judges that black arts *mattered* was the most important product of the event for him. At the end of the evening he announced that funds for a second annual contest were already in hand—Casper Holstein, king of Harlem's numbers racket, had promised Johnson the money.

This was, at the time, the largest gathering of African American writers in history. Almost all the young bloods and many of the established figures of Manhattan's black intellectual world were there, including the poets Countee Cullen and Jean Toomer, the sociologist E. Franklin Frazier, the writer and politician James Weldon Johnson, the philosopher Alain Locke, and the actor Paul Robeson. But also among the 316 guests were representatives of practically every major New York publisher and such white literary luminaries as humorist Robert Benchley, poet Witter Bynner, playwright Eugene O'Neill, theater critic Alexander Woollcott, literary critic Van Wyck Brooks, bestselling writer and activist Dorothy Canfield Fisher, and the Van Doren clan (Carl, Dorothy, and Mark, all prominent writers). The scholar Arnold Rampersad has gone so far as to call it "the greatest gathering of black and white literati ever assembled in one room."

It could be said, however, that the real stars of the evening were Zora Neale Hurston and Langston Hughes. For they won two prizes and two honorable mentions each, an achievement unequaled by any of the others. Zora was thirty-four but passing for twenty-four; Langston was actually twenty-four. Newcomers to the Manhattan literary scene, they were taking it by storm.

▼▼▼

By 1925, the "Harlem Renaissance" (then known as the "Negro Renaissance")—a flourishing of African American art and writing that would soon reach its peak—was already well underway.

This renaissance—which might be more properly called a *naissance*, since it really represents the birth of a conception of black American literary culture as fundamentally different from its white counterpart, as well as the first time the black influence on American culture became a widely recognized fact—offered African Americans a venue for social advancement theretofore denied to them. By the end of World War I, African Americans were suffering from appalling political, economic, and social conditions. The triumphant return of black soldiers from the war in Europe had been followed by a Ku Klux Klan resurgence,

widespread antiblack riots, brutal lynchings, and general xeno-
phobia. Since progress in race relations had been stymied for so
long, and since it was so difficult for black people to get respect-
able positions, a number of black progressive thinkers suggested
that if black Americans could prove themselves in the arts, it
could have a radical impact on the way whites thought of them,
and that this in turn would lead to increased political, economic,
and social power. Chief among these progressives was sociologist, publisher, and organizer Charles S. Johnson; he was joined
by James Weldon Johnson, Alain Locke, *Crisis* editor Jessie Fauset, W. E. B. Du Bois, librarian and socialite Regina Anderson,
and writer Gwendolyn Bennett, and was abetted by prominent
white intellectuals, including Carl Van Doren, publishers Hor-
ace Liveright and Alfred and Blanche Knopf, and art collector
Albert C. Barnes. So the press, cultural institutions, white philanthropists, and black leaders all actively encouraged the development of black arts. (While this effort did indeed put black arts
on the map, as it were, the hoped-for increase in political and
economic power would not take place. The Great Depression
would wipe out any gains that black people may have made.)

African American music and theater was in its heyday in 1925,
and New York City was its epicenter. *Shuffle Along*, the all-black
musical that opened in 1921, had been a runaway success among
both races, and had helped propel the careers of choir director
Hall Johnson; composers William Grant Still, Eubie Blake, and
Noble Sissle; comics Miller and Lyles; and actors Florence Mills
and Josephine Baker. Singers Paul Robeson, Bessie Smith, and
Ethel Waters were becoming stars. The jazz of Louis Armstrong
and Duke Ellington was beginning to electrify the nation.

In literature, poems by Langston Hughes, Claude McKay, and
Countee Cullen had been published in *The Crisis, Opportunity,*

and the Marxist magazine *The Liberator.* James Weldon Johnson's 1912 *Autobiography of an Ex-Colored Man* had predated the era by a decade, but showed the way; in 1922 Johnson edited *The Book of American Negro Poetry*, the first anthology of African American literature. Claude McKay's first book of poems about black life in the United States, *Harlem Shadows*, had also come out in 1922, followed closely by his essay collection *Negroes in America*. Several important African American novels had been published in the last two years: Jean Toomer's *Cane*, which consisted of a series of vignettes and poems set in the Deep South; Walter White's *The Fire in the Flint*, about the lynching of a black physician, a veteran of World War I; and Jessie Fauset's *There Is Confusion*, about middle-class black families in New York and Philadelphia.

To put this in perspective, probably only seven novels by African Americans had been published in the United States between 1910 and 1920—Johnson's *Autobiography*, two by W. E. B. Du Bois, three by Oscar Micheaux (self-published), and Joel Augustus Rogers's *From "Superman" to Man* (also self-published). The explosion of black writing that began around 1922 was truly a renaissance in the making.

The 1925 *Opportunity* contest was not the first major event celebrating these young writers—that had been the Civic Club dinner, also organized by Charles Johnson, on March 21, 1924. (The Civic Club was one of the few New York City social clubs that welcomed both black and white members.) If the Harlem Renaissance had needed an official launching, the Civic Club dinner would have been it. Many, if somewhat fewer, of the great names of the Renaissance had attended that dinner too, though not Langston, who was in Europe, and not Zora, who was in Washington, D.C., and had barely begun to publish.

Tonight, however, something new was in the air. A year earlier, the chief instigators of the Renaissance—Charles Johnson, Jessie Fauset, and Alain Locke—had wanted "highly polished stuff," according to historian David Levering Lewis, "preferably about polished people, but certainly untainted by racial stereotypes or embarrassing vulgarity. Too much blackness, too much street geist and folklore—nitty-gritty music, prose, and verse—were not welcome." But now it was 1925, and the younger generation of black writers were up to something else. When elder statesman James Weldon Johnson read Langston's "Weary Blues" to the assembled, they heard a more earthy, more genuinely vernacular literary voice than any they had yet encountered. Langston and Zora were the two new stars in the firmament and looked and sounded quite different from the others.

And they were drawn to each other, too.

▼▼▼

Opportunity's contest had been announced the previous fall, and there had been over seven hundred submissions. Awards were given in five categories, and the judges comprised many of the greatest literary figures of the age, both black and white. The nine judges for the short stories included Carl Van Doren, editor of *The Century* magazine; Zona Gale, who had recently become the first woman to win the Pulitzer Prize for drama; Fannie Hurst, one of the most famous fiction writers in the country; three other well-known female novelists; and Alain Locke, the Howard University professor who would play a major role in both Langston's and Zora's lives. First prize was given to John Matheus for his story "Fog," in which a collection of stereotypes—white racist miners, money-grubbing Jews, dance-oriented African Americans, German and Slavic immigrants, a pair of young lovers—nearly meet their deaths on a train when a bridge over the Ohio almost gives way, and, in light of their survival, renounce their more evil urges. Third prize went to the Caribbean writer Eric Walrond, who would shortly publish a story collection, *Tropic Death*, one of the more florid productions of the era.

But Zora's "Spunk," which won second prize, put the others to shame. It tells a simple story. The large, handsome, and dashing Spunk has taken Lena from her husband Joe and openly belittles him. Joe tries to kill Spunk with a razor, but Spunk shoots and kills him first. He is haunted by Joe's ghost, and two days later, the ghost pushes him in front of a circular saw and kills him. The artistry here is not so much in the story but in the telling—almost all of it through the words of the gossipy men who hang around the general store. Zora keeps her own narrative voice pithy, but vivid. The story ends thus: "The women ate heartily of the funeral baked meats and wondered who would be Lena's next. The men whispered coarse conjectures between guzzles of whiskey."

There were only four judges in the poetry category: Clement Wood, a prolific writer from Alabama whose works by then included two novels, *Nigger* and *Mountain*, three books of poetry, and a critical work entitled *Poets of America*; Witter Bynner, one of America's best-known poets and former president of the Poetry Society of America; John C. Farrar, editor of *The Bookman* (he would soon found the Bread Loaf Writers' Conference and two major publishing firms); and the great poet, novelist, historian, and anthologist James Weldon Johnson, author of the Negro national anthem "Lift Every Voice and Sing." They awarded first prize to Langston's "The Weary Blues." A sympathetic rhymed portrait of a blues singer written two years earlier, after a visit to a Harlem cabaret, it was the first of Langston's poems—or, for that matter, perhaps anyone's—to quote from the lyrics of a blues song. Rhythmic, taut, spontaneous, plainspoken, and utterly original, it heralded something new for Langston, and for American writing in general: the adaptation of the blues into literature.

While second prize went to Countee Cullen's love poem "To One Who Said Me Nay," with its nineteenth-century prosody and vocabulary, the third prize was split between Cullen's "A Song of Sour Grapes," an equally traditional hate poem, and Langston's "America." With its repeated assertions "You are America. / I am America," "America" is about the kinship between Jewish and African Americans, and its affirmation of blackness as American was striking and important.

Langston's two honorable mentions were "The Jester," a brief but brilliant poem that tackles the prevailing view of black people as alternatingly comic and tragic (a view that black critics would later accuse Zora of encouraging), and "Songs to the Dark Virgin," a clever, heartfelt, and effective love poem, but something of a departure for Langston, who rarely used archaisms like "thy," "thou," and "would that."

As for the plays, the four judges were Montgomery Gregory, who directed the drama department at Howard; Alexander Woollcott, drama critic for the *New York Times*; Robert Benchley, theater reviewer for *Life* magazine; and Edith Isaacs, the editor of *Theatre Arts* magazine. Zora again won second prize, here for *Color Struck.* The play's main character is Emma, whose paranoid jealousy destroys her life, as well as her boyfriend's and daughter's; her constant and obsessive worry is that her boyfriend John would prefer practically any lighter-skinned woman to her. Although overwrought and melodramatic, it showcases Zora's skill in writing comic badinage, especially in the opening scene, set on a train from Jacksonville to St. Augustine. Joe

Clarke, the mayor of Eatonville (Zora's hometown), makes his first appearance here, though a minor one, at the cakewalking contest around which the play revolves; he would reappear in Zora's fiction sporadically for the next dozen years, playing major parts in her play *Mule Bone* and her novel *Their Eyes Were Watching God* (as Jody Starks).

Spears, for which Zora received an honorable mention, is a two-scene sketch about an African tribe facing both famine and war. In it, the young warrior Uledi incurs the wrath of a neighboring tribe by stealing its food and killing its fighters; he successfully argues against the advice of the cowardly elder, a councilor named Bombay, and leads the hungry warriors of his tribe to victory. Although the costumes and setting are stereotypical of contemporaneous imaginings of Africa, the message is one of uncompromising defiance, quite unlike the ridiculous Africa portrayed in most Broadway musicals of the day (and in Zora's own play *Meet the Momma*, which she copyrighted two months later).

Africa also figures in "Black Death," one of Zora's early Eatonville stories and another honorable mention, which centers around the killing power of Old Man Morgan, the town's hoodoo man. When Mrs. Boger goes to hire Morgan to kill Beau Diddely, who had seduced and abandoned her daughter, "all Africa awoke in her blood. . . . Africa reached out its dark hand and claimed its own. Drums, tom, tom, tom, tom, tom, beat her ears. Strange demons seized her. Witch doctors danced before her, laid hands upon her alternately freezing and burning her flesh. . . ." Zora's visions of savage Africa seem to have come straight out of comic books; thankfully, neither *Spears* nor "Black Death" saw publication in her lifetime.

▼▼▼

Of all of the prizewinning works of that night, only Zora's short story "Spunk" would reappear in *The New Negro*, a landmark anthology edited by Alain Locke and published seven months later, but whose contents were already mostly in place. A large number of the most important writings of the era also appeared in it, including eleven of Langston's poems.

The son of a teacher at the Philadelphia School of Pedagogy, Alain Locke had grown up in high Victorian surroundings, and had inherited their fastidiousness. He wore bespoke suits, spoke in a high pitch, and walked quickly, despite his seeming frailty. He graduated from Harvard in 1907 and was the first African American Rhodes scholar, studying first in Oxford and then in Berlin. He received a PhD in philosophy from Harvard in 1918, after which he was chair of the Department of Philosophy at Howard University in Washington, D.C. In 1924 he first met Zora, who was a student there. They were quite a contrast. "Zora was patronizingly fond of him," Bruce Nugent told Zora's biographer Robert Hemenway, because "he was small and she was large. He was a man with rather effete gestures and a quiet way of speaking and she was robust and you know she could have snapped him in half."

Locke intently promoted black writers, artists, and musicians, encouraging them to depict African and African American people and history. *The New Negro* has defined the Harlem Renaissance ever since. Yet he was a pompous, supercilious, and frustrated man, holding himself above the rest of his race. His pontifications on the "peasant mind and imagination" of black spirituals, for example, or his effusions on what he found "primitive in the American Negro—his naïveté, his sentimentalism, his exuberance and his improvizing spontaneity," are condescending, reminiscent of the kind of whites who considered a visit to Harlem an expedition into an uptown jungle.

By this time Locke was thirty-nine years old, but had published relatively little. At the 1924 Civic Club dinner, Paul Kellogg, the editor of the monthly magazines *Survey Midmonthly* and *Survey Graphic*, which were dedicated to social causes, had called for a special issue of the latter devoted to the "New Negro"; Charles Johnson regarded Alain Locke, who was master of ceremonies at the dinner, as "a sort of 'Dean' of this younger group," and asked him to edit it. (According to Jessie Fauset, the dinner had been planned in honor of the publication of her novel *There Is Confusion*, and that is certainly how the press treated it. But one could hardly have expected *Opportunity* to honor its competitor, and scholar George Hutchinson has shown that the honor was only an initial suggestion. Fauset was understandably furious that she had been passed over in favor of Locke—he had published less and was less acquainted with the current crop of Harlem writers. Moreover, Locke despised her, and she knew it.) Fortunately, Locke embarked upon his task with an assiduousness and energy he had rarely displayed before, traveling to New York frequently not just for meetings with established writers like James Weldon Johnson and W. E. B. Du Bois, but to make friends with the younger generation as well. The special issue was published in March 1925, entitled "Harlem: Mecca of the New Negro"; 42,000 copies were printed—double its normal circulation. Locke then expanded it into what he would view as the definitive anthology of the movement. Although it has ever since been cited as the landmark publication of the Harlem Renaissance, *The New Negro*, unlike the *Survey Graphic* issue, was *not* specifically focused on Harlem; Locke himself had never lived there, nor did many of the contributors, and the book included a great deal of material from and about other places (as well as a truly out-of-place reiteration of hoary stereotypes of black people in an essay ostensibly on Negro art penned by the white collector Albert Barnes). Instead it focused on what Locke—and many others—called the "Negro Renaissance," taking a more or less middle-class approach (for example, it devoted a great deal of space to spirituals and none at all to blues). The book, which came out from a major publisher, Albert and Charles Boni, put Locke on the map, as it were, despite his own voluminous and condescending essays in it (Fauset would aptly describe them as "stuffed with a pedantry which fails to conceal their poverty of thought").

Zora and Langston were singular contributors to the volume, their rhythms and prose far more vernacular than most of the rest. By comparison, the other writers (with the exceptions of poet Angelina Grimké, James Weldon Johnson, Bruce Nugent, and playwright Willis Richardson) aimed for a sophisticated, complex style either indebted to traditional poetic forms or in a more modernist mode. They all aspired to elevated diction; they all used vocabulary or syntax the man in the street might find difficult to understand. Zora and Langston eschewed this, sticking to words and rhythms more typical of everyday African American usage.

▼▼▼

During the hubbub of the *Opportunity* dinner, Carl Van Vechten came up to congratulate Langston. Van Vechten was not only an important modernist literary critic and novelist, but was the former music critic at the *New York Times*, a friend and publisher of Gertrude Stein and Wallace Stevens, an early proponent of modern music, purportedly the first New York man to wear a wristwatch, and the first American dance critic. Largely inspired by that night's dinner, he would soon become the most vital white abettor of the Harlem Renaissance, a champion of the blues, Langston's steadfast patron, and one of his and Zora's closest friends.

Van Vechten asked Langston, whom he had met before, if he had written enough poetry to make a book. Langston told him he had. Van Vechten then apparently invited him to join him in Harlem that evening. After leaving the Fifth Avenue that night, Van Vechten and his entourage stopped in at the heiress A'Lelia Walker's residence on West 136th Street, then went to the Manhattan Casino on Eighth Avenue and West 155th Street, where the YMCA was sponsoring a dance, and where, according to Arnold Rampersad, Langston joined him. The next stop was the Bamville Club on West 125th, where they saw some of the performers from the whites-only Cotton Club, and at 4:30 a.m. they adjourned to a party at the exclusive Vaudeville Comedy Club in the basement of the palatial Savoy Ballroom on Lenox Avenue.

On each of the next two days, Langston visited Van Vechten, who lived in a large, elegant apartment at 150 West 55th Street. Practically every inch of the entrance hall, drawing room, and dining room was covered with art and artifacts, from first editions crowding the towering bookcases to modernist oil paintings. The vases were full of lilies, carnations, and roses, and the oriental rugs were even more colorful. Langston gave Van Vechten his poems on May 2, Van Vechten secured him a contract on May 19, and the result would be published as *The Weary Blues* the following January. Van Vechten would also see to it that *Vanity Fair* purchased prepublication rights to some of the book's poems.

Zora would soon follow Langston's example, visiting Van

Vechten later that May and impressing him with her "bright, rangy, intelligent Negro personality"; she immediately became one of his frequent companions on his all-night visits to Harlem parties and nightclubs.

Zora's introductions to white novelists the night of the *Opportunity* dinner were no less consequential. She met Annie Nathan Meyer for the first time there, and Meyer would quickly secure Zora a scholarship to Barnard College, which she had founded, and where Zora would be the only black student. Zora also met the bestselling writer Fannie Hurst at the banquet when she handed Zora her second-place prize; Hurst soon engaged Zora as a personal secretary at Meyer's urging.

Zora, with her distinctively high cheekbones and colorful clothes, radiated energy and insouciance—she loved nothing better than telling stories and putting on a show. Her accent was deeply Southern—like many Georgians and northern Floridians, she never pronounced her *r*'s or the final *g* of gerunds, and *dead* and *can't* often had two syllables—and her voice was deeptoned, like a blueswoman's; when she sang she sounded like a contralto Bessie Smith. Langston, equally at ease with uneducated workers, intellectuals, and Manhattan socialites, was tall, thin, muscled, and enviably handsome in his dark suit and vest, even though he had barely recovered from a bout of malaria contracted in Washington. His English was impeccable, his accent generic. They were each inimitable characters and terribly attractive, especially to certain wealthy white Negrophiles. And both of them had been writing almost exclusively about the Negro, drawing heavily on black folk tales and popular music not just for the rhythm but for the content of their work.

Zora's flamboyance would soon become legendary. After the *Opportunity* dinner she arrived at a party wearing a long, brightly colored scarf. As soon as she'd been noticed, she flung the end of the scarf around her neck and declaimed the title of her second-prize play in loud, long tones: "Color Struck!" She smoked Pall Malls in public, a rare sight for a woman; wore "lots of bangles and beads," according to a friend; and sang spirituals, played harmonica, and told racy stories of Southern life. Unlike most of the prominent artists of the Harlem Renaissance, Zora not only hailed from the Deep South but had spent substantial time there; compared to the rest of the crowd, she embodied the "folk." The black writer Arna Bontemps later recalled of Zora at that time, "She was really not a showoff but she just drew attention in that way. In appearance, Zora was a pleasant, ordinary, brown-skinned young woman; not stunning, . . . a little above average in appearance, but she had an ease and somehow projected herself very well orally, and almost before you knew it, she had gotten into a story. She had a wealth of them." She possessed "the gift," or so Fannie Hurst said, "of walking into hearts." In short, she was not only the object of considerable attention, and the life of every party, but a woman who inspired great fondness— especially among her white admirers.

Carl Van Vechten was one of them. He would later write, "Zora is picturesque, witty, electric, indiscreet, and unreliable. The latter quality offers material for discussion; the former qualities induce her friends to forgive and love her." He insisted that Zora regarded appointments as provisional at best. And Zora showcased her disregard for convention by coming to one of Van Vechten's parties in a Seminole Indian skirt made entirely of patches, and to another in a Norwegian skiing outfit.

As for Langston, he had, perhaps, an impact upon black youth in Manhattan similar to that Bob Dylan would have on white youth there thirty-odd years later. (The parallels are striking:

both were very young when they arrived from the Midwest, handsome, intense, and penniless. Both generated immense attention and precocious adulation. Both were elusive characters prone to shifting gears. The literati regarded both as outside the bounds of American literary poetry—their verse, it was said, was better listened to than read. Both worshipped Carl Sandburg. Both shifted from folk-based material to political diatribe, and then back again. Both suffered hiatuses in which they produced work of negligible quality. And both became elder statesmen who led long, productive lives.)

Bruce Nugent, a flamboyant black teenager at the time, later described his first impression of Langston in Washington that year: "He had done everything—all the things young men dream of but never get done—worked on ships, gone to exotic places, known known people, written poetry that had appeared in print—everything. I suppose his looks contributed to the glamorous ideal, too . . . as did his voice and gentle manner." Nugent, who bore a strong resemblance to Langston, is a perfect example of the kind of effect Langston could produce: after meeting Langston—the biggest thing that had ever happened to him—Nugent followed him to New York, got to know Van Vechten, and became close friends with both.

Both Zora and Langston were practically broke. Zora had arrived in New York in January with $1.50 in her purse, not knowing a soul. She had been employed as a manicurist in Washington, D.C., where she'd been a part-time student at Howard for the previous five years. Charles Johnson had helped her get by over the last few months with a series of odd jobs. Langston had been living with his mother in Washington, D.C., doing a variety of low-paying work. He had borrowed the train fare from Jessie Fauset, the first person to publish his poems. But their

impecunious state, they both knew, was the price of their freedom. While Zora and Langston shared a willingness to work
hard, they also shared a lifelong aversion to commitment—and
to a "career."

Their backgrounds, however, were quite different. Zora had
grown up in an all-black Florida town named Eatonville, and had
attended all-black schools all her life. She had traveled widely,
but only in America. Langston, on the other hand, had grown
up in mostly white Lawrence, Kansas, the product of a middle-
class family with venerable roots, and had gone to mostly white
schools. By this point he had traveled through much of the world,
even visiting Africa as a crew member of a freighter. While Zora
was solidly a product of black America, Langston had necessarily found himself at a distance from his people. However, he was
beginning to bridge that distance.

And they were drawn to each other, despite—or perhaps
because of—their differences. She "is a clever girl, isn't she?"
Langston wrote to Van Vechten in early June. "I would like to
get to know her." He certainly got his wish.

2

1891–1924

I Laugh, and Grow Strong

Zora Neale Hurston had lived a full life by the time she arrived in Harlem. She had been born on January 7, 1891, the fifth child of John Hurston and Lucy Potts. Zora would never admit to her birthdate, claiming at times to have been born in every year from 1899 to 1903, but the 1900 census gives her birth year as 1891, as does the Hurston family bible. Nor would she admit to having been born in Notasulga, Alabama, rather than in Eatonville, Florida, where her family moved when she was three.

Adjacent to Maitland and just six miles from bustling Orlando, Eatonville was, as Zora put it, a "city of five lakes, three croquet courts, three hundred brown skins, three hundred good swimmers, plenty guavas, two schools, and no jail-house." According to census records, there were only 125 people in Eatonville in 1900, while Orlando's population was near 2,500 (though these numbers have to be adjusted for the tendency of the US census to undercount black residents).

Eatonville was "a Negro town," Zora emphasized, "a pure

Negro town—charter, mayor, council, town marshal and all."
The black people in Maitland, under the leadership of "a mus-
cular, dynamic Georgia Negro" named Joe Clarke, had left, with
the backing of Maitland's whites, to incorporate their own town
next door in 1887. It was perhaps the nation's first incorporated
all-black town.

Maitland and Eatonville are contiguous; the eastern border is
simply East Street, with the houses on each side belonging to different towns. Yet their character is strikingly different. Eatonville
was, and remains, a town of inexpensive bungalows. Maitland
was "a center of wealth and fashion," as Zora put it—a vacation
town of lakeside mansions with large lawns, spreading trees, and
names like Pine Crest Villa and Chadbourne Hall. The streets in
Eatonville are all north-south or east-west; the streets in Maitland curve luxuriously around its twenty-one lakes.

The Reverend John Hurston, Zora's father, was one of Eatonville's most prominent citizens; he would later be elected mayor.
A strong, brave leader, he preached powerful sermons and wasn't
afraid to use his fists. He built a solid eight-room house for his
family on five acres of land, and always managed to put food on
the table. Zora's mother Lucy was just as tough as her cheating
husband—she once horsewhipped one of his female admirers. As
for Zora, she was one of eight children (six boys and two girls), an
"extra strong" child (in her words) who would rather play with
boys than girls and spent hours in the woods. She would later call
herself "the one girl who could take a good pummeling without
running home to tell."

The community was rich in stories. One of Zora's earliest
memories was being sent down to Joe Clarke's store in the evening and staying as long as she could to hear the stories swapped
on the front porch. The store "was the heart and spring of

the town," she wrote. "Men sat around the store on boxes and benches and passed this world and the next one right through their mouths." What Zora enjoyed the most were the "lying sessions," when "God, Devil, Brer Rabbit, Brer Fox, Sis Cat, Brer Bear, Lion, Tiger, Buzzard, and all the wood folk walked and talked like natural men."

But just as important were the stories Zora read: fairy tales by Hans Christian Andersen and the brothers Grimm; myths from Greek, Roman, and Norse antiquity; short stories by Rudyard Kipling and Robert Louis Stevenson; and Jonathan Swift's *Gulliver's Travels*. Stories became, quite early, Zora's raison d'être. Most people enjoy hearing, reading, and telling stories, but for Zora they became more important than anything else. She craved them, lived in them, and told them constantly. But she also learned that often she had to keep her stories secret, telling them only to herself.

This was even truer of Zora's visions. A series of twelve scenes came to her one day when she was six or seven years old. "Like clearcut stereopticon slides, I saw twelve scenes flash before me, each one held until I had seen it well in every detail, and then be replaced by another. There was no continuity as in an average dream. Just disconnected scene after scene with blank spaces in between. I knew that they were all true, a preview of things to come, and my soul writhed in agony and shrank away. But I knew that there was no shrinking. These things had to be." The visions came back to her again and again until each one came to pass, at which point it vanished. "As this happened, I counted them off one by one and took consolation in the fact that one more station was past, thus bringing me nearer the end of my trials." They darkened the remainder of Zora's childhood. "I consider that my real childhood ended with the coming of the pronouncements. True, I played, fought and studied with other children, but always I stood apart within. Often I was in some lonesome wilderness, suffering strange things and agonies while other children in the same yard played without a care. I asked myself why me? Why? Why? A cosmic loneliness was my shadow."

Throughout her life, Zora continued to exhibit tremendous faith in the supernatural. Ghosts, superstitions, prophecies, conjuration, visions, possession by spirits, and telepathy were all fundamental to her beliefs and her art.

▼▼▼

Lucy Hurston died in September 1904. Before she passed, she gave Zora "certain instructions," Zora wrote in her autobiography, rejecting Eatonville's superstitions and folkways. Zora was to make sure that the pillow under her mother's head was not removed until after her death, and to see that nobody covered the clock or the mirror. But the child's pleas were ignored by the adults.

> Papa held me tight and the others frowned me down. . . .
>
> I was to agonize over that moment for years to come. . . . I was old before my time with grief of loss, of failure, of remorse of failure. No matter what the others did, my mother had put her trust in me. She had felt that I could and would carry out her wishes, and I had not. And then in that sunset time, I failed her. . . .
>
> That hour began my wanderings.

Zora's father soon remarried, and her dislike of her stepmother, who was only six or seven years older than she was, loosened her ties to her father—as did being sent to school in Jacksonville, where she found out for the first time what it meant to be "colored" in America. For the next ten or twelve years, her life became peripatetic—in and out of school; living now with her father and now with an older brother or other relatives, even going as far away as Memphis; working for white people as a maid, but unable to retain such a subservient position very long. She learned what real solitude meant, with its pleasures and pains; she began to know poverty, and to get used to it.

During one of Zora's sojourns in Eatonville, she had a near-fatal fight with her stepmother. Zora wrote,

> She called me a sassy, impudent heifer, announced that she was going to take me down a buttonhole lower, and threw a bottle at my head. The bottle came sailing slowly through the air and missed me easily. She never should have missed.
>
> The primeval in me leaped to life.... I looked at her hard.... I didn't have any thoughts to speak of. Just the fierce instinct of flesh on flesh—me kicking and beating on her pudgy self—those two ugly false teeth in front—her dead on the floor—grinning like a dead dog in the sun. Consequences be damned! If I died, let me die with my hands soaked in her blood. I wanted her blood, and plenty of it. That is the way I went into the fight, and that is the way I fought it.

Soon Zora pinned her against the wall and pummeled her with her fists, ignoring the scratching of her stepmother's fingernails. "In a few seconds, she gave up. I could see her face when she realized that I meant to kill her. She spat on my dress, then, and did what she could to cover up from my renewed fury." Zora's father, in response to his wife's cries, asked Zora to stop, but Zora kept going: "Her head was traveling between my fist and the wall, and I wished that my fist had weighed a ton." The Reverend's pistol was kept in the dresser drawer, but Zora stopped her stepmother from reaching it. "I was so mad when I saw my adversary sagging to the floor I didn't know what to do. I began to scream with rage. I had not beaten more than two years out of her yet. I made up my mind to stomp her, but at last, Papa came to, and pulled me away."

Zora's revenge wasn't over. She later portrayed her stepmother, in her novel *Jonah's Gourd Vine*, as a slut who had only convinced John Hurston to marry her by using conjure. And in her autobiography, she wrote that she paid her a visit in the 1930s in order "to finish the job, only to find out she was a chronic invalid. . . . I couldn't tackle her under such circumstances."

▼▼▼

Zora claimed to have often gone hungry during those years of wandering. As a result she developed a lifelong voracious appetite. Fannie Hurst would testify that Zora always snacked between meals and got so impatient waiting for dinner that she would eat it off the stove or out of the refrigerator. "I was hungry for so many years of my life," Zora told her, "I get going nowadays and can't stop."

Those years were often nightmarish. In the seventh of her visions she had seen a shotgun house with peeling white paint; despite knowing that torture awaited her, she felt she had to go in. Zora never described what actually happened in that house, admitting in her autobiography only that this one vision, which was so painful she used to wake up drenched in sweat, had come true, and that she had then run away.

Soon afterwards, she applied for a job that finally gave her what she was looking for: she became a wardrobe girl in a Gilbert and Sullivan repertory theater company sometime around 1915 or 1916, when she was in her mid-twenties. With that position came the chance to travel the country. During the eighteen months she spent with the troupe, Zora's eyes were opened to "the ways of white folks," as Langston Hughes would later phrase it—as well as to the opportunities a decent education could present. She read book after book loaned to her by the company's tenor, a Harvard graduate who had been to Europe. She learned a lot about music and theater, lessons that would prove invaluable much later when she staged her own musical and theatrical events. She later reflected on those months, "I had been in school all that time."

Zora began to hunger for more schooling, but she had no money. After she left the troupe, she moved to Baltimore, where she worked as a waitress and ran a confectionery. But she could never save much. She took a few night classes, including a particularly inspirational one in which the teacher's reading of Coleridge's "Kubla Khan" inspired her to decide that literature was her calling. Finally she figured out how to get into school without funding: lie about her age. The Maryland Code specified that admission to public schools be free for anyone between six and twenty years of age. Zora shaved ten years off her age and, in 1917, pretended to be sixteen years old. She enrolled at Morgan Academy, a high school in Baltimore. Zora was so poor that she had only one dress and one pair of shoes, but school officials offered her jobs. In class, she memorized poems, took exams to get credit for two years of schooling, and then took college preparatory courses.

That summer, her father, who had just moved to Memphis,

was struck by a train and died. Zora didn't react, not even attending the funeral. Perhaps it was liberating to be an orphan.

Instead she moved to Washington to attend Howard University, which was to black students what Harvard was to whites. She supported herself as a manicurist, waitress, and maid; during her first year there she took courses at Howard Prep to fill in the areas her unconventional education had omitted, and earned her high-school degree in May 1919. In her second year she found a beau, Herbert Sheen, who had come to Washington from Decatur, Illinois, planning to be a congressional page, but who instead became a hotel waiter and a Howard student. Zora and Herbert were both children of ministers. "He could stomp a piano out of this world, sing a fair baritone and dance beautifully." Sheen later told Robert Hemenway, "At the time I was going around with Zora I had so many other girlfriends that it was almost confusing. It was just, you might say, too hard to turn them down. . . . I don't remember having any difficulties with Zora about this. Zora was always magnanimous—whatever pleased me was alright with her." Their open relationship became a long-distance one after Sheen moved to New York in 1921 to work for a physician. In 1922, Sheen's sister Genevieve, who lived in Washington and was a close friend of Zora's, was murdered by her husband. Zora took on the responsibility of handling a lot of the necessary legal arrangements while Herbert took the body back to Decatur; in doing so, she made a positive impression on the whole family. Sheen then went to the University of Chicago to complete his BS and entered medical school, but he would, much later, play an important part in Zora's romantic history.

Zora could probably have joined him if she'd so desired. Largely due to health and money troubles, she completed only eighteen months of college coursework at Howard between 1919 and 1924, with wildly inconsistent grades. She left with only an associate's degree, granted in 1920. But she was one of the few students professors Montgomery Gregory and Alain Locke selected for Howard's literary club, the Stylus, whose membership was granted via writing competitions; Locke would write to Charles Johnson that Zora was the best and brightest student he'd had in years. And in 1921 she published her first short story, "John Redding Goes to Sea," in the Stylus's literary magazine.

Zora fit into the black Washington literary community well. She attended a literary salon hosted by poet Georgia Douglas Johnson, which is likely where she first met such Harlem Renaissance luminaries as W. E. B. Du Bois, Jessie Fauset, Angelina Grimké, Bruce Nugent, Jean Toomer, and the scholar and poet Sterling A. Brown. (Coincidentally, Langston Hughes would also attend Johnson's literary salon, but probably not until early 1925, after Zora had moved to New York; it was likely there that he too first met Bruce Nugent.) And she began writing poems, publishing a half dozen of them in 1922 in *Negro World*, a newspaper put out by the black nationalist leader Marcus Garvey's Universal Negro Improvement Association. The 1923 Howard University yearbook stated that Zora's "greatest ambition is to establish herself in Greenwich Village where she may write stories and poems and live an unrestrained Bohemian."

Those stories the yearbook referred to were being read. Locke recommended them to Charles Johnson, who asked Zora to submit her work to *Opportunity*. In December 1924, that magazine published "Drenched in Light," an autobiographical story that showcased one of Zora's attitudes toward race relations. In it, the protagonist, a little girl named Isis, finds true joy when she performs for white folks. She feels no self-consciousness or shame until her grandmother appears, and the kindness of white folks is the only form of approbation she gets. Zora had long perfected the art of "making the white folks laugh," to quote Richard Wright's derisive critique, and playing to white folks' expectations would be a constant throughout her life.

Then, in January 1925, with Charles Johnson's encouragement, Zora Hurston moved to Harlem and very quickly became the center of attention of not only the white folks, but also the black literary world.

▼▼▼

James Langston Hughes was, mathematically speaking, an American of approximately three-eighths European descent, three-eighths African, one-eighth Jewish, and one-eighth American Indian. Such an accounting appears reductive, but it was important to Langston, who never tried to hide his complicated racial makeup. In his autobiography, *The Big Sea*, he wrote, "I am not black. There are lots of different kinds of blood in our family. . . . I am brown. My father was a darker brown. My mother an olive-yellow." Nevertheless, like Frederick Douglass before him and Amiri Baraka after, Langston tried to establish himself in his writing as the voice of his people, a sort of African American everyman, even though he was acutely conscious that his genetic heritage was quite different from that of his African brethren. His statement "I am not black" can be read as "I am not African: I am an *American* Negro."

His mother, Carolyn Langston, was born into one of the most prominent African American families of her era. Her paternal grandfather was a Revolutionary War captain and Virginia planter who sired several children with his slave Lucy; he soon freed Lucy and her children and, in his will, funded their education. Charles Langston, Lucy's son and Carolyn's father, was secretary of the Ohio Anti-Slavery Society and worked as an abolitionist for three decades; Charles's brother, John Mercer Langston, was the first dean of the law school at Howard University, the first president of the Virginia Normal and Collegiate Institute (now Virginia State University), and the first black Virginian to be elected to the US House of Representatives. Carolyn's mother, Mary, had been previously married to Sheridan Leary, a member of John Brown's army who had been killed during the raid on Harper's Ferry. She wed Charles after she was widowed. Langston's ambitiousness came, in part, from his mother's and grandmother's pride in such a heritage.

Langston always believed that he was born on February 1, 1902. But in 2018, convincing evidence appeared that he was alive and well the previous May. It seems likely that his mother made him a year younger than he actually was.

Langston's father, James Nathaniel Hughes, had become embittered by the American racism that wouldn't allow him to go to law school nor, after studying law through correspondence courses, to take the bar exam. So, in October 1903, when Langston was only two years old, James left the United States for Mexico. Thereafter, Langston seldom lived with either parent. When he was in the second grade, Mary Langston, his septuagenarian maternal grandmother who lived in Lawrence, Kansas, took care of him: "My grandmother never took in washing or worked in service or went much to church. She had lived in Oberlin and spoke perfect English, without a trace of dialect. She looked like an Indian." It was hardly a typical African American household. But Langston would travel a great deal to other cities to spend months with his mother, months during which he would become familiar with urban African American culture.

When he first arrived in Lawrence, he was sad and lonely,

being away from his mother and friends. As he later wrote, "Then it was that books began to happen to me, and I began to believe in nothing but books and the wonderful world in books." It was a hardscrabble existence, often with nothing to eat but "salt pork and wild dandelions." It was also a childhood without much familial tenderness. When he was thirteen, his grandmother died, and he went to live with some friends, the Reeds, also in Lawrence, where he was better fed and looked after. (Today, unfortunately, neither Langston's grandmother's house nor that of the Reeds still stands.)

It's hard to imagine a more bucolic setting for an American childhood than Lawrence, with its high hills, the wooded campus of the University of Kansas, and its thriving downtown full of small businesses. But the town, which had been founded by abolitionists, was, by the time of Langston's childhood, largely segregated. While schools had both black and white pupils, black patrons had to sit in the balconies at the theaters and were excluded from some restaurants and nightspots.

Langston left Kansas in 1915 to join his mother, her new husband, and a two-year-old stepbrother. After a year in Lincoln, Illinois, the family moved to Cleveland, where Langston attended all four years of Central High School, and was one of only ten black students to graduate. He read widely, attended left-wing political events, and wrote poetry. A popular student, he was on the track team and the honor roll, was a lieutenant in the military training corps, was elected to the student council, became class poet, and served as secretary, treasurer, and president of various clubs. In short, he was a success—despite the fact that during most of his sophomore and junior years he lived alone, his mother and step-father having temporarily relocated to Chicago.

While in high school, Langston fell in love with Carl Sandburg's poetry; its influence on his work cannot be overstated. Compare, for example, two of their most famous poems, Sandburg's 1918 "Grass," about dead soldiers, and Langston's 1922 "The Negro" (named "Proem" in *The Weary Blues*), which tries to encapsulate pan-African history. Both use conversational prose and line breaks, both end in an echo of their beginning, both treat history as a list, both use repetition at the beginnings of lines, both eschew metaphor, both rely on extreme simplicity for their effect, both are concerned with generalities rather than specifics, with history in headline form rather than observation. Over and over again, Langston followed Sandburg's lead: the narrator will exemplify a character at different historical points; the poet champions the *people*—"the people will live on," Sandburg wrote—avoiding anything too high-class or intellectual, socialist to the core. Sandburg's 1919 "Jazz Fantasia" was one of the first American poems about African American music and undoubtedly influenced Langston's many poems on the subject. Indeed, at the age of fifteen, Langston wrote a poem that ran,

> Carl Sandburg's poems
> Fall on the white pages of his books
> Like blood-clots of song
> From the wounds of humanity.
> I know a lover of life sings.
> I know a lover of all the living
> Sings then.

Langston's poetry, like Sandburg's, was powerful, expressive, direct, and extremely effective. But it was only when he wrote "The Weary Blues" in early 1925 that he found a truly original voice, one that echoed not Sandburg but the song-poetry of black people.

▼▼▼

After his junior year in high school, Langston spent a summer
with his father in Toluca, Mexico. He was unutterably miserable.
His father felt only contempt for "the people," particularly Mexican and black; his sole concern seemed to be money. "My father
hated Negroes," Langston wrote. "I think he hated himself, too,
for being a Negro. He disliked all of his family because they were
Negroes. . . . My father had a great contempt for all poor people.
He thought it was their own fault that they were poor." He often
left Langston alone on his ranch with nothing to do but practice
bookkeeping, typing, and Spanish. Langston turned suicidal,
then came down with an illness he would later diagnose as psy-
chosomatic; in a Mexico City hospital, he found some relief from
his misery.

It was the "red summer" of 1919, a tense season of race riots in
many major US cities, and when Langston returned, the hostility toward his fellow Negroes was particularly acute. But this
hardly affected him. He threw himself back into his high school
studies in Cleveland, becoming editor of the yearbook and class
poet. His mother was pushing him to get a job upon graduating so that he could help take care of her; his father was pushing
him to go to college, which was far closer to his inclinations. He
threw his lot in with the latter and went back to Mexico, writing
one of his most famous poems, "The Negro Speaks of Rivers,"
on the train ride down. He had a somewhat better summer there
than the previous one, being more proficient in Spanish now, and
enjoying the companionship of his father's German housekeeper
and her daughter. And he firmed up his resolve to go to college at
Columbia, where he could learn about literature and be close to
Harlem, which was already legendary among African Americans

nationwide. "I was in love with Harlem long before I got there," Langston would later admit.

Unfortunately, his father did not support Langston's plan. He wanted Langston to study mining engineering—that's where the money was. So Langston stayed in Mexico—for fifteen months in all—teaching English, writing, and waiting for his father to give in. He finally did, agreeing to pay for Langston's education at Columbia.

Near the end of Langston's stay in Mexico, he was almost murdered. A German brewer had fallen in love with his own German servant girl and suspected her of having an affair with Langston. He went to Langston's father's house, shot the girl three times (she miraculously survived), and would have killed Langston if he had been there. Luckily, he wasn't, and the would-be killer gave himself up to the police. Langston, who barely knew the girl, evinced no emotion.

▼▼▼

In the summer of 1921, Langston sailed from Veracruz to New York City. "At last!" he wrote in *The Big Sea*. "The thrill of those towers of Manhattan with their million golden eyes, growing slowly taller and taller above the green water, until they looked as if they could almost touch the sky! Then Brooklyn Bridge, gigantic in the dusk! . . . All this made me feel it was better to come to New York than to any other city in the world."

Four years after his arrival, he would write, Whitmanesque,

Manhattan takes me, is glad, holds me tightly. Like a vampire sucking my blood from my body, sucking my very breath from my lungs, she holds me. Broadway and its million lights. Harlem and its love-nights, its cabarets and casinos, its dark, warm bodies. The thundering subways, the arch of the bridges, the mighty rivers hold me. . . . I cannot tell the city how much I love it. I have not enough kisses in my mouth for the avid lips of the city. I become dizzy dancing to the jazz-tuned nights, ecstasy-wearied in the towered days. . . . The fascination of this city is upon me, burning like a fire in the blood.

When a white southerner named Josephine Cogdell visited Harlem in 1927, she listed the sights there in her journal. Langston would have probably seen them all: "The octoroon choruses at the Lafayette, the black sheiks at Small's, the expert amateur dancing to be seen at the Savoy, the Curb Market along the 8th Avenue 'L,' with its strange West Indian roots and flare of tropical fruits." Cogdell described the chitterlings and pigsnouts on display in the windows of restaurants, how the black upper crust lived in "stately houses behind stately trees" on Strivers Row, the panoply of skin colors on display among the children in the tenements of 142nd Street, and the babel of European languages spoken in their African and Caribbean permutations by black immigrants. In short, Harlem was not a black ghetto but a cosmopolitan delight—one of the reasons Langston was so in love with the place.

If Langston had any lifelong passion, it was for Harlem. That passion was born when he arrived in September 1921. He wasted no time becoming acquainted with the place. Getting off the subway at 135th and Lenox, he went straight to the Harlem YMCA, then to the Harlem Branch Library, and that evening to the Lincoln Theater to hear a blues singer. "Everybody seemed to make me welcome," he later wrote. "The sheer dark size of Harlem intrigued me. And the fact that at the time poets and writers like James Weldon Johnson and Jessie Fauset lived there, and [comedian] Bert Williams, Duke Ellington, Ethel Waters, and Walter White too, fascinated me."

Columbia was unpleasant, with its haphazard racism. Langston far preferred the lectures he attended at the socialist Rand School of Social Science in Lower Manhattan. Instead of studying, he spent his time reading and going to talks and shows. He would withdraw from Columbia after his freshman year and spend as much time in Harlem as he possibly could. After all, by mid-decade Harlem would be billed as the "Nightclub Capital of the World," with over a hundred different places to hear music and to dance. But he had another good reason to be there—his mother, now separated from her second husband, had moved to Harlem for a few months, and Langston was funneling some of his father's money her way.

He was also making a name for himself in Harlem. By the end of 1922, fifteen of his poems had been published in *The Crisis*. These poems included some of his most famous—"The Negro Speaks of Rivers," "Negro," and "My People"—poems that attempted in their own way to redefine the history and identity of the American Negro, quite in keeping with the editorial stance of *The Crisis*, which was in essence that what was most American was the African American. It was around this time that Langston was first introduced to the Harlem literati, whom he had thus far avoided due to his fear of "learned people." Jessie Fauset had managed to track him down and persuade him to lunch with her at the Civic Club; Langston was so shy he brought his mother along.

But making a name for himself was no way to make a living. Jobs for African Americans were scarce in New York City, and after stints growing vegetables on a Staten Island farm and as a delivery boy for the House of Flowers in Manhattan, he landed a job as a mess boy on an old ship (a "mother ship," it was called) moored at Jones Point, twenty miles north of Harlem, that served as quarters for a crew of immigrants who took care of a fleet of decommissioned freighters.

Langston's job wasn't very demanding, and he had plenty of time for writing (it was at Jones Point that he started work on "The Weary Blues"), reading, and conversing with his shipmates about distant lands. These talks increased his wanderlust, so in May 1923 he found a similar job on the SS *Malone* and was on his way to Africa.

▼ ▼ ▼

Langston described his many adventures on "the big sea" in his 1940 memoir of that name. It begins,

> Melodramatic, maybe, it seems to me now. . . . I leaned over the rail of the S.S. *Malone* and threw the books as far as I could out into the sea—all the books I had had at Columbia, and all the books I had lately bought to read.
>
> The books went down into the moving water in the dark off Sandy Hook. Then I straightened up, turned my face to the wind, and took a deep breath. . . . And I felt that nothing would ever happen to me again that I didn't want to happen.

Langston was, perhaps unconsciously, staging a precise reversal of the trope of the talking book, which Henry Louis Gates Jr. has called the "ur-trope" of the Anglo-African tradition. A number of black-authored texts of the eighteenth and nineteenth centuries repeat a story told in the first English-language slave narrative in which a slave on board a ship coming from Africa to the New World sees a white man reading a book and thinks that the book is talking to him; the book, however, refuses to speak to the slave, which inspires a desire to make it speak in a black voice. Here Langston is also on a ship, but going to Africa, the continent of some of his ancestors, and he throws all his talking books, all his *instruction*, overboard. As he would write to his patron Charlotte Osgood Mason in 1929, "All my childhood, lonely, I spent reading, up until the time I went to sea. Then . . . suddenly, the very sight of books made me ill." (In fact, he kept *one* book: Walt Whitman's *Leaves of Grass*.)

That he would choose to *begin* his memoir with this symbolic act makes it even more weighty. Langston was declaring his allegiance to the preliterate—or, as his contemporaries put it, the "primitive"—and turning his back definitively on the Enlightenment idea of liberation through literacy. Liberation, for Langston, would arrive through the *abandonment* of literacy. Of all the great writers of the time, he was the one who went the farthest in eschewing literary references and conventions: his poems were meant to be declaimed, not read in silence—they were oral first and foremost.

Shortly after his return to New York in November 1923, Langston sailed across the Atlantic again, this time to Europe. He spent a good part of 1924 in Paris, penniless in Montmartre, where he had a brief love affair with an Anglo-African woman, Anne Coussey. He worked as a dishwasher at a nightclub and kept company primarily with other African Americans, so he didn't bother to visit the famous English-language bookstore Shakespeare and Company, hobnob with the white American expatriate set, or pay a call upon Gertrude Stein. In fact, he found Montparnasse more pretentious than Greenwich Village. Nor did he attend the Olympics, which were being held just outside Paris, in Colombes. He did meet with art collector Albert Barnes, who bored him; Paul Guillaume, a collector of African art; Kojo Tovalou Houénou, a Dahomey-born intellectual and self-proclaimed prince; and the bestselling Caribbean-born novelist René Maran. Otherwise he showed no interest in the radical literary and artistic culture fomenting in Paris. His best American friend in the city was likely Ada Smith, an African American blues singer who would later become famous as Bricktop. In keeping with the beginning of his autobiography, he shunned "literary" culture.

The poems he was producing hewed to his maxim "that poetry should be direct, comprehensible and the epitome of simplicity." "I, Too" (renamed "Epilogue" in *The Weary Blues*)—the most powerful and famous poem he wrote in Europe that year—begins with a nod to Walt Whitman's "I Hear America Singing." But while Whitman used archaisms and positioned himself as experimental, Langston's language was purely of the moment; while Whitman stretched his lines to the breaking point, Langston's were short, like those of his contemporaries William Carlos Williams, Marianne Moore, E. E. Cummings, and H.D. While the line breaks of those poets often called attention to themselves by their unconventionality, Langston's seemed natural, as if he were simply speaking; while most of his contemporaries used "poetic" diction, Langston stuck to words familiar to five-year-olds:

I, too, sing America.

I am the darker brother.
They send me to eat in the kitchen
When company comes,
But I laugh,

And eat well,
And grow strong.

Tomorrow,
I'll be at the table
When company comes.
Nobody'll dare
Say to me,
"Eat in the kitchen,"
Then.

Besides,
They'll see how beautiful I am
And be ashamed—

I, too, am America.

Few if any of the great American poets have written so plainly yet so effectively, and with such an utter lack of pretense.

▼▼▼

Alain Locke had a complicated relationship with Langston Hughes. Early in 1923, when Langston was only twenty, Countee Cullen, then a close friend of both, decided that, since Langston seemed impervious to Cullen's charms (Cullen had serenaded him with the sensuous poem "To a Brown Boy," to no avail), and since Cullen had reservations about embracing his own homosexual proclivities, he would try to arrange for Locke to seduce Langston in his stead. "Write to him," he urged Locke, "and arrange to meet him. You will like him; I love him; his is such a charming childishness that I feel years older in his presence." He described Langston as "looking like a virile brown god."

Langston teased Locke in his letters, pretending not to understand Locke's "infatuation with Greek ideals of life," asking him if he liked the (homosexual) poems in the Calamus section of Walt Whitman's *Leaves of Grass*, then sighing, "how wonderful it would be to come surprisingly upon one another in some Old World street! Delightful and too romantic!" Meanwhile he asked Cullen if Locke was married, likely just to confirm Locke's homosexuality. But Langston backed off when Locke pressed harder. Their relationship was conducted entirely through the mail; Langston was curious about the professor, but refused to meet him in person. He would later write that he was "afraid of learned people in those days"; doubtless the confessional nature of Locke's letters increased his own shyness. Locke was wounded, and Cullen let Langston know this; Langston didn't care and pretended not to understand. Locke swore he would have nothing more to do with Langston, only to melt when Cullen encouraged him and Langston approached him—Langston was anxious to attend Howard, and knew that Locke could get him a place. But after sending a telegram reading "MAY I COME NOW PLEASE," Langston backed off two days later with an apology, explaining, "I had been reading all your letters that day and a sudden desire came over me to come to you then, right then, to stay with you and know you. I need to know you. But I am so stupid sometimes." The next day he sailed for Europe, and soon settled in Paris. Locke was heartbroken, accusing Langston of "whoredom," writing him, "I do not recognize myself in the broken figure that says 'come,—come when you can, come soon.' . . . I cannot describe what I have been going through . . . it has felt like death."

One day in July 1924, around noon, Langston was awoken by a gentle knock on his Paris door. It was Locke. Eighteen months after their correspondence had begun, they had finally met in person, and they were both charmed. "We've been having a jolly time," Langston wrote his friend Harold Jackman, Countee Cullen's gay soulmate. "I like him immensely." Locke took Langston everywhere: the Louvre, the Opéra-Comique, a ballet, gardens. And after spending a few weeks with Langston, Locke wrote Cullen, "See Paris and die. Meet Langston and be damned." He was deeply in love. He wrote Langston about two days in which "every breath has the soothe of a kiss and every step the thrill of an embrace. . . . I needed one such day and one such night to tell you how much I love you in which to see soul-deep and be satisfied." It seems as though Langston had granted Locke some measure of sexual intimacy, and Locke was hungry for more.

They came to a compromise of sorts. Locke would help Langston get into Howard and help pay his tuition; Langston would live in Locke's house. Then Langston left for Italy, where, a few days later, a letter from Locke reached him. It was a love letter, but it amounted to an ultimatum. It suggested that if Langston did not gratify Locke's desire for intimacy, the Howard promise would be rescinded. So they spent five days in Venice, where Langston got fed up with Locke's touristic proclivities and pontifications on high culture. He started wandering the back alleys, looking for signs of poverty. They had planned to sail back to the United States together, but Langston was robbed of his passport and all his money on the way to Genoa, and Locke had to abandon him in order to catch the ship—or so Langston believed. In fact, Locke spent the next few weeks in a tiny town on the seaside, San Remo. He could have asked Langston—who was sleeping in a flophouse, roaming the Genoa waterfront, and starving—

to join him there. But things had soured between them, and he would never show much kindness to Langston again.

▼▼▼

Langston arrived in New York in November 1924, almost a year after he'd left. He immediately became enmeshed again in Harlem. His first day back he spent with Countee Cullen, who wrote, dressed, and spoke in a Victorian manner; Harlem's best-known poet, he represented the aspirations of the cultured black bourgeoisie. Langston then went to an NAACP benefit dance at Happy Rhone's nightclub on 143rd and Lenox, featuring performances by Florence Mills, Alberta Hunter, Noble Sissle, Bill "Bojangles" Robinson, and Fletcher Henderson and his orchestra—definitely the leading lights of New York's black music scene. There he was introduced to Walter White, future head of the NAACP and a published novelist; James Weldon Johnson; W. E. B. Du Bois (although it's possible that they had already met); and, most importantly, Carl Van Vechten. Just a few days later Cullen introduced him to Arna Bontemps, who would in time become his best friend and closest collaborator, at a soiree on Edgecomb Avenue also attended by Jessie Fauset, Charles Johnson, Alain Locke, and Eric Walrond. There Langston, looking dapper in a plaid mackinaw, "galvanized" the gathering, according to Bontemps, reading his latest poems and accounts of his voyages from his pocket notebook.

Shortly thereafter, Cullen and Langston made a decisive break. Langston later wrote elliptically that something had happened to make him "lose my boyish faith in friendship and learn one of the peculiar prices a friend can ask for favors." His biographer Arnold Rampersad surmises that Cullen propositioned Langston, then revealed that he knew about the intimacy Locke had enjoyed with Langston in Europe, which knowledge Langston was unable to forgive.

Anyway, Langston couldn't afford to stay in New York. His mother had been begging him to visit her in Washington, D.C., where he still hoped to attend Howard University with Alain Locke's help.

But that help didn't come through, and Howard was beyond his means. Surrounded by wealthy and snobbish relatives of his late great-uncle, the congressman John Mercer Langston, he felt ill at ease and out of place with the crème de la crème of Washington black society. "Never before," he wrote, "had I seen persons ... quite so audibly sure of their own importance and their high place in the community. So many pompous gentlemen never before did I meet. Nor so many ladies with chests swelled like pouter-pigeons whose mouths uttered formal sentences in frightfully correct English."

He found a job in a laundry, but was able to save nothing towards college, and couldn't find a scholarship. His mother worked as a domestic. They lived in an unheated tenement through a harsh winter, barely making ends meet.

In March 1925, Dr. Carter G. Woodson offered Langston a job as his personal assistant. Woodson was a well-known scholar, founder of the Association for the Study of Negro Life and History, and editor of the *Journal of Negro History*. Among other duties, Langston alphabetized the thirty thousand slips of paper that would make up Woodson's book *Thirty Thousand Free Negro Heads of Families* and checked the proofs. The work was long and dreary.

It was only a few weeks later that Langston received the invitation to the *Opportunity* magazine banquet that would literally change his life. For one thing, it was there that he met the woman who became his very best friend.

3

SUMMER 1926

The Niggerati

By the summer of 1926, a year after the *Opportunity* dinner, Zora had helped organize a Harlem-based group she jokingly named the "Niggerati," composed of an accomplished group of young writers and artists who were by and large opposed to the literary conventions of the older generation of the black elite. Among them were Gwendolyn Bennett, poet, art teacher, and the assistant editor of *Opportunity*; John P. Davis, who would soon be an editor at *The Crisis*; Aaron Douglas, whose illustrations and paintings were just beginning to be celebrated; and Wallace Thurman, editor of *The Messenger* (Thurman would soon leave this position in order to take one as editor at the pacifist Christian journal *The World Tomorrow*). A half-dozen others also partook in the group's social and literary activities, including Countee Cullen and Dorothy Peterson, a teacher and arts patron who held a literary salon in her father's house in Brooklyn. Except for Zora and sculptor Augusta Savage, all of them were in their late teens or twenties, but Zora can't really be considered an exception since everyone thought she was just as young.

Iolanthe Sydney, a successful black employment agent, had offered a house she owned rent-free to Thurman, Nugent, and a graduate student at Columbia named Harcourt Tynes (Thurman's white male lover also lived there for a time). It was to be the center of activity for the Niggerati. At 267 West 136th Street, a block from the steep hill of St. Nicholas Park, it was within two blocks of the offices of the *New York Age*, *Messenger*, Brotherhood of Sleeping Car Porters, and National Urban League; the swanky apartments of musicians Eubie Blake, Will Marion Cook, W. C. Handy, Fletcher Henderson, Noble Sissle, and Ethel Waters, most of whom lived in the elegant townhouses known as "Striver's Row"; and the huge new nightclub Small's Paradise, where the waitresses glided from table to table on roller skates, singing, dancing, and spinning their trays. Within five blocks lived James Weldon Johnson, Fats Waller, and A'Lelia Walker (Harlem's richest woman and the president of the Madame C. J. Walker Manufacturing Company). Langston moved into this "Niggerati Manor" in July, along with Bruce Nugent, and immediately joined the group. The shared artists' house was unprepossessing from the outside, but on the inside—at least, according to Thurman's roman à clef *Infants of the Spring*—the draperies and bed covers were red and black and Nugent painted the walls with brightly colored phalluses.

Langston had returned to Washington after the *Opportunity* banquet and proved himself a master of self-promotion. He was working as a busboy at the Wardman Park Hotel when, in December, perhaps America's most famous poet, the white Midwesterner Vachel Lindsay (his signature poem was the primitivist paean "The Congo"), visited. Langston placed a few of his poems next to Lindsay's dinner plate and, at the reading in the hotel auditorium that night, Lindsay read the poems to the whites-only audience. The next day Langston was besieged by all the newspapers—the "bus boy poet" who had been "discovered" by Vachel Lindsay. It was Langston's "first publicity break," as he called it. But even better fortune quickly followed. In January, his first book, the overtly romantic *Weary Blues*, was published to widespread acclaim—that is, acclaim by white critics (black critics were not quite so kind). Then Amy Spingarn, a poet, painter, and heiress who was married to the treasurer of the NAACP, Joel Elias Spingarn, agreed to loan Langston money to pay for his college education. Although he could have gone back to Columbia or transferred to Harvard (a potential patron had offered him a full scholarship), Langston had had enough of white schools, so in February he enrolled in Lincoln University, then an all-black college with all-white teachers in the rolling hills forty miles west of Philadelphia (one of his classmates was Thurgood Marshall, who quite admired Hughes). He continued to spend some of his weekends and holidays in New York.

As for Zora, she moved out of her Harlem apartment (at 108 West 131st Street) in June or July 1926, for it was simply too expensive. Since her arrival in New York City in early 1925, she seems to have lived in seven different apartments, if one judges from her return addresses. Perhaps she was always behind with her rent (at one point she only had eleven cents to her name). Rents for black tenants were, in general, forty to sixty percent higher than those for whites in comparable apartments, and Harlem was especially expensive. It was difficult for African Americans to find apartments to rent outside certain neighborhoods. But Zora got lucky.

Her new apartment was at 43 West 66th Street, just half a block from Central Park, which would be her primary address

for most of the remainder of the decade (the building no longer exists); calling herself "Queen of the Niggerati," she often
entertained the group there, with a stew on the stove that visitors
would each contribute something to—when she wasn't serving
a specialty like Florida eel. Since she lacked money and posses-
sions, she threw a "furniture party," and each guest was required
to bring something. Her friends quickly filled up her apartment
with quirky objects, including silver birds perched in the linen
closet. Zora reigned over the tight-knit group, singing spirituals, playing harmonica, and telling tall tales. Her apartment was
always open to everyone, and her visitors included Columbia
students, songwriters, and authors. She always had something
ready to feed them: fried okra and shrimp, perhaps, or simply
gingerbread and buttermilk.

▾▾▾

Despite the activity at Zora's West Side apartment, the bulk of
the action was in Harlem.

Carl Van Vechten, who described himself as "violently interested in Negroes," was hardly alone among white New Yorkers
in viewing the neighborhood as the ultimate playground. In fact,
he served as the primary chaperone of the group of whites Zora
referred to as "Negrotarians"; Bruce Nugent called him "the Livingstone of this Empire-State Africa . . . the big white discoverer
of High-Harlem." As his biographer Emily Bernard memorably
describes him, "Photographs from around 1924 reveal a large,
imposing [man], with thin graying hair and generous lips that
barely reached over a famously protruding pair of front teeth.
His odd looks were complemented by a one-of-a-kind wardrobe
that included jade bracelets, ruffled blouses, and silk lounging
robes." His views had changed since the summer of 1924, when

he wrote H. L. Mencken, "Jazz, the blues, Negro spirituals, all stimulate me enormously for the moment. Doubtless, I shall discard them too in time." He never did discard them, remaining faithful to the African American cultural cause to the end of his long life.

The motives of the other Negrotarians were a mixed bag. In his history *When Harlem Was in Vogue*, David Levering Lewis enumerates them clearly. Some, like Hart Crane and Waldo Frank, looked to Harlem for "personal nourishment" and "cultural salvation," in Lewis's words. Some, like Muriel Draper and Max Eastman, hoped that African Americans would overturn the established social and political order. Some, like Eugene O'Neill and Alfred Stieglitz, took a more Freudian position, thirsting for the unleashing of the id. Some, like Albert Barnes, Florenz Ziegfeld, George Gershwin, and H. L. Mencken, hoped to reap benefits—financial or in cultural capital—from African American culture. Still others had philanthropic motives.

As for Van Vechten, it wasn't unusual to see him with Zora, Langston, and a group of his other friends in a Harlem nightclub or speakeasy, and he went out with one or both of them to parties, dinners, and clubs once or twice a month, not just during that summer but ever since he'd started his Harlem partying in May 1925. His motive was distinct from the others. Yes, he was devoted to breaking down all barriers between Harlem-dwellers and the crème de la crème of New York society. But he also simply liked to be with his friends, and his friends all lived in or loved to visit Harlem. The conviviality of the atmosphere was magical. They would go to Small's, the Nest, the Vaudeville Comedy Club, the New World Cabaret, or Philadelphia Jimmie's, but rarely to only one of those. If he threw a party at his house (invariably interracial), it was often either preceded or followed by a visit to Harlem, and he frequently stayed out until after dawn.

▼▼▼

Perhaps nowhere else and never before in the United States had sexuality of every variety been so open and accepted as it was in Harlem in the 1920s. "You just did what you wanted to do," Bruce Nugent related. "Nobody was in the closet. There wasn't any closet." The sexual act was public in places and private in others, promiscuous in race and gender, freely talked about and freely practiced. If you wanted something sexual, there was no shortage of ways to get it. One example out of many was millionaire A'Lelia Walker's extravagant "funny parties," where, as one partygoer recalled, "There were men and women, straight and gay. They were kinds of orgies. Some people had clothes on, some didn't. People would hug and kiss on pillows and do anything they wanted to do. You could watch if you wanted to. Some came to watch, some came to play."

Langston Hughes was by no means celibate. He had had a serious romance with a young African-English woman in Paris and visited prostitutes in various seaports; he also had quite passionate love affairs with several women in the 1930s, and came down with gonorrhea from his sexual activities. He had at least one homosexual experience—with a fellow seaman on his African voyage—and his friendships with homosexual men were some of his closest (though most of those men swore that Langston never expressed any interest in homosexual relations).

Still, there was something mysterious about Langston, especially where his friends were concerned. As Van Vechten, a married man who made little secret of his queer predilections, would confess after a friendship of thirty years, Langston "seemed to thrive without having sex" in his life. Langston was living with two flamboyant queers, Thurman and Nugent; Thurman later boasted that his friendship with Langston was more than Platonic, but Nugent denied it. As social historian Ann Douglas cleverly puts it, Langston "obscured and shielded his sexual identity from clear scrutiny by anyone, probably including himself."

This was not out of shame. Langston was proud of being disreputable. His elusive sexuality was simply part of his elusive nature—he was constantly in motion, never staying in one place too long, never devoting his attentions exclusively to one person. Just as he refused to confine himself to poetry—fiction, plays, essays, letters, and reminiscences flowed from his pen—he refused to confine himself to anything else either. His elusiveness was a deliberate strategy. As he wrote, "Silence is as good as the next best thing in the face of wrath. (And the next best thing is to evaporate! Get away, leave.)"

Wallace Thurman was quick to notice Langston's elusiveness too. In his satire of the Harlem Renaissance, *Infants of the Spring*, Thurman characterized Langston, whom he named "Tony Crews," as

> smiling and self-effacing, a mischievous boy, grateful for the chance to slip away from the backwoods college he attended. Raymond [Thurman's alias for himself] had never been able to analyze this young poet. . . . Even an intimate friendship with Tony had failed to enlighten [Raymond]. For Tony was the most close-mouthed and cagey individual Raymond had ever known when it came to personal matters. He fended off every attempt to probe into his inner self and did this with such an unconscious and naïve air that the prober soon came to one of two conclusions: Either

Tony had no depth whatsoever, or else he was too deep for plumbing by ordinary mortals.

And years later, the great writer Arthur Koestler, who came to know Langston in Turkestan, of all places, wrote, "Behind the warm smile of his dark eyes there was a grave dignity, and a polite reserve which communicated itself at once. He was very likeable and easy to get on with, but at the same time one felt an impenetrable, elusive remoteness which warded off all undue familiarity."

Zora seems to have shared Langston's sexual and emotional solitude. During those first few years in New York City she apparently cultivated no romantic ties. Her biographer Robert Hemenway relates a characteristic story: "Once, dressed for a party in a flowing white dress and a wide-brimmed hat, she found herself sharing an elevator with a would-be Casanova. As they approached the first floor, he made his pass, and Zora responded with a roundhouse right that put him flat on the floor. She stepped out of the elevator, never looking back at the man laid out behind her."

But there was one thing about which neither Langston nor Zora would ever be elusive. Their identities as African Americans were unshakable, as was their devotion to the race.

▼▼▼

Zora had begun studying anthropology under Franz Boas at Columbia in the fall of 1925, which involved a momentous shift of perspective. All her life Zora had been immersed in black folkways and had never even thought of separating her identity from those of the folk. She used to tell this story: when a policeman stopped her from crossing on a red light, she told him that since she saw all the white people crossing on green, she thought the red light was for colored folks. Here, as she often did, she was taking a common black folktale and applying it to herself. Zora defined folklore as "the arts of the people before they find out that there is any such thing as art, and they make it out of whatever they find at hand"; as a corollary, the folklore that Zora had always drawn on was suddenly *art* to her: it had changed its nature.

Therefore, now that she was embarking on a course of studying the folk, she could no longer be one of them. As she would write at the beginning of *Mules and Men*, "From the earliest rocking of my cradle, I had known about the capers Brer Rabbit is apt to cut and what the Squinch Owl says from the house top. But it was fitting me like a tight chemise. I couldn't see it for wearing it. It was only when I was off in college, away from my native surroundings, that I could see myself like somebody else and stand off and look at my garment. Then I had to have the spy-glass of Anthropology to look through at that." Suddenly African American culture was a thing to research rather than to roll around in and play with.

In this new endeavor she could not have asked for a better guide than Franz Boas, whom she idolized, calling him "the greatest anthropologist alive" and "the king of kings." She even convinced Bruce Nugent, who hated schools, to attend Boas's classes. Boas was sixty-seven at the time and had been at Columbia since 1899. He was without doubt America's preeminent anthropologist, almost singlehandedly responsible for debunking scientific racism, defining cultural relativism, and establishing folklore as a subject worthy of scientific study. He unflaggingly encouraged Zora's work, and urged her to become a professional anthropologist herself; undoubtedly he recognized that Zora could well become America's foremost authority on black folkways.

But that would never do for Zora—her creative urges were too strong for her to deny them in favor of the pursuit of scientific objectivity. She was simply too ambitious and imaginative, and she recognized it. In a letter to Annie Nathan Meyer written in January 1926, she exclaimed,

> Oh, if you knew my dreams! my vaulting ambition! How I constantly live in fancy in seven league boots, taking mighty strides across the world, but conscious all the time of being a mouse on a treadmill.... The eagerness, the burning within, I wonder the actual sparks do not fly so that they be seen by all men. Prometheus on his rock with his liver being continually consumed as fast as he grows another, is nothing to my dreams. I dream such wonderfully complete ones, so radiant in astral beauty. I have not the power yet to make them come true. They always die. But even as they fade, I have others.

Zora's unstated goal was not the study of folklore but its conversion into a creative form that could appeal to the general public without losing its essential character. One of her first attempts to do this was the publication of "The Eatonville Anthology" in three parts in the September, October, and November 1926 issues of *The Messenger.* This miscellany of fourteen short sketches of Eatonville life and "lies" introduced many of the characters and tales that would appear in Zora's later works, including *Mule Bone, Mules and Men,* and *Their Eyes Were Watching God.* And they were all strongly based both on Zora's observations of her hometown and on its folklore. In these sketches Eatonville becomes not just an all-black Southern town but a repository of legends and traditions, as rich in its own way as the Arthurian Camelot.

Zora realized what so many people forget: that folkways are not simply tales and songs and sayings that can be easily jotted down and reproduced. Instead they inform every aspect of daily life—they make up the warp and woof of deed and doer.

▼▼▼

In late 1925, while studying with Boas, Zora also worked as a secretary (or amanuensis) for Fannie Hurst, who lived at 1 West 67th Street. Hurst had by then published five collections of short stories and two novels and was one of the most highly paid writers in the country. She had scandalized New York by living in a separate apartment from her husband, maintaining her own name, making her marriage contract renewable every five years, and allowing him to see her only three nights a week. Four years Zora's junior, she was, in Zora's own word, a "stunning" woman; Zora wrote a profile of her for the *Saturday Review of Literature* in 1937 in which she called her "a person of the most contradictory moods and statements of anyone in public life" and "a little girl who is tall for her age." Zora suspected that one reason Hurst liked her so much was because the contrast between their skin colors drew attention to Hurst's fair complexion.

Hurst seems to have hired Zora partly out of pity; Zora was barely making do. At first, as Hurst wrote in 1960, Zora's "shorthand was short on legibility, her typing hit-or-miss, mostly the latter, her filing, a game of find-the-thimble." She would interrupt Hurst's dictation with interjections, suggestions, and clarifications. When she got bored, she would yawn and say, "Let's get out the car, I'll drive you up to the Harlem bad-lands or down to

the wharves where men go down to the sea in ships." Soon Hurst
had had enough. One morning when Zora said she'd rather take
a drive through the countryside than dictation, Hurst lost her
temper, called her "the world's worst secretary," and fired her.

Zora's employment had only lasted a few weeks. But Hurst
kept her on as her sometime chauffeur for years, and saw her frequently. Zora was "all in greased curls, bangles, and slashes of
red," as Hurst wrote to Van Vechten in April 1926. "She drove with
a sure relaxed skill"—once taking her employer all the way down
to Eatonville. In 1937, Zora wrote an amusing sketch of a 1931 road
trip they took together, setting out in Hurst's "little Chevrolet"
for Maine, "with my foot in the gas tank splitting the wind," stopping in Saratoga Springs to drink the water and take Hurst's two-
pound Pekingese for a brisk walk of five feet, changing course and
driving to Niagara Falls, then touring Ontario, where they met
up with Hurst's lover, the Arctic explorer Vilhjalmur Stefansson.

Hurst became one of Zora's greatest friends and benefactors,
introducing her to a host of writers and other people in the arts,
helping her to get through the exigencies and expense of Barnard (other students became much friendlier to Zora because of
her friendship with the famous novelist), and penning the foreword to her first novel, *Jonah's Gourd Vine.*

▾▾▾

That summer of 1926, Zora and Langston planned their first
collaboration—an opera based on black popular music. This was
hardly unprecedented: a number of black writers and composers,
including Scott Joplin, Paul Laurence Dunbar, and Will Marion
Cook, had already created black culture–inspired operas. But
Langston thought Zora's knowledge of Southern folklore would
immeasurably enrich the form. Zora had a composer in mind

too—Clarence Cameron White, director of music at West Virginia State College. When he came to New York in August, Zora introduced him to Langston and Van Vechten, who wholeheartedly supported the project.

Not much came of this effort—except, perhaps, for a few of the blues-based poems that would soon be published in Langston's second book. Langston would explain to Charlotte Mason in 1929 that *The Weary Blues* had belonged to "a period of solitary wandering, looking out of myself at the rest of the world, but touching no one, nothing"; in *Fine Clothes to the Jew* "many of the poems are outward, rather than inward, trying to catch the moods of individuals other than myself."

In March 1926, Zora had commented to Countee Cullen, "Hughes ought to stop publishing all those secular folk-songs as his poetry. Now when he got off the 'Weary Blues['] (most of it a song I and most southerners have known all our lives) I said nothing for I knew I'd never be forgiven by certain people for crying down what the 'white folks had exalted', but when he gets off another '*Me and mah honey got two mo' days tuh do de buck*' [from Langston's 'Negro Dancers'] I dont see how I can refrain from speaking." Now, however, Zora was fully aiding Langston's efforts. And by the end of the summer, the two friends had turned to a new collaboration.

▼▼▼

In a June issue of *The Nation*, Langston published the essay "The Negro Artist and the Racial Mountain," a polemic decrying the staid, middle-class values of the black bourgeoisie and proposing that black art should never be beholden to white cultural norms. *The Nation* had commissioned it in response to black critic George Schuyler's "The Negro-Art Hokum," which had been published in the same magazine a week earlier, and which had argued that "the Aframerican is merely a lamp-blacked Anglo-Saxon." The "racial mountain" of Langston's title was one which stood in the way of the Negro artist—the "urge within the race toward whiteness, the desire to pour racial individuality into the mold of American standardization, and to be as little Negro and as much American as possible," much as Schuyler had advised. To avoid this, Langston urged artists to ask, "Why should I want to be white?" and to answer, "I am a Negro—and beautiful."

"I want to be a poet—not a Negro poet." These words, which we still often hear today with "black," "Hispanic," "Jewish," or "woman" in place of "Negro" and a variety of career choices in place of "poet," formed the opening quotation of the essay, put in the mouth of "one of the most promising young Negro poets"— quite transparently Countee Cullen, who had complained about Langston's preoccupation with race in his review of *The Weary Blues* for *Opportunity*, and who would soon write that "Negroes should be concerned with making good impressions." Langston argued that "I want to be a poet—not a Negro poet" was the equivalent of saying, "I would like to be white." This poet, Langston wrote, came from "the Negro middle class," which Langston contrasted to "the low-down folks," whose "joy runs, bang! into ecstasy.... Work maybe a little today, rest a little tomorrow. Play awhile. Sing awhile. O, let's dance!... Perhaps these common people will give to the world its truly great Negro artist, the one who is not afraid to be himself."

Langston praised writers who truly wrote in the Negro idiom— Charles Chesnutt, Paul Dunbar, Jean Toomer, W. E. B. Du Bois, Rudolph Fisher—along with blues singers and jazz musicians. These writers were producing an honest African American body of literature despite the efforts of white editors and "Nordicized

Negro intelligentsia" to make them conform. Negro art, dance, and music was either on the cusp or thriving. But still to come was "the rise of the Negro theater." The essay ended, "We build our temples for tomorrow, strong as we know how, and we stand on top of the mountain, free within ourselves." Langston's call to arms helped energize the Niggerati.

Zora would echo "The Negro Artist and the Racial Mountain" in one of *her* finest essays, "How It Feels to Be Colored Me," which was published in the progressive Christian magazine *The World Tomorrow* (edited by Wallace Thurman) in 1928, but was likely written a year or more earlier, as well as in her 1934 essay "The Race Cannot Become Great Until It Recognizes Its Talents." These essays, published for a wide audience, defended black comic and "low" culture and provided a kind of blueprint for Zora and Langston's shared vision of black art and identity.

Yet their points of attack were different. Langston scorned black artists who tried to imitate whites. Zora, on the other hand, scorned black artists who wrote about racial injustice: "I am not tragically colored. . . . I do not belong to the sobbing school of Negrohood who hold that nature somehow has given them a low-down dirty deal and whose feelings are all hurt about it. . . . No, I do not weep at the world—I am too busy sharpening my oyster knife."

Zora was hardly the only writer concerned with this issue. In 1926, *The Crisis* devoted many of its pages to a symposium run by W. E. B. Du Bois dedicated to the questions of "propaganda" and "decadence," the former term connoting literature devoted to racial uplift and the latter a more art-focused depiction of Negro life. In "Criteria of Negro Art," Du Bois wrote, "All art is propaganda and ever must be, despite the wailing of the purists. . . . I do not care a damn for any art that is not used for propaganda." Du Bois even looked down his nose at jazz, blues, and black dance—unless they were transformed into serious art.

Alain Locke took the other side in the debate, publishing three responses in 1927 and 1928 that defended the kind of nonpropaganda work that Langston and Zora were publishing. In "Beauty Instead of Ashes" he argued that "the folk temperament raised to the levels of conscious art promises more originality and beauty" than any sort of group psychology. And in "Art or Propaganda?" he answered Du Bois directly: black "genius and talent . . . must choose art and put aside propaganda."

▼ ▼ ▼

"We do *not* hate white people," Zora once wrote. "We certainly have no wish and desire to kill off the pink-toed rascals. Even if they were not useful as they are, we'd keep 'em for pets." Throughout her life, Zora largely shunned public display of resentment of white folks (her resentment of certain black folks she readily flaunted). The one unforgivable sin for her was self-pity. As her biographer Valerie Boyd points out, "It was, Zora knew, like drinking poison and expecting the other person—the resented one—to die."

Langston, on the other hand, never shrank from writing about racial injustice, and had by this time devoted a number of poems to the subject—"The Little Frightened Child," "The White Ones," "Lament for Dark Peoples," and "I, Too"; in fact, this may have been the biggest ideological difference between the two friends. At the root of this difference was an important difference in their experiences. Zora was very comfortable around those of both races; Langston, however, would admit in 1929, "Only now am I beginning to be at all at ease and without any self-consciousness in meeting my own people." His defense of African Americans against racial injustice stemmed, perhaps, from his own discomfort around them—his fear that he wasn't black enough, and his envy of those who were. As he told the Cuban poet Nicolás Guillén in 1930, "Yo quisiera ser Negro. Bien Negro. ¡Negro de verdad!" ("I'd like to be black. Really black. Truly black!")

By contrast, Zora roundly condemned black writers who wrote about the suffering of their race. Her essay "Art and Such" paints a satirical portrait of a black poet who wants to write "a song to the morning" but can't, because what is expected of him, the "one subject for a Negro," is "the Race and its sufferings." Instead, he writes a poem about a lynching.

A story that both Zora and Fannie Hurst told exemplifies Zora's attitude toward white race prejudice. On their road trips together, they frequently encountered discrimination. Zora was often directed to the servants' quarters at hotels—on the occasions when she wasn't told that there were no vacancies. If Hurst responded that she would also forgo accommodations, Zora quickly responded that it would be impossible for them to travel together if Hurst took that stand. "This is the way it is and I can take care of myself as I have all my life," she told Hurst. "I will find my own lodging and be around with the car in the morning." Hurst later confessed that she was puzzled by Zora's "lack of indignation." So she determined to do something about it.

One day, the two of them stopped at a well-known Westchester County hotel and Hurst, discombobulating the headwaiter, introduced her colorfully dressed companion as "Princess Zora." They were shown to the best seats in the place and given an excellent meal. But later, Zora turned to her companion and said, "Who would think that a good meal could be so bitter."

Telling this tale after an interval of over thirty years, Hurst still failed to grasp the humiliating nature of what she had done.

There was, perhaps, little Zora was prouder of than being an African American woman. To pretend, even for the space of a meal, that she was an African princess so that she could obtain the privileges of a white American was decidedly worse than going hungry because of racial discrimination. Being subject to the injustices perpetrated by white folks did not require Zora to change her identity—in fact, it reinforced it. Her acceptance of separate accommodations, like her proclivity for playing up racial distinctions for white people, was not just second nature to her, but a strategy she employed to hew close to and affirm those distinctions.

One of the main reasons Zora's writing was so savagely criticized by African Americans during her lifetime was the perception that she deliberately avoided anything that smacked of resentment against whites in her published work. In fact, however, each of her first three novels include instances of whites acting superior to African Americans or treating them unjustly and the latter recognizing their mistreatment and dealing with it in their own ways. In addition, Zora contributed three strongly worded essays against discrimination to *Negro Digest*: "My Most Humiliating Jim Crow Experience" (1944); "Crazy for This Democracy" (a forthright and highly sarcastic attack on US imperialism and Jim Crow laws, 1945); and "What White Publishers Won't Print" (1950). If, on the whole, white oppression makes few appearances in Zora's published work, whenever it does she views it through the lenses of humor and protest rather than self-pity, bitterness, or resentment. As she wrote in "How It Feels to Be Colored Me," "Sometimes, I feel discriminated against, but it does not make me angry. It merely astonishes me. How *can* any deny themselves the pleasure of my company! It's beyond me."

Zora claimed, in *Mules and Men*, that the Negro storyteller is "lacking in bitterness . . . in circumstances that ordinarily would call for pity." This observation challenged that of Sterling A. Brown, who had taught in the South. He disapproved of *Mules and Men* for leaving out the anger and hostility so characteristic of the black men and women he knew there. He ended his review of the book by noting that Zora's characters were "naive, quaint, complaisant, bad enough to kill each other in jooks, but meek otherwise, socially unconscious." He mentioned the ills that the people she wrote about faced daily—disease, poverty, filth, violence, lack of education, and the exploitation of their labor. To write about them as if they harbored no resentment seemed false to Brown. He cited his own experience: "These people brood upon their hardships, talk about them 'down by the big-gate,' and some times even at the big house. . . . *Mules and Men* should be more bitter; it would be nearer the total truth." This vein of criticism would be echoed by many of the black writers who encountered Zora's work during her lifetime.

Zora argued that in black folklore "there are no bitter tragic tales at all. When Old Massa won, the thing ended up in a laugh just the same." She could have added that the same is true of the blues. Zora would likely have agreed with Ralph Ellison when he wrote that "the blues are not primarily concerned with civil rights or obvious political protest; they are an art form and thus a transcendence of these conditions."

Moreover, what Zora's black critics failed to grasp was the reason behind Zora's lifelong practice of minimizing the resentment of African Americans in her work. It was a simple one, really: "Bitterness," as she put it in *Dust Tracks on a Road*, "is the graceless acknowledgment of defeat." Zora recognized that those who are bitter and resentful are seen by themselves and others as victims, and the very existence of victims justifies, in a real way, the acts of the victimizers. If you are intent on oppressing a people, you want and expect them to be bitter and resentful; if, instead, they react with good humor and heroism, taking matters into their own hands and ignoring your oppressive acts, you feel frustrated that those acts have failed to crush your intended victims. "I am in the struggle with the sword in my hands," she wrote, "and I don't intend to run until you run me. So why give off the smell of something dead under the house while I am still in there tussling with my sword in my hand?" Whether fools or sages, tricksters or saints, villains or heroes, her characters, by refusing to be victims and by asserting their complete independence from the white world, attained a freedom that the resentful and bitter characters of, say, Richard Wright were forever unable to attain. Having grown up in an all-black town, Zora wanted to show the world that an autonomous black community, led and organized by black people, had no need for bitterness or resentment. They already lived in a kind of utopia.

Zora took pains to explain her stance in a 1943 letter to Countee Cullen:

> Why dont I put something about lynchings in my books? As if all the world did not know about Negroes being lynched! My stand is this: either we must *do* something about it that the white man will understand and respect, or shut up. No whiner ever got any respect or relief. If some of us must die for human justice, then *let us die....* But my own self-respect refuses to let me go to the mourners bench. Our position is like a man sitting on a tack and crying that it hurts, when all he needs to do is get up off it.... I shall never join the cry-babies.

Besides, it was a lot more fun advancing than complaining. As

Zora wrote in "How It Feels to Be Colored Me," "The game of keeping what one has is never so exciting as the game of getting."

▼▼▼

Underlying Langston's and Zora's defiant views of black literary production was their belief in fundamental differences between the Negro and the Nordic, to use terms in contemporaneous use. This belief was widespread among both groups in the 1920s, and backed by many of the latest scientific theories. The idea of the racial superiority of whites was promoted by the likes of the racial anthropologist Lothrop Stoddard (*The Rising Tide of Color Against White World-Supremacy*) and the amateur historian Madison Grant (*The Passing of the Great Race*). Their highly influential beliefs in the threat of "inferior" races to American civilization had a tremendous impact, including the passage of the Immigration Act of 1924, which drastically curtailed immigration quotas. Arnold Rampersad has posited that most of the black writers of the 1920s "accepted the notion of black racial and cultural inferiority compared to the highest standards of European civilization." But Zora and Langston turned this belief on its head, positing that the distinctive characteristics of black expression were in fact superior to those of the "Nordics." They then used this belief to classify black people into two groups. One acted "white"; it included black political leaders, whom they roundly despised. The other was exemplified by "the poor Negro, the real one in the furrows and cane breaks," as Zora put it.

Naturally, these theories of racial difference were countered by the work of other, more sage scientists, in particular her mentor Franz Boas. She had read and admired his work, in which he explained that perceived racial differences are the result of cultural rather than physical differences, in contrast to the pre-

vailing idea that different cultures were at different stages of biological evolution; she was familiar with his studies of American
Indians, which showed that their belief system was as sophisticated and complex as any other, and knew that he thought the
same of African Americans. Yet she chose to ignore the conclusions in his 1911 masterwork *The Mind of Primitive Man*, where, as
he later wrote, he argued that "there is no fundamental difference in the ways of thinking of primitive and civilized man. A
close connection between race and personality has never been
established."

For the majority of Americans of the time, "primitive" societies, including African American, were characterized by a lack of
impulse control and a short attention span, and governed more
by emotion than by reason; Zora shared these ideas, as evidenced
in her essay "The Characteristics of Negro Expression." Boas
had spent his career disproving theories such as these; Zora paid
little heed.

Primitivism was by then a well-established ideology. It had
its roots in colonialism, which reached its apex in the eighteenth
century, with the slave trade funding expansion and empire.
It was blended with exoticism, which glorified the *other,* but it
applied that other to the self: for the primitivists, the exotic
was innate, part of our instincts, and just needed to be set free.
Primitivism was—and remains—part of a nostalgia for a pre-
industrial world.

By the 1920s, primitivism was inextricable from Negrophilia.
The love of everything "Negro"—a category that paradoxically
included jazz, Brazilian rhythms, African carvings, Eskimo art,
and Aboriginal Australian poetry along with Harlem Renaissance literature and art—was sweeping high culture. In post–
World War I France, art, music, literature, and dance were

all utterly suffused with Negrophilia, informed by the latest anthropological findings, and these ideas traveled swiftly to New York.

Primitivism, like racism, promulgated racial differences based on colonialist fantasies. From the bananas that decorated the costumes of Josephine Baker to the jungle rhythms Duke Ellington played at the for-whites-only Cotton Club in Harlem and the jungle-based illustrations of Niggerati members Aaron Douglas and Bruce Nugent, it indulged in tropes associated with the tropics. But the very things that racists denigrated African Americans for, primitivists celebrated. And that celebration became, in the early twentieth century, a central tenet of modernism. In Emily Bernard's words, "Primitivism *was* the avant-garde; it offered artists in a variety of media an exciting new way to think about culture."

In "How It Feels to Be Colored Me," Zora memorably describes a kind of out-of-body experience at the New World Cabaret, a club she frequented with Langston and Van Vechten, among others:

> This orchestra grows rambunctious, rears on its hind legs and attacks the tonal veil with primitive fury, rending it, clawing it until it breaks through to the jungle beyond. I follow those heathen—follow them exultingly. I dance wildly inside myself; I yell within, I whoop; I shake my assegai above my head, I hurl it true to the mark *yeeeeooww!* I am in the jungle and living in the jungle way. My face is painted red and yellow and my body is painted blue. My pulse is throbbing like a war drum. I want to slaughter something—give pain, give death to what, I do not know.

Zora here not only identifies African American culture with hoary stereotypes of the jungle, as did Locke, Charlotte Mason, Cullen, and so many others, but becomes the metaphor herself.

Langston wrote something very similar in his 1923 "Poem"— "All the tom-toms of the jungle beat in my blood. / And all the wild hot moons of the jungles shine in my soul." (Countee Cullen would take the same experience as the main subject of his famous poem "Heritage," written in 1925.) This metaphor had already appeared in Langston's 1922 "Danse Africaine" (both poems were republished in *The Weary Blues*) and would again in "The Negro Artist and the Racial Mountain": "the eternal tom-tom beating in the Negro soul—the tom-tom of revolt against weariness in a white world, a world of subway trains, and work, work, work; the tom-tom of joy and laughter, and pain swallowed in a smile."

Compare Zora's and Langston's descriptions to this one by their friend Carl Van Vechten. In May 1926, Zora took him and a few friends to "a sanctified church in a real estate dealer's office [in Harlem], where there is shoutin', moanin', yelling during & praying hours on end to the music of a cornet & guitar & jumping and dancing. Exactly like the jungle. The guitar plunks a rhythm like a tom-tom."

That's the major difference between primitivists like Zora and Langston and their exoticist contemporaries like Alain Locke, Van Vechten, and the white tourists that the latter shepherded to Harlem. The exoticists take safaris and point at the wildlife, while the primitivists enter the jungle and become its denizens.

And for the African Americans among them, hearing the jungle tom-toms beating in their blood wasn't a matter of proliferating stereotypes but of linking themselves with the mythical home that slavery had robbed them of.

▼ ▼ ▼

Although widely published in the three primary black magazines—*The Crisis, Opportunity,* and *The Messenger*—the writers of
the Niggerati, Langston foremost among them, felt that these
outlets were largely hidebound and stale. Besides, their circulation was tiny: *Opportunity* sold only 11,000 copies per month, with
only about 7,000 to black readers. As Zora put it in a letter to
Alain Locke, " 'The Crisis' is the house org. of the N.A.A.C.P. and
'Opportunity['] is the same to the Urban League. They are in
literature on the side, as it were." A new magazine was called for,
one that would capture their voices—for truly, with their earthy
and unconstrained visions, they were at the vanguard of the new
Negro art. And Langston was to be at the vanguard of this new
magazine, *Fire!!* "Always guiding unobtrusively," as Nugent put
it, it was Langston who suggested that Wallace Thurman be editor, he who insisted that Aaron Douglas do the cover artwork—
in black on red. On "sweltering summer evenings," as Langston
later wrote, the Niggerati met and plotted.

At the end of July, Van Vechten's novel *Nigger Heaven* was published. Its title was taken from the term for the section of the
theater (the balcony) in which black people were forced to sit;
as the balcony was to the theater, Harlem was to Manhattan. It
was far from the first well-intentioned white literary work to use
the "n-word" in its title: it was preceded by Joseph Conrad's 1897
novella *The Nigger of the Narcissus,* Edward Sheldon's 1909 play *The
Nigger,* Clement Wood's 1922 novel *Nigger,* and Ronald Firbank's
1924 novel *Prancing Nigger* (whose title had been suggested by
Van Vechten himself). A literary effort to portray and promote
the infinite variety of Harlem's culture, *Nigger Heaven* was successful: it received high praise from literati like H. L. Mencken,

Sinclair Lewis, and F. Scott Fitzgerald; it sold 100,000 copies, more than any other Harlem Renaissance novel, and not only to white readers. Langston wrote to Alain Locke that "colored people can't help but like it," and his mother pronounced it "our people to a 'T'"; Charles Johnson and James Weldon Johnson gave it laudatory reviews. (A few months later, after a lawsuit was filed against Van Vechten for using a copyrighted song without permission, Langston wrote over a dozen lyrics for the seventh and subsequent printings of the novel.) But W. E. B. Du Bois savaged it in *The Crisis,* writing, "Life to [Van Vechten] is just one orgy after another, with hate, hurt, gin, and sadism," and recommending that the book be dropped in the sewer. Harlem newspapers refused to advertise it, criticizing it for its mangling of black dialect and its obsession with the most sordid aspects of Harlem's nightlife; a rumor went around that Van Vechten had been hanged in effigy on Lenox Avenue; and to his great chagrin he was barred from Small's nightclub—though they let him back in when Zora accompanied him. Van Vechten biographer Edward White writes, "As many black people saw it, a wealthy white man from downtown had come up to tear around Harlem and then taunted its inhabitants with a book portraying black life as dripping in sex and drugs and violence, capping it off with the most offensive word possible."

Nigger Heaven is a clumsy and sensationalist novel about the clash between the black middle-class and the new hedonists of the Harlem scene. Its message is clear: no compromise between the two camps is possible. In that, it affirmed one of the central premises of Langston's "The Negro Artist and the Racial Mountain" and Zora's "The Characteristics of Negro Expression." There was an uncrossable divide between the generation of W. E. B. Du Bois and that of Josephine Baker.

David Levering Lewis argues that the "unmistakable message" of the novel is encapsulated in the words spoken by a character named Lasca Sartoris: "Negroes aren't any worse off than anybody else. They're better off if anything. They have the same privileges that white women had before the bloody fools got the ballot. They're considered irresponsible like children and treated with special fondness." Certain of the Niggerati shared that point of view—particularly Zora, who gloried in, cultivated, and considered herself deserving of the advantages of differential treatment. The black critic Emily Bernard, on the other hand, says that the novel's "central lesson" is that "blacks must hold on to their true savage selves or risk something worse than neurosis—annihilation." This affirmation of primitivism— "a birthright that all the civilized races were struggling to get back to," in Van Vechten's words—was catnip to the Niggerati, who had placed themselves in opposition to the more "civilized" members of their race.

The Niggerati rallied around Van Vechten. After all, they had been to so many of his parties that Walter White, who would soon be head of the NAACP, referred to Van Vechten's apartment as the organization's midtown branch; it was a place where black and white editors, writers, artists, and philanthropists could mix freely with each other, and the Niggerati—especially Zora and Langston—attended frequently. Moreover, Van Vechten had done far more for the Harlem Renaissance writers, artists, and musicians than any other of his race, getting them published, publicizing them in *Vanity Fair,* and introducing them to white high society—all without condescension or sycophancy. The attacks on Van Vechten were attacks on everything the Niggerati believed in—the validity of native black expression; the refusal to idealize black life; the freedom to live, create, and behave in ways that the black middle class frowned upon. The new magazine, *Fire!!*, would be their vindication.

As Langston would later relate, seven of the Niggerati—Langston, Zora, Aaron Douglas, Bennett, Davis, Thurman, and Nugent, in the order they would be listed on *Fire!!*'s Board of Editors' letterhead—gathered one night to found "a Negro quarterly of the arts to *épater le bourgeois*, to burn up a lot of the stereotyped Uncle Tom ideas of the past, and to provide us with an outlet for publishing not existing in the hospitable but limited pages of *The Crisis* or *Opportunity*." (It's unclear exactly where they gathered. Langston wrote that it was at Aaron Douglas's apartment at 409 Edgecombe in Sugar Hill, but Douglas didn't move there until 1934.) Each was to contribute fifty dollars toward production expenses—no small amount in those days.

Thurman was an inspired choice as editor. "Strangely brilliant," as Langston described him, he "had read everything ... because he could read eleven lines at a time." He criticized everything he read, yet could take nothing truly seriously. His energy, dedication, high standards, and insouciance were critical to *Fire!!*'s publication.

Two days before the magazine was to go to press, Bruce Nugent visited Zora. They had a philosophical conversation about subjectivity and objectivity; Nugent said, "Over collards and black-eyed peas and things, Zora would have these philosophical conversations sometimes." That day Nugent discovered that Zora's brother Everett had accidentally burned up the proofs of his story "Smoke, Lilies and Jade," which had been lying around her apartment; she did her best to comfort him, and then he "took a roll of toilet paper and several paper bags and got on the subway and wrote the thing over again." He would never have done this without Zora's encouragement, he said, "because

I wouldn't have believed I could have done it. But with Zora, there was no question. You can do it." He was only nineteen, and Zora and Langston were the only people he knew "who could say that this was good, bad, or indifferent, and I would listen, I mean really listen."

In the end, only $150 was collected (none coming from Zora, who was broke), and *Fire!!*, subtitled "A Quarterly Devoted to the Younger Negro Artists," was finally published in November, costing Thurman $1,000, for which he was dunned on his subsequent earnings. "We got carried away with ourselves," Langston wrote, "and our taste proved extremely expensive"—the issue was printed on "the best cream white paper" with "a rich crimson jacket on de luxe stock." Zora's work was more heavily represented in the journal than that of any other writer; Thurman had even considered putting a pseudonym in place of her name at the top of her play *Color Struck* so that *Fire!!* wouldn't seem too "Zora-ish." The magazine only lasted one issue due to lack of funds, and hundreds of unsold copies would literally go up in flames; but it was one of the most exciting publications of the Harlem Renaissance.

For in *Fire!!* the Niggerati were showcasing their literary innovations, which followed Langston's and Zora's lead. Indeed, Bruce Nugent believed that of all the magazine's contributors, only Zora and Langston had a sense of its historical importance. For them, black language, whether derived from traditional dialect or urban slang, was no longer to be used only for local color, humor, and stagy effects. It could be the foundation of a new art, a way to express the most profound visions. By basing their art on black folklore and music, Zora and Langston were reinventing black culture on their own terms, avoiding dependence on white literary models. Certainly not all the Niggerati followed this impulse—Countee Cullen's prosody and vocabulary were practically indistinguishable from Edna St. Vincent Millay's (he wrote his master's thesis on her work and called her his "goddess"). But Langston and Zora were leading the charge toward change.

Fire!!'s value, however, lay not only in its prosody, but in its subject matter. The journal opened with a foreword penned by Langston and Thurman (though unsigned) that ran, in part, "FIRE...weaving vivid, hot designs upon an ebon bordered loom and satisfying pagan thirst for beauty unadorned...the flesh is sweet and real" (ellipses in original). Immediately following the table of contents was Nugent's drawing of a nude black woman leaning against a palm tree; facing it was Thurman's story "Cordelia the Crude," about a licentious sixteen-year-old would-be prostitute. Nugent's "novel" "Smoke, Lilies and Jade," the very long prose poem that he wrote on toilet paper and paper bags, describes in part the physical ecstasy enjoyed by two male lovers, and quotes eight lines from a poem about a mercurial and attractive man that he attributes to Langston (if Langston indeed wrote it, it would be his most openly homosexual poem). Bennett's story "Wedding Day" was about a black man in Paris who hated white Americans and habitually beat and shot them, but was then seduced by a heartless white American girl. Zora's chilling story "Sweat" was about the revenge of a mistreated wife, and was as earthy as its title.

In other words, *Fire!!* was mainly about black sex and black sin. Steven Watson, one of the most perceptive of Harlem Renaissance historians, puts it this way: "It celebrated jazz, paganism, blues, androgyny, unassimilated black beauty, free-form verse, homosexuality—precisely the 'uncivilized' features of Harlem proletarian culture that the Talented Tenth propagandists preferred to ignore. *Fire!!* offered an alternative manifesto to *The New Negro*, undiluted by sociopolitical issues and race-building efforts."

As Nugent would later testify, its editors aimed to get *Fire!!* banned in Boston. "Wally and I sat around figuring out," Nugent told Hemenway, "what two things just will not take. Well, we'll write about a street walker or a whore, and we'll write a homosexual story. . . . So we flipped a coin to see which one of us would do which."

As for Zora's contributions, *Color Struck* was less incendiary than "Sweat." The story centers around a married couple, Delia and Sykes, who have come to hate each other; after Sykes brings home a rattlesnake to torture Delia, she gets her deadly revenge when she leaves the escaped snake in the bed. Delia's murderous inaction is fully justified by her mistreatment; indeed, though she may not know it, the whole town has taken her side. Women, this chilling tale seems to say, are better off without men around.

And when it came to attacking the black Americans who had attacked Van Vechten's *Nigger Heaven*, *Fire!!* minced no words. Its penultimate piece was Arthur Huff Fauset's essay "Intelligentsia," a frontal attack on that class. (Fauset, Jessie Fauset's twenty-eight-year-old half-brother, had studied African American anthropology under Alain Locke and had collected animal tales in the Mississippi Delta; his scholarly work might have served as a model for Zora's.) This was followed by Thurman's "Fire Burns," a sarcasm-laden dismissal of those who attacked the novel. As Emily Bernard writes, *Nigger Heaven* "had done more for [the writers of *Fire!!*] than it had done for its author. It enabled members of the younger generation to distinguish themselves from their predecessors. It had become their cackling chuckle of contempt."

When the magazine was published at the end of October 1926, its reception was predictably mixed. Publicly, W. E. B. Du Bois said little about it, acknowledging its receipt and calling it "a beautiful piece of printing... strikingly illustrated"; privately, however, he took it as a personal attack (one journalist made the mistake of mentioning *Fire!!* first thing when he visited Du Bois, which "hurt his feelings so much that he would hardly talk to me"), and Langston was under the impression that he had "roasted it." The *Baltimore Afro-American* began its review, entitled "Writer Brands 'Fire' as Effeminate Tommyrot," "I have just tossed the first issue of *Fire!!*—into the fire and watched the crackling flames leap and snarl as though they were trying to swallow some repulsive dose," and went on, "Langston Hughes displays his usual ability to say nothing in many words." The Civic Club, on the other hand, invited Langston, Zora, Thurman, and Bennett to read from the magazine at a tea party. And Alain Locke published a largely positive review in *The Survey*: "A good deal of it is reflected Sherwood Anderson, Sinclair Lewis, Dreiser, Joyce and Cummings, recast in the context of Negro life and experience."

All that would happen later. Back in September, Langston had to return to Pennsylvania for another year at college, but not before doing some serious partying. For example, on the 14th, Carl Van Vechten and his wife Fania Marinoff were dining at his friend Eddie Wasserman's house when Zora dropped by, followed by Langston accompanied by the socialite and impresario Caroline Dudley Reagan. Van Vechten proceeded, in his words, to get "very drunk & abusive & finally I passed out." Then they all went back to Van Vechten's place and stayed until three.

Four days later, Zora cooked a dinner in Langston's honor—and Zora was, in Bruce Nugent's words, "a phenomenally good cook." The guests included her brother Everett, a cousin of hers, Van Vechten, Marinoff, Reagan, and the composer J. Rosamond Johnson (James Weldon's brother; he had set some of Langston's songs to music, and they were planning to write a revue together). Then, two nights later, Langston and some classmates threw a party at Small's to help raise funds for their tuition; Van Vechten was there, of course, as were Ethel Waters, Countee Cullen, and likely Zora.

Did they say goodbye that night? We don't know. But Langston would come back to New York on weekends quite frequently. It would have been impossible for him to stay away.

4

SPRING 1927

Enter Godmother

Charlotte Osgood Mason seemed to strike almost everyone who met her as some sort of goddess. She instructed people to call her "Godmother," and indeed, if one split that word into its constituent parts and joined them with an ampersand, it would describe well how her acolytes regarded her. (In fact, Zora once called her "My Mother-God," and another time her "true conceptual Mother—not a biological accident.") Zora was given to flattery in her letters, but her worshipful missives to Mason read as if they had been addressed to a pagan idol. "You renew your promise to the world," she wrote her on Mason's birthday in May 1930, and compared her to Persephone, the Greek goddess of spring, not to mention Jesus:

> May I, on your emergence day sing with my broken harp the small song of love that I am able to sing? . . . Oh, my lovely just-born flower, if back there when you fluttered pink into this drab world—if they had but known how much joy and love you would/should bring! How much of the white light of God

you would diffuse into soft radiance for the eyes of the primitives, the wise ones would have stood awed before your cradle
and brought great gifts from afar. I am not very wise but let me
lay the gift of eternal devotion within your little manger. . . .

It is you who gives out life and light and we who
receive. . . .

I wish I knew how many you have dragged from ever-
lasting unseeing to heaven!

Zora was hardly alone in her effusions; numerous beneficiaries
of Godmother's generosity shared Zora's sense of devotion to a
miraculous presence.

Even back in 1923, before Mason began bankrolling the major
black writers and artists of her time, the white Chicago writer
Blanche Matthias described their first encounter like this:

> The little figure of ivory face and white, white hair with lilac
> dress and softest film of lace about the throat was very exqui-
> site, very serene and outpouring. . . . Gently she stroked my
> hand and face and then our eyes met and I saw the flame
> leap up, blue as the mysterious color which springs first from
> the burning log before it changes to violet and orange and
> then vanishes up the chimney to be lost in a gray wandering
> wraith of spent energy. That blue flame is the Godmother. . . .
> I was fortified and inspired when I left, and . . . I carried the
> thought of her sweetness and strength with me like a magic
> talisman which I could touch at will, and with it open the
> door to some of life's great visions and activities.

But this devotion wasn't just what Mason inspired—it was what
she demanded. If they treated her like a god, she behaved like one

too. She was not just a god of love, "never forgetting a minutiae of their daily lives and . . . interesting herself fully in every detail of their struggles," as Carla Kaplan, whose *Miss Anne in Harlem* includes the fullest depiction of Mason's extraordinary career, puts it. She was also a jealous god, controlling and wrathful.

▾▾▾

Mason was born Charlotte van der Veer Quick in 1854, the product of a wealthy family. In 1886, she married Rufus Osgood Mason, a famous physician twenty-four years her senior. He practiced parapsychology and hypnotherapy; his books include *Telepathy and the Subliminal Self.* Many of his patients believed he had cured them through psychic healing, and his wife adopted his beliefs and practices. Moreover, she viewed him, especially after his death in 1905, as a messianic figure, and published an allegorical, religious, and lyrical essay about him, "The Passing of a Prophet," two years later.

She also believed that American Negroes and Indians were "younger races unspoiled by white civilization" whose primitive creativity and spirituality would energize and renew America. After Dr. Mason died, leaving to her his vast wealth, she spent months traveling the Southwest and living with Native Americans. One acolyte, Louise Thompson (who would play a major role in Zora and Langston's lives) wrote that Mason "used to secretly listen to some of the rituals and ceremonies that no outsiders were supposed to witness[;] she told me about crawling through the shrubbery . . . and listening to these ancient rites." Mason also helped Natalie Curtis publish *The Indians' Book*, a groundbreaking and enduring study of Native American culture and music, in 1907. The book concludes with a paragraph that Mason wrote herself; it encapsulates her philosophy perfectly.

Let us recognize in all things the value of our opposites. Old age seems justly to be the summing-time of life, the only philosophic decade; yet should we never forget the child nor the child-race who live so near to God that truth flows to them from a still untainted channel. For of such is the Kingdom of Heaven. Do we tend to become a people continually busy with the world's affairs, let us remember that the sources of spiritual truth have arisen oftenest among the contemplative peoples of the Orient, and let us then turn to the contemplative dark-skinned natives of our own land. If not in the hope and expectancy that are born of friendship, at least with tolerance and without scepticism let us stop long enough to hear the broken fragments of a message which they might have brought in its entirety to all their brethren in the world.

Primitivism, the cure for the ills of civilization, was one of Mason's passions; the other was controlling the lives of her "godchildren." She even went so far as to ask them to record, in intimate detail, "all things financial, domestic, nutritional, and digestive . . . every penny spent, every piece of linen purchased, every calorie consumed, each bodily waste emitted." As Kaplan writes, "She *craved* people. She lived for the moments when she could see into someone's soul and divine just how his or her life should be lived."

After *The Indians' Book*, Mason dedicated herself for a time to the education of Katherine and Cornelia Chapin, sisters of eighteen and fifteen when Mason entered their lives in 1908. The three would live together for the next thirty years, with occasional separations. Cornelia was a sculptor and Katherine a poet; Katherine's husband, Francis Biddle, whom Mason introduced to her, would soon be chairman of the National Labor Relations Board, and in 1941 would become US Attorney General. The Chapins and the Biddles were from the old Philadelphia aristocracy. They were so close to Charlotte Mason that she even accompanied Katherine and Francis on their honeymoon in 1918 and wore a matching third ring. Katherine and Cornelia behaved around Mason like cultists behave around their messiah figure. All of Katherine's friends had to listen to the advice of Godmother, whom she nicknamed "Precious." Kaplan writes, "She hated to be separated from 'Precious' even for a night. They often shared a bed, lying awake for hours to talk, read, and plan Katherine's life, down to the last detail of the linen she would order and how it would be stored." When Kaplan interviewed their relative Schuyler Chapin, who had been the Metropolitan Opera's general manager and Columbia University's dean of the arts, he repeatedly mentioned Godmother's "unusual personal powers" and "how intimidating he had found [her] and how impossible it seemed to him to so much as disagree with her."

Mason told Matthias in 1923, "That is the reward of being a godmother, to share the ecstasy of first moments with her children." Apparently, Mason had cultivated numerous godchildren by then—"lovely brown-eyed Cornelia [Chapin], and the artist who paints bashful fancies which come to him in the candle light; there is a handsome African of royal family, a full-blooded Indian from some place in Arizona, and before her death, there was Natalie Curtis"—each earning her trust and financial support through their hard work and seeking spirit, each the recipient, one supposes, of florid letters and telegrams like those Mason sent Matthias and, later, Langston.

By 1927, she was ready for a new avenue for her philanthropy—

she had for the past few years been sending money to black
schools in the South, but that was without personal connections.
She was craving more godchildren. And that was when Alain
Locke entered her life.

▾▾▾

On February 6, 1927, Charlotte Mason attended a lecture Locke
was giving to open an exhibit of African art in a gallery on West
57th Street. Locke's views on this art were quite different from
those of most white patrons, who had for decades been excited
about its capacity to evoke a savage, jungle race. For Locke, there
was nothing "primitive" about African art—it was "rigid, controlled, disciplined, abstract, heavily conventionalized, . . . sophisticated, laconic and fatalistic." The *American* Negro, he wrote, was
a different beast altogether: "free, exuberant, emotional, senti-
mental and human." Locke believed that African American artists had a great deal to learn from African art, and thought they
should "move in the direction of a racial school of art."

Mason was by then a major collector of African art. In her
apartment were weapons, masks, drinking vessels, and head-
dresses; other artworks were in her safe-deposit box. That day—
which they would both celebrate as their anniversary—she was
introduced to Locke after his lecture. Immediately she felt a "tremendous rapport." Locke asked Mason for permission to call on
her and, a few days later, on February 16, had tea with her in her
twelve-room apartment at 399 Park Avenue. There, after inviting
him to sit in a chair that belonged to her great-great-grandfather
and giving him a $500 check so that he could start working on
opening a museum of African art in Harlem, she asked him to
introduce her to some of the young black artists and writers he
was telling her about.

He did so immediately. At Carnegie Hall, where Langston and Carl Van Vechten were attending a performance of Negro spirituals that day, Locke presented Langston to this short, elderly, white-haired, beautifully dressed white woman.

Mason and Locke quickly developed a long list of African Americans to rescue. Jean Toomer, the author of *Cane*, was one prospect (Toomer had by then turned his back on both literature and his race and was now on a quest for a higher state of consciousness via methods taught by the mystic George Gurdjieff, but Mason thought it her duty to bring him back to his true "flowing spirit" and "miraculous power"). Locke was to offer assistance to actor Paul Robeson and tenor Roland Hayes, though they hardly needed it, considering their success (both steadily resisted receiving any assistance from Mason, Robeson rightly thinking she wanted to control his career). Other choices, however, came to fruition, among them the anthropologist Arthur Huff Fauset, the composer Hall Johnson, the illustrator Miguel Covarrubias, and the writer Claude McKay, all of whom came to see her—and accepted her checks. Altogether, Mason would end up giving between $50,000 and $75,000 to her black protégés (multiply that by ten to get today's equivalent). Mason did not, however, approve of *all* of Harlem's black literati. James Weldon Johnson, W. E. B. Du Bois, and sculptor Richmond Barthé were all too closely allied to the white world for her taste.

It wasn't long before Mason would conceive of *herself* as black—"I am eternally black," she would write to Locke, who couldn't fulfill his potential unless he too could "slough off this weight of white culture." Locke held whatever distaste he may have had for her pronouncements in reserve; he was unfailingly deferential, and his reverence for her—over the course of almost twenty years—was profound. He had, in Bruce Nugent's words, an "almost arbitrary way . . . of selecting who was good and who wasn't good" for Godmother. Among the Niggerati, Locke was called the "mother hen."

And while Mason's beneficiaries initially shared Locke's reverence, Godmother would become an object of satire just a few years later, even among those who had loved her the most.

▼▼▼

Around the same time as Locke met Godmother, Zora was turning to a subject she had rarely before written about: Harlem. She composed four stories set there for the black weekly *Pittsburgh Courier,* one of the two leading black newspapers in the country (the other was the *Chicago Defender*), which were published in February and March 1927. And one of the stories, "The Back Room," not only was a vivid portrait of Harlem high society but also, in part, seems like a self-portrait. It is one of her most revealing—and saddest—stories. (Unfortunately, it was inadvertently omitted from *The Complete Stories by Zora Neale Hurston*, and has never been republished in the United States.)

The *Courier* billed it as "A Gripping Story of the Life of New York Society from Twilight to Dawn and a Woman Who Had Reached the 'Dangerous Age.'" This woman is named Lilya Barkman, "born Lillie Barker," and these names, like her character and situation, clearly echo "Lily Bart," the protagonist of Edith Wharton's 1905 novel *The House of Mirth*, whose fruitless attempts to get married end in tragedy. (Barkman was also the name of a friend Zora made in 1925.) "The Back Room" is very clearly fiction, not autobiography, but certain parallels between Lilya Barkman and Zora Hurston (such as the same last letters of their names) are telling. Lilya, like Zora, shaved years off her age—Lilya "was thirty-eight, though she never declared a day over twenty-five." Both were unmarried, and Lilya, at least, was ready for that to change—she had waited long enough. Her plans, though, as developed over the course of the evening, come to nought but heartbreak. In the end, as she looks at a portrait of herself painted years before, it seems to say to her, "I am youth, and beauty. I know nothing, feel nothing, except the things that belong to me." On the other hand, Lilya, now older, feels too much, and has lost too much.

Like Lilya, Zora rarely let her lonely side show; this story is one of the very few suggestions we have of it. But there is another suggestion too, from around the same time. In December 1926, Zora had sent Langston a Christmas card—her first correspondence with him. On it, she wrote, "Thank you, thank you dear Langston. You warmed me tremendously in my dark hour. I shall never forget."

Was it that loneliness, that fear of ending up like Lilya Barkman, that prompted Zora in May 1927 to marry Herbert Sheen, the medical student she had dated when she attended Howard seven or eight years earlier? They tied the knot in St. Augustine, Florida, where she was attempting to collect folklore, and where Sheen joined her from Chicago, where he was studying. She immediately regretted it. As she wrote him years later, the night before he arrived a dream "cast a dark shadow" over her. "A dark barrier kept falling between us, and I sat up with the voice of your sister Mildred calling my name in most unfriendly terms commanding me to leave you alone. Leave you alone or suffer severe penalties. It was as vivid as noon, and it haunted me for a very long time.... We appeared like shadowy figures seen through an opal. It was terrible. Therefore, I was not surprised when something came between us." According to her autobiography, she wondered on her wedding night, "Who had cancelled the well-advertised tour of the moon? . . . What I had taken for eternity turned out to be a moment walking in its sleep." After a few days, Sheen, who had no taste for folklore collecting, went back to Rush Medical College. The marriage was all but over. Though he would visit her in September, and even played piano at Carl Van Vechten's, by early January 1928, as she wrote to Langston, she had definitively broken off relations. And she told few people about the whole affair.

No evidence suggests that Langston played a part in Zora's disappointment. But, given her Christmas card, it's possible that at this point her emotional attachment to him was stronger than that to her husband. And only two or three months after her wedding, that attachment would be firmly cemented.

▼▼▼

Langston, meanwhile, was undergoing a whipping of sorts at the hands of the black intelligentsia. His *Fine Clothes to the Jew* had just been published in January; it was a collection of lyric poems, many of them straightforward blues lyrics, about lower- and working-class black men and women. The blues, as Langston knew very well, was one of the few unalloyed modes of African American expression. Spirituals were in part derived from Methodist hymns; ragtime owed a great deal to European pianism; jazz came, to some extent, out of military bands. But the blues owed next to nothing to white culture. In writing his blues-derived poetry, Langston was taking his own advice in "The Negro Artist and the Racial Mountain," as well as reenacting his symbolic action on board the boat to Africa—he was rejecting white conventions of literacy and creating a purely black art.

The book's title, likely suggested by Van Vechten (the dedicatee of the volume), was unfortunate: the book's second poem is a blues about a man who had to pawn his clothes, and in black parlance of the time a pawnbroker was "the Jew." Samuel Knopf, publisher Alfred A. Knopf's father, insisted in vain that it be changed, and Langston later regretted not doing so. (Langston was by no means anti-Semitic, and, as noted earlier, was part Jewish himself.) But the book itself was a triumph: beautifully organized, clear-eyed and empathetic, simple yet profound in its affirmation of the black *volksgeist*. As Arnold Rampersad writes, *Fine Clothes* "was Hughes's poorest selling but perhaps most important single work, a breakthrough in black literary culture on a par, in its own way, with the effect of Whitman's 'scandalous' *Leaves of Grass* of 1855." The book remains largely ignored, though, and is currently out of print.

Predictably, the black, not the Jewish, press opened fire on Langston. The story in the New York *Amsterdam News* was headlined "LANGSTON HUGHES—THE SEWER DWELLER"; his book was "100 pages of trash." The *Chicago Whip* called it "unsanitary, insipid and repulsing"; the *Philadelphia Tribune* called it "a study in the perversions of the Negro"; and it made the historian who reviewed it for the *Pittsburgh Courier* "positively sick." Benjamin Brawley, perhaps the most respected black critic in America, would soon write, "It would have been just as well, perhaps better, if the book had never been published. No other ever issued reflects more fully the abandon and the vulgarity of its age." There were exceptions: Locke published a rave in the *Saturday Review of Literature*, *The Crisis* called it "the outstanding book of the month," and sympathetic reviews appeared in the *Chicago Defender*, *Washington Eagle*, *New York Age*, and *Messenger*. But the overall reception was hostile.

Langston was quick to respond, writing an essay entitled "These Bad New Negroes: A Critique on Critics." In it he not only offered a point-by-point defense of his book, but also defended the work of Zora, Jean Toomer, Rudolph Fisher, Eric Walrond, John F. Matheus, Wallace Thurman, Countee Cullen, and poet Edward Silvera, along with Locke's *New Negro* anthology, Van Vechten's *Nigger Heaven*, and DuBose Heyward's *Porgy*. His argument was similar to the one he had made in "The Negro Artist and the Racial Mountain": he called his critics *nouveau riche* and defended the New Negro writers as "humble people." The essay would be published in the *Pittsburgh Courier*, which had labeled his poems "trash," on March 22.

In the midst of such a shellacking, it's no wonder Langston would be more receptive than ever to anyone who would defend his affinity for, as he would put it in *The Big Sea*, "the masses of our people." Ten days after Langston had first met Mason at Carnegie Hall, Alain Locke brought him up to her apartment, "with attendants in livery at the door and a private elevator-landing." (Mason also had at least two maids and probably a butler too, all white.) "I found her instantly one of the most delightful women I had ever met, witty and charming, kind and sympathetic, very old and white-haired, but amazingly modern in her ideas, in her knowledge of books and the theater, of Harlem, and of everything then taking place in the world." There, with a view of practically all of New York spread beneath them, she spoke to Langston about her project: "a mystical vision," as she later wrote, "of a great bridge reaching from Harlem to the heart of Africa, across which the Negro world, that our white United States had done everything to annihilate, should see the flaming pathway . . . and recover the treasure their people had had in the beginning of African life on the earth."

The meeting was a success. Langston found himself just as

spellbound as Locke had been. Mason showed him her art collection—"every piece was rare and beautiful"—then spoke of socialism, the Negro, American culture. And Langston impressed Mason too: his Native American lineage, inherited from his maternal grandparents; his innocence; his fine looks. As Langston was about to leave, she handed him a fifty-dollar bill, "a gift for a young poet." He turned to Locke as they went out the door and asked him, "Who is this woman? How does she know so much about us?"

Langston came back to New York for the long Easter weekend and went to Mason's apartment on April 16, again accompanied by Locke. As they left, Locke whispered to Langston, "Mask in one pocket, thick white envelope in another," a cynical comment on the kind of hustle he believed he'd introduced Langston to. Mason—or, more likely, one of her companions, since she was somewhat deaf—overheard the remark, and she was rather upset with Locke. So the next time Langston visited, a month later, on May 22, he came alone. They dined on duck, wild rice, and ice cream with fresh strawberries; they talked for hours. Langston wrote that Mason asked him "about my plans for the future, my hopes, my ambitions, and my dreams. I told her I wanted to write a novel. She told me she would make it possible."

Mason would later remember this visit as "our first real hours together," doubtless since Locke wasn't present. As she wrote in a letter to Langston on June 5 (her earliest dated letter to him), he was, for her, "my winged poet Child who as he flies through my mind is a noble silent Indian Chief—a shining messenger of hope for his people—and then again a precious simple little boy with his pocket full of bright colored marbles—looking up at me with his dear and blessing eyes."

She also wrote him an undated note, probably early in their relationship, that reads in full:

> My precious Boy,
>
> The holiness of that beautiful light you gave me so graciously and generously before you left the car still moves near me. Nothing touches its amazing beauty. But now—Dear Child—comes this magical wonder you wrought last night through the radiant sustaining force of your presence!!
>
> What can "Godmother" say!

As Carla Kaplan has justly observed, "If Locke was her designated lieutenant, Langston Hughes was Mason's first true black love. She considered him flawless."

Godmother's letters would continue to be just as effusive for years, and in exactly this vein. Langston was in every way her child, and she was full of motherly advice, including on how he could make time to write and on what he ate (plenty of fresh fruits and vegetables); but Godmother was even more given to high-flown praise. "The Gods be praised Langston your work is wonderful! . . . It is the same thing as when the Navajos induced the Colorado River to cut the Grand Canyon. And then it is made whole by the negro warmth and tenderness at the loves of your Precious Heart." Occasionally her adoration of Langston would go far beyond her usual effusion: "You know your 'Godmother' becomes a very little girl when she listens to any [illegible] you may drift across the pages of your letters. Have you any idea how good Godmother is when she is so hungry? But all the hunger in the world cannot compare to my belief & hope in this precious Child of my old age."

The letters are so numerous and so much in this vein that even when she opened a letter with "I greet thee Morning Star with a full heart of love & belief as you rise this morning still unknown in the hearts of your audience," it could not have surprised him.

By the time her June 5 "winged poet Child" letter reached him, though, Langston was in the South.

5

SUMMER 1927

The Company of Good Things

Ornate and imposing, the century-old Gulf, Mobile and Ohio Passenger Terminal in downtown Mobile, Alabama, resembles a cross between a Venetian palace and a Spanish mission. Here, on St. Joseph Street, on July 23, 1927, one of the more fortuitous meetings in American literary history occurred, a chance incident that would seal the friendship of two of its most influential writers. "No sooner had I got off the train" from New Orleans, Langston wrote in *The Big Sea*, "than I ran into Zora Neale Hurston, walking intently down the main street. I didn't know she was in the South [actually, he did, having received a letter from her in March, but he had no idea she was in Alabama], and she didn't know I was either, so we were very glad to see each other."

Zora was in town to interview Cudjo Lewis, purportedly the only person still living who had been born in Africa and enslaved in the United States. She then planned to drive back to New York, doing folklore research along the way. In late 1926,

Franz Boas had recommended her to Carter Woodson, whose Association for the Study of Negro Life and History, together with Elsie Clews Parsons of the American Folklore Society, had decided to bankroll her to the tune of $1,400. With these funds, Zora had been gathering folklore in Florida all spring and summer. As the first Southern black to do this, her project was, even at this early stage, clearly of immense importance. It had, however, been frustrating. "I knew where the material was, all right," she would later write. "But I went about asking, in carefully accented Barnardese, 'Pardon me, but do you know any folk-tales or folk-songs?' The men and women who had whole treasuries of material just seeping through their pores, looked at me and shook their heads. No, they had never heard of anything like that around there. Maybe it was over in the next county. Why didn't I try over there?"

Langston, meanwhile, had been touring the South for months, penniless as usual, making some public appearances and doing his own research. He read his poems at commencement for Nashville's Fisk University in June; he visited refugees from the Mississippi flood in Baton Rouge; he strolled the streets alone in New Orleans, ducking into voodoo shops; he took a United Fruit boat to Havana and back; and his next stop was to be the Tuskegee Institute in Alabama. It was his very first visit to the South.

When Zora invited him to join her expedition in her little old Nash coupe, nicknamed "Sassy Susie," Langston happily accepted. (The car looked a lot like a Model T Ford, and could only seat two.) Langston adored the company of entertainers, and Zora was as entertaining as they came. Langston did not know how to drive, but Zora loved driving and didn't mind a whit. They decided to make a real trip of it, "stopping on the way to pick up folk-songs, conjur [*sic*], and big old lies," as Langston wrote. "Blind guitar players, conjur men, and former slaves were her quarry, small town jooks and plantation churches, her haunts. I knew it would be fun traveling with her. It was."

The road trip provided the perfect opportunity for Zora and Langston to compare notes from their Southern travels, exchange ideas, and explore, along the back roads, the characteristics of African American culture that informed their greatest work. They had both kept meticulous records of songs, sayings, turns of phrase; they related their impressions of conjure wisdom, including the names of potions and powders; they delighted in the cultural riches of their Southern black brethren. Zora told Langston all about her terribly disappointing marriage in St. Augustine two months earlier to her old flame Herbert Sheen; perhaps she also told Langston that her second thoughts had begun the moment she said, "I do." Langston told Zora all about his infatuation with Godmother. As they drew closer, the writers shared not only their knowledge, ideas, and feelings, but also their food and money. True traveling companions, they had the time of their lives.

▾▾▾

Misconceptions about the South of the 1920s come naturally to us. We imagine it strictly segregated; while that was true of schools, hotels, and practically everything to do with transportation, the races lived in much closer proximity to each other than in the North, and it was rare to find an all-white or all-black community. "Sundown towns," where no black people were allowed after sundown, became increasingly common all over the United States between the end of Reconstruction and the end of segregation, but in the 1920s there weren't yet many in the South. In general, black and white neighbors attended each others' churches, played ball together, visited each others' homes, and helped each other through crises of sickness and death—even as white southerners maintained political, social, and economic control over most black lives through lynchings, disenfranchisement, and unfair labor practices. We imagine black southerners as poor sharecroppers, chain-gang workers, and itinerant bluesmen, and certainly the disparity in income between the races was enormous—not to mention the constant threat of white-on-black violence. But the majority of black southerners, who comprised some eighty percent of the nation's African American population, were not prisoners, fugitives, or roustabouts. They were churchgoing, upstanding citizens, as interested in their children's education and the possibilities of economic advancement as any white person might be. In the 1930s, Zora would play a major role in canonizing black Southern folklore, and the picture she painted of rural Southern life would be reinforced by Hollywood's image of Southern Negroes in rags, the rural focus of the Federal Works Progress Administration in the 1940s, the search for forgotten bluesmen in the 1950s, and the murders of civil rights workers in the 1960s. As a result of this focus on the rural and the downtrodden, we sometimes forget about the myriad black educators, businessmen, theatergoers, ministers, jazz musicians, doctors, dentists, carpenters, and skilled workers that filled Southern cities and towns.

Across the South, the summer of 1927 was marked by a growing recognition that the great exodus of African Americans to the North represented an economic threat that had to be dealt with. Alabama enacted a statute prohibiting the inducement of workers to leave the state "through grandiose promises of economic and social betterment"; Georgia already had a similar law on the books; and the labor commissioner of Louisiana warned of a crisis in the building trade in New Orleans if the exodus continued.

The Great Mississippi Flood, the most destructive river flood in US history, had begun the previous summer and lasted until August 1927, breaking over a hundred levees along the Mississippi River, which at one point stretched to sixty miles wide. It had displaced over 600,000 people in Mississippi, Arkansas, and Louisiana; 25,000 of them went to St. Louis alone, adding more than twenty-five percent to that city's African American population. But the emigration was widespread all over, for the conditions in which many black people lived, especially in rural communities, were insupportable. They were essentially under mob rule, with constant threats of lynchings and whippings. The land they had gained at the end of the Civil War had been stolen, the hardships of sharecropping kept them impoverished, and peonage and prison farms effectively re-enslaved many of them.

Six years later, Zora would pen one of the most vivid descriptions of this great exodus in her first novel, *Jonah's Gourd Vine*:

Do what they would, the State, County and City all over the South could do little to halt the stampede. The cry of "Goin' Nawth" hung over the land like the wail over Egypt at the death of the first-born.... Railroads, hardroads, dirt roads, side roads, roads were in the minds of the black South and all roads led North.

Whereas in Egypt the coming of the locust made desolation, in the farming South the departure of the Negro laid waste the agricultural industry—crops rotted, houses careened crazily in their utter desertion, and grass grew up in streets.

Earlier in 1927, Langston had published some poems that took place in the South, poems like "Song for a Dark Girl," about a lynching, and "Mulatto," about the rape of a black woman by a white man. Yet his demonstrated awareness of the dangers of being black in this area of the country he'd never been to did not for a moment deter him from going there. To Zora, on the other hand, the South was her home, and conditions for Negroes in the North were hardly better. And both of them loved taking risks.

Also, Zora had her gun, which she wore on a shoulder holster. There's a picture of her taken in Mobile that summer, pistol under her left arm, hands on her wide, low-slung ammunition belt, head cocked under a wide-brimmed hat; if it weren't for her white dress and stockings, she'd look like a Wild West gunslinger.

▼▼▼

Langston had jotted down a few observations in his pocket notebook on the train from New Orleans: "The palm trees / The pecan groves on both sides of Ocean Spring / The little boys with their derbies and box band[s]." When he got off the train in Mobile, it was either for a break or a pause between two trains on his way to Tuskegee, where he had made arrangements to visit the college. He had spent $13.34 on his ticket, the equivalent of about $175 today—the biggest single expense he noted for his trip.

Right after meeting Zora, Langston wrote, "we went to eat some fried fish and watermelon." Watermelon is, of course, a food loaded with negative associations for African Americans, and Zora and Langston were aware of its connotations. But they rejected them. Zora's biographer Valerie Boyd writes, "Once, at a ritzy interracial party in New York, Zora had angered some of her fellow New Negroes by going straight for the watermelon.

They viewed its inclusion on the buffet as a test of sorts, almost an insult, and had collectively vowed to abstain from the forbidden fruit. 'And leave all this good watermelon for the white folks?!' Zora dissented." As for Langston, he recorded buying watermelons for thirty to fifty cents each several times in the detailed expense notebook he kept on his trip. (Another repeated expense noted there was for cigarettes, fifteen cents a pack.)

After the watermelon, the two of them went to Dr. H. Roger Williams's home, likely a two-story brick row house, where Zora had probably been staying, and met with the doctor and his daughter Lucy Ariel, "a talented pianist and poet." Dr. Williams had opened, in 1901, the Live and Let Live Drug Store, the first black-owned drugstore in Mobile, in an 1891 row house right across fashionable Dauphin Street from his home in the heart of downtown. (The drugstore is now part of Wintzell's Oyster House, and where Williams's own house stood is now its gravel parking lot.) He had graduated from Meharry Medical School and was a published poet and one of Mobile's best-regarded citizens. Lucy Ariel had just graduated with a degree in music from Fisk and her brilliant dialect poem "Northboun'" had tied for first prize in the 1926 *Opportunity* contest. It's not known how Zora and Langston knew them, but they certainly moved in the same literary circles.

In his notebook that evening, Langston wrote, "Mobile July 23. / Zora Hurston / Mr. H. Roger Williams / 'I'm a sojourner in truth since I got religion so I just calls ma self Sojourner Truth.' / The slave walk, which came from hoeing and planting. / The 'Big House' explanation for Negro jealousy of those who come up. / Zora's bare front. / The chicken seller." I have to assume that the lines about Sojourner Truth and slavery came from conversations Langston was having with Zora. As for "Zora's bare front," I can draw no conclusions except that the sight must have provoked some feeling in him. That Zora might, even inadvertently, reveal her "bare front" to Langston does not seem out of character.

▼▼▼

Mobile was Alabama's second largest city (after Birmingham), with a population of about 65,000. Founded as the capital of *La Louisiane*, it was colonized in turn by the French, the British, and the Spanish before becoming part of the United States in 1813; it retained a distinctive culture not unlike that of New Orleans (it was the first US city to feature a Mardi Gras carnival, and that of New Orleans was imported from Mobile). Because of its port, it had been an important slave-trading center; now it was a bustling, cosmopolitan city.

Cudjo Lewis, the reason for Zora's presence in Mobile, was idealized at the time as the last true connection between Africa and America. (Zora later found an even older woman who had been on board with him.) The *Clotilda* was the last known slave ship to bring captives from Africa to the United States: it was secretly commissioned by a wealthy Mobile businessman and arrived in 1859, over fifty years after the United States had abolished the African slave trade. Lewis and his fellow shipmates were slaves only a few years. After the Civil War, they established an extensive community called Africatown a few miles north of Mobile, with shotgun shacks dispersed over a large wooded area. Unlike in Mobile, there were no sidewalks, paved roads, electricity, or gaslights. (Home to lumber mills from the time of its inception, the community has been continually plagued by industrial pollution, and even now its poverty is shocking. "We're still burying most of our people between the age of 40 and 50 right now," a resident stated recently.)

Cudjo's house had no windows, so he left the door open in the summer. He grew sugarcane and clingstone peaches in his garden. Speaking in a thick West African accent, he was somewhat cagey about his past. Zora helped him sweep out the church he attended and drove him to Mobile to buy turnip seed. But she was unable to obtain sufficient information from her interviews to complete the kind of report Carter Woodson expected. So she padded her article with lengthy uncredited excerpts from the 1914 interviews with Lewis that Emma Langdon Roche had published in her book *Historic Sketches of the Old South*, and submitted the resulting piece to Woodson, likely with no intention of having it appear in print. Woodson, however, unaware of her plagiarism (the last seven pages were taken almost verbatim from Roche), published the report under Zora's name as "Cudjo's Own Story of the Last African Slaver" in the *Journal of Negro History*. Zora never told anyone what had happened, and it wasn't until long after her death that her copying was discovered and revealed. Biographer Robert Hemenway believed that her plagiarism was a kind of subconscious academic suicide attempt, since Zora was at this point tired of being beholden to academic standards. Certainly if Woodson had discovered her source, it would have been the end of her academic career. Zora would, however, go back to interview Lewis again, much more successfully, later that year and the next, and would use those interviews as the basis for a book, *Barracoon*, completed in 1931 and finally published in 2018. In it, she heavily fictionalized her own experience, presenting her visit as having lasted from June to October, all under Godmother's auspices. But Zora told Cudjo's story faithfully, backing it up with copious research.

▼▼▼

The first road over Mobile Bay, a complicated multimillion-dollar project that included five bridges and a causeway, was completed in June 1927, just in time for Zora and Langston to cross it on their way to Montgomery, probably taking the roads now labeled US 90 and US 31. It should have been tremendously exciting to traverse that brand new series of spans, one of them an enormous vertical lift bridge, across the twenty-four-mile-wide bay. They then probably drove through such thick timberlands that the road resembled the bottom of a canyon. Perhaps they stopped in Brewton, with its brick storefronts and cast-iron balconies, or Castleberry, which even then was the strawberry capital of Alabama. But perhaps they motored right through them.

Langston and Zora spent Saturday night in Montgomery. Langston wrote of the "Distance from station / The churches with yelling ministers" on Sunday morning. It's possible that one of these churches was the Dexter Avenue Church, built in the 1880s very near the capitol, quite a distance from the station, where Martin Luther King Jr. would help kick off the civil rights movement in 1955.

Then they pushed on to Tuskegee. Booker T. Washington, a proponent of vocational training, had founded the Tuskegee Normal School for Colored Teachers in 1881. In addition to training teachers, the school taught a variety of agricultural and industrial trades. It did not teach liberal arts, political subjects, or any of the theoretical sciences. While white guests were put up in a spacious guesthouse, Langston and Zora stayed in a dormitory. Neither of them expressed any reservations about Tuskegee's program at the time of this visit. In fact, Langston wrote a poem of praise for and remembrance of Washington, an anthem for Tuskegee called "Alabama Earth," which was published on the cover of *The Tuskegee Messenger* the following summer. When

Langston returned to Tuskegee in 1932, however, he responded with the poem "Red Flag on Tuskegee," a lengthy and rousing call to Tuskegee students to join the Communist Party, and an explicit repudiation of Washington's vision of black and white social life as "separate as the fingers" on a hand.

Tuskegee's campus is reminiscent of Harvard's—red brick, traditional, with the clean lines of academic American architecture; the primary architect, Robert R. Taylor, was the first black graduate of MIT, and the campus was built entirely by its students, who even fired the bricks. Situated on rolling hills, it's picturesque, but not to a fault; the central quadrangle is especially impressive. In 1915 the campus had over a hundred fully equipped buildings (it now has about seventy-five).

Zora and Langston arrived on July 24. In his notebooks, Langston noted practically all the people he met with over the next few days, but it would be hard to tell exactly who several of them, mentioned by last name only, were. Some are identifiable, though: on the 25th, he saw Jessie Fauset, who had come from New York. Fauset, whom Langston once described as "my own brown goddess," had been watching over Langston for years, publishing most of his greatest poems while unsuccessfully trying to steer him away from free verse, Lincoln University, and what she considered the baleful influence of Carl Van Vechten (she wanted him to go to Harvard and write more like Countee Cullen). She had even more or less propositioned him in a letter she wrote him when he was in Paris. She no longer worked at *The Crisis*, having had a bitter falling out with her boss and sometime lover W. E. B. Du Bois. Langston also met Mary Williams, the nurse in charge of the Tuskegee Institute Health Center, that day, and they had dinner that night and took a drive together the next day in Fauset's company. On the 27th, Langston had lunch with Sadie Peterson, who had helped develop the African American collection at the New York Public Library in the early 1920s and then the library at the Veterans Administration hospital in Tuskegee; he had dinner at the house of Albon Holsey, personal secretary to Tuskegee's president. He also received a check for $100 that day from Godmother, along with a letter. Mason expressed her joy that he was making a "pilgrimage through the South at the moment you extend your own field of freedom," then asked him not to tell anyone in New York about his trip, but instead to use the material he was gathering later, when "the flame of it can burn away the *debris* that is so rampant" in the city. He replied with a long letter (now lost), detailing his travels.

On July 29, he wrote to Gwendolyn Bennett, who would publish an excerpt from his letter in *Opportunity* in September: "I am having the time of my life down here. Everybody's fine to me and the South isn't half bad. Tuskegee is wonderful. Jessie Fauset is here, Marie [*sic*] Peterson and gangs of delightful folks. . . . I am going to the country tomorrow for a while and then on to Georgia."

▾▾▾

What Langston meant by "going to the country" was a journey with Tuskegee's Movable School, or the Booker T. Washington Agricultural School on Wheels, an exemplar of rural outreach. The Movable School worked through county agents who would arrange stops throughout the area. Alabama was the only state that had one. It had been Washington's idea, and had first operated using mules, then a Ford truck; by Langston's time it was housed in a White Motor Company truck (the 1920s equivalent of a heavy-duty pickup). It carried a Delco-Light "electric plant" (a generator), motion picture projector, electric sewing machine,

iron, churn, gasoline stove, tool chest, ax, shovel, fireless cooker (a
wooden bucket with an inner metal pail surrounded by sawdust;
it functioned like a modern crockpot when one put a heated brick
or rock in it), and water cooler, along with volleyball equipment,
flour, baking powder, sugar, pots, pans, and more. Langston left
Tuskegee at 7 a.m. on July 30 with three teachers and arrived in
Decatur, Alabama, near the Tennessee border, at 8:30 p.m.

The week was mainly spent in Berkley, about twelve miles
from Huntsville. Langston was staying with a family of black
landowners. They had a five-room house and a riverside farm
with three mules where they grew mostly cotton, but also some
corn, peanuts, pears, sweet potatoes, cane, and sorghum; they
also kept pigs, cows, and chickens. The Parkers had ten children,
who went barefoot most of the time, and who, for one week out
of the year, attended the Movable School.

During that week, the big project for the men and boys was
the construction of an outdoor toilet. They also cleared a yard
and laid down a walk through it, and built a roof and a concrete
base for a well. They learned how to use surveying equipment;
care for, breed, and judge livestock; build a chicken house; and
make whitewash. The women and girls, meanwhile, learned how
to frame pictures, make rugs, care for and feed typhoid patients
(with one girl playing the part of the sick woman and the others bathing her, feeding her, and cleaning her teeth), bake bread,
raise egg-laying hens, store sweet potatoes, bathe babies, prepare
salad, can beans and vegetables, and set tables.

The school's aim was clearly to bring a bit more "civilization"
to these country folk. Children were taught the importance of
baths and cleanliness, and Langston spent a memorable afternoon delivering a lesson on "Great Men," especially "Great
Negroes," to the boys. Most of them had never heard about "Great

Negroes"; one knew about the poet Paul Laurence Dunbar and one the boxer Jack Johnson, while others thought that Abraham Lincoln was black. One evening the school showed educational films, which attracted about a hundred and twenty spectators, most of whom had never seen a movie before. They cried, "Look a yonder" and shouted at every movement. The show ended with a lecture on sanitary toilets, flies, and their effect on health.

Langston participated as much as he could. He especially enjoyed working with the littler children, teaching them how to blow bubbles with spools, or swimming with them in the river. He also appreciated the local food, on which he kept meticulous notes. One breakfast consisted of ham, cornbread, buttermilk, and molasses; another of catfish, chicken, cornbread, applesauce, peach preserves, and sweet milk. Dinner was served at noon, and might comprise chicken, ham, cabbage, corn muffins, mashed potatoes, tomatoes, buttermilk, and custard pie; then again the menu might be rolls the girls had baked, chicken cooked in the fireless cooker, okra, stringbeans, mashed potatoes, tomatoes, apple cobbler, and iced tea. Supper was usually a bit lighter: ham, applesauce, preserved tomatoes, and hot biscuits; or chicken, biscuits, and sorghum. The meals each cost him between a quarter and forty cents, which was significantly cheaper than similar meals elsewhere during their trip.

Langston came back to Tuskegee on his own, stopping overnight in Montgomery, and arriving August 7. He found a note from Charlotte Mason: "How wide open the door of your being is—how I love for you this experience that you are going through now—rising with the sun in the back country of the Alabama hills! You will know, dear child, so much better what lies deeply hidden in your poetic soul and in the far reaches of your ancestral dreams." Mason had somehow recognized that Langston was experiencing a sort of rebirth. Indeed, as he was leaving Berkley, Langston had written a few lines for a song to be sung at a 4-H Club concert in December: "Out of death and darkness going toward the sun— / The sun, the sun." And he also wrote a beautiful poem then, which has never been published, and which gives a good impression of his emotional state:

> There is no weakness here
> But only strength
> Bursting the grave asunder
> Seeking stars.
> There is no weakness here
> But only strength
> To smash iron bars.
> O, here in Alabamy earth
> The strength of stars.

▾▾▾

Langston and Zora stayed another week at Tuskegee, during which he had a long talk with Thomas Monroe Campbell, the first African American agricultural extension agent, the first manager of the Movable School, and, at the time, the supervisor of over four hundred black extension agents throughout the South. At some point, Langston also visited the pioneering black scientist George Washington Carver in his laboratory, a massive brick building on the edge of the campus. And on the morning of August 10 he gave a reading to a "rather mixed audience composed of school teachers attending summer school, faculty members of Tuskegee Institute and not a few visitors," as the *Tuskegee Messenger* reported. The reading was part of Tuskegee's summer session, which was for high school and junior college teachers; besides Jessie Fauset and Langston, Alain Locke and Benjamin Brawley had also participated that summer. Langston talked about how he became interested in poetry while in high school and how he always tried to write "of things within his experience." He read a number of his poems, and described his travels in France and Africa. The audience "was captivated by his pleasing voice, his assured, unaffected manner and the sincerity and feeling which he put into his verse."

What Zora did during those two weeks remains a mystery. She might have visited her birthplace, Notasulga, which is only six miles north of Tuskegee, but she probably remained in Tuskegee the rest of the time. She was most likely working on her Cudjo material. An undated note she wrote Langston reads, "Dear Langston—Finished work and got my check today. Woodson cut me a week. I thought I'd get pay for the month but he only paid me for two weeks. Have only $100°°. Rather depressed. I hate that improperly born wretch. / Shall we drive, or shall I sell car? shall see you in five days at the outside. / Zora." She probably sent it to him while he was in Berkley with the Movable School.

There are three photographs of Zora and Langston at Tuskegee. In one they're with Jessie Fauset standing at the center of Tuskegee's campus in front of Charles Keck's statue *Lifting the Veil of Ignorance*, which shows Booker T. Washington uncloaking a newly freed slave. In another they stand in full sun, brightly lit, with a number of trees behind them. From left to right are Colonel Joseph Ward, vice-president of the VA Hospital in Tuskegee, in his World War I uniform; Langston in shirt sleeves and a loosened tie; Zora in a white dress with a long string of beads around her neck; an unidentified heavy, light-colored man with a bowtie; and a distinguished-looking young African American man—perhaps a student—with a much tighter tie than Langston's. None of them smile, but they look comfortable. In the third, again in full sun, the two writers stand with Sadie Delaney, the librarian at the VA hospital, who wears a simple white dress, and two very elegantly dressed young African American men. Zora is wearing a different white dress in each of the photographs, but the same long string of beads; Langston wears the same jazzy tie in the two sunny photographs. These are the only photographs that exist of Langston and Zora together.

▼▼▼

When the two friends finally left Tuskegee on August 15, they crossed into Georgia. Langston wrote in his notebook, "Saw man driving goat cart in Columbus. Passed many gourds for bee-martins high on poles." It's impossible to imagine anyone driving a goat cart anywhere near Columbus today, and it couldn't have been common in 1927 or else Langston wouldn't have remarked on it. The gourds are practically the only things Langston wrote about in his notebooks that haven't changed. (They are put up as houses for purple martins; Langston was mistaken about the bee-martins, another name for kingbirds.) Some poles sport as many as two dozen gourds arranged symmetrically; in other cases a line of half a dozen poles will sport one or two gourds each, put up haphazardly, like inverted Calder mobiles.

On August 20, the *Chicago Defender*, one of the main black newspapers of the era, ran an article, "Barbecue in Georgia," on its editorial page. They reported that the white citizens of Talbot County had hosted an integrated barbecue the previous Sunday in order "to show that good feeling exists between the races, and that white people are their friends." With thousands attending, one speaker there shouted, "'We must stop this migration. . . .

There will be no more lynching in this county, and no more in this state if we can help it. We have decided to remove all inequalities between the races; henceforth there shall be no more use of 'nigger' in this county if we have to build more jails to house those who violate this rule.'"

This utopian satire gives a good indication of how desperate the Great Migration had made the South. And coincidentally, Zora and Langston drove right through Talbot County on the day after this fictional barbecue. "Passed a town last night named Tallbottom," Langston wrote to Van Vechten, deliberately misspelling Talbotton. "Maybe that's where the Blackbottom started. Anyhow the Georgia Grind seems prevalent." Langston was referring, jokingly, to two popular dances of the day.

Their next stop was Fort Valley, Georgia, where they visited Henry and Florence Hunt, who lived in a large, elegant white house next to the Fort Valley High and Industrial School, a high school and junior college which they ran (the house is still there on the campus of Fort Valley State University, and is now called the Anderson House). Henry Hunt, a light-skinned man with small glasses and a gray goatee, was one of the most important black educators in the South, "advancing" at Fort Valley "the vanguard of civilization on a front where the resistance has been most bitter," as *The Crisis* would put it in 1930. An expert carpenter, who had helped build the state capitol building, he had come to Fort Valley High and Industrial School in 1904 with the idea of making it the equal of other black Southern schools like Hampton and Tuskegee. His wife Florence raised funds to build the area's first infirmary, which treated both black and white patients. Unfortunately, it was summer break so the school wasn't in session. Langston and Zora's connection to the Hunts was their daughter Dorothy Hunt Harris, who was secretary to

Charles S. Johnson and lived in Greenwich Village, where she had hosted the Niggerati on occasion.

The Peach Capital of Georgia (and also a major producer of pecans, with towering orchards just outside of town), Fort Valley hosted a Peach Blossom Festival every spring from 1922 to 1926, with 40,000 visitors descending upon the town of 4,000 people for musical performances, dancing, pageants, and barbecue; but no festival had taken place in 1927, as it had simply become too overwhelming for a town of that size. From Fort Valley, Langston and Zora sent a telegram to Van Vechten, inviting him to join them; Langston also posted a letter to him from there, telling him that the Hunts' home was "marvelous."

That night, as Langston related to Van Vechten, they drove out of town to a "backwoods church entertainment given by a magician. It closed with his playing on a large harp and singing the Lord's Prayer in a very lively fashion. And his version began like this: / Our Father who art in heaven, / Hollywood be Thy name!" In a postscript, Langston added, "There are so many amusing things to do here and the Hunts are delightful." And he outlined their plan for the next day: to visit the old Toomer plantation.

Jean Toomer's 1923 *Cane* had been set in rural Georgia. His father had once been a slave on John Toomer's small plantation not far from Fort Valley, and a number of his relatives still lived there. Jean Toomer had never actually been there himself, having grown up mostly in Washington, D.C. His account of Georgia in *Cane* is based on his three months in Sparta, more than eighty miles away, where he had been a substitute principal at the Sparta Agricultural and Industrial Institute.

The Toomer plantation was in Houston (pronounced house-ton) County, Georgia. I couldn't locate it precisely, but on Toomer Road there I found an old C.M.E. (Christian Methodist Evangelical) church, set a little bit away from the road in the woods, white, with the windows all boarded up with plywood painted black, and no driveway, just driven-over grass. In the graveyard are seven Toomer graves, the oldest dating from the 1950s: they are the only stones painted white. The churchyard is surrounded by pine timber farms. The plantation was likely nearby.

Langston and Zora talked there with some of Toomer's distant relatives, and according to his autobiography, Langston became enamored of an old hat that one of the men there wore, "a marvelous patchwork hat of felt, patched over and over with varicolored bits of leather, linoleum, canvas, and baize where the holes of time had worn through. The entire hat was wonderfully weather-stained and dirty. The old Negro looked like something out of Uncle Remus. Indeed like Uncle Remus himself." Langston wanted that hat because it reminded him of "the quaint soul of labor in the Old South"; he then referred to some lines from *Cane* about "caroling softly souls of slavery" and "early dawn on the Georgia plum trees and sunlight in the cotton fields." In the end, Zora paid the man three dollars for it, and Langston brought it back to New York.

Langston's fondness for Uncle Remus and "the quaint soul of labor in the Old South" isn't just retrograde, it echoes age-old white justifications for the horrors of slavery. Perhaps thirteen years after his trip he wanted to give an impression of it that would amuse and flatter his white readers. His writings of the 1920s are altogether different. Here's how he described the same visit in his journal: "Homestead now occupied by Tom Buff (73 years old) [probably the man who sold him his hat] and his grandchildren. Old man knew Toomer well, aunt and cousin of

Gene's [*sic*] now living on place. Aunt (Fannie Coleman) looks like ghost of past; pale, dry, and white,—didn't know Gene was writer." (Jean Toomer was also fair-skinned, and would later refuse to identify as black.) "Cousin (Fred Toomer) much like Gene. Wife ill. House in midst of cotton fields and peach trees. Chickens running under house and two dogs alive with fleas. Pecan, and English walnut trees. Grape vines and brambles. A very deep, cloudy well. / Came back to town and went looking for a guitar player named Bugaboo but couldn't find him." The simple lyricism I find stunning.

The next day, August 17, Langston and Zora sent Van Vechten a postcard joking about the slowness of Zora's car. (The top speed for the era was about 35–40 miles per hour; Sassy Susie likely chugged along at a more moderate pace.) It read, "We are charging home in a wheezy car and hope to be home for Xmas. We are being fed on watermelon, chicken, and the company of good things. Wish you were with us. Lovely people not spoiled by soap-suds and talcum."

▼▼▼

Langston described their visit to the "famous conjur-man away off in the backwoods" at great length in his autobiography; Zora talked about it in a letter to Van Vechten; and Langston listed the "Herb Doctor's routine" in his notebook. Apparently he was so popular that on the weekends his cabin yard would be filled with visitors, both black and white. But neither Langston nor Zora revealed his name or the town he lived nearest, only that one had to drive over red clay roads to reach him (these kinds of roads were common, but they had been driving mainly on gravel or chert roads), and that everyone they asked on the way knew him. They arrived in the early afternoon and were received by "a tall, red-skinned, middle-aged man.... There was nothing especially distinguished about the man either in appearance or personality. He was quiet and pleasantly serious and asked us, in a southern drawl, what our trouble was." Zora told him a lie about a cousin of hers, and named Tom R. Smith as the one who placed the curse they wanted the herb doctor to lift. (Smith was a white New York friend of Van Vechten's who had edited *The Century* magazine in the teens and was now editor in chief at the publisher Boni and Liveright.) Ten days later she explained to Van Vechten that they had nothing against Smith, "but we had to have a victim and since he is free[,] single, and childless we thought he was the best one to use. If he should turn up one day with his limbs all tied up in a knot don't tell that we conjured him." As Imani Mtendaji, an African American storyteller in Savannah, pointed out to me, "Zora and Langston *had* to conjure a white man; conjuring a black one would have been too risky."

The conjurer read to them from chapter six of the Book of Tobit in his "huge apocryphal Bible," including the passage that explains that "if a devil or an evil spirit trouble any," smoke the heart and liver of a fish, "and the party shall be no more vexed."

The conjur-man then "darkened the room, after having laid out various chalks and powders on a nearby table." He took a piece of chalk and made white marks on Zora's forehead and breast in the shape of a cross. Then he sprinkled water on them from a green bottle, anointed them with "Palm of Gilead," "mumbled an incantation," gave each of them a small rock, and touched the rocks with a lit match. They began to burn. He told them to make the sign of the cross with the stones, which he described as "Burning of hell fire and brimstone." "After the stones had burned a while, he spoke in tongues, performed other simple rites behind our backs, and then raised the curtains and opened the door." Zora paid him two dollars.

Zora, who had visited a lot of other conjure men, told Langston that this one "was a poor one without power, using tricks like the burning sulphur-stones to amaze and confound people." They were both baffled as to why he was so well known in the area: apparently some of the doctors had been complaining that he'd robbed them of patients.

That day, Zora told Langston many things she'd picked up from her research. He jotted down some of them in his notebook: "A black woman so evil she sleeps with her fists doubled up"; "Threat: 'I can make all four of yous strip buck naked and dance right here till sun down.'" Then she told him a how to cast a black-magic spell. "Take a black cat on a black night deep in the woods and boil him alive," she said. To find the lucky bone, you throw all the bones in a stream and choose the one that floats upstream. With this bone, "you can give yourself to the devil. Put it in your mouth and you can disappear, become invisible."

▼▼▼

They had found out while in Fort Valley that Bessie Smith was performing in Macon, and made sure to get there in time to see her. Langston was a devoted fan of the great blues singer, who became known as "The Empress of the Blues" in 1923 when her song "Down Hearted Blues" sold 760,000 copies in six months. He wrote a blues song for her in 1925, which he sent to Carl Van Vechten to give her; he had seen her perform several times; and he listened to her records probably more than those of any other musician. Famously foul-mouthed, violent, and frequently drunk, she was a powerful woman whom nobody messed with.

Langston had first met her backstage in Baltimore in 1926,

where she told him about her summer traveling tent shows down South and how lucrative they were. She remembered the Van Vechtens but didn't exactly appreciate Carl's *Vanity Fair* article on the blues (which Langston had helped write), and the only thing that interested her in "the art of the blues" was the money to be made from it. Smith attended a few of Van Vechten's parties; at one, she told a Metropolitan Opera diva, "Don't let nobody tell you you can't sing." She was fond of telling the story of how, at a party he gave in 1928, she downed three shots of whiskey, performed a set of blues, and, when Van Vechten's wife Fania Marinoff threw her arms around her and tried to kiss her goodbye, exclaimed, "Get the fuck away from me!" and threw her to the floor. As for Zora, she had not yet met Smith, but had accompanied Van Vechten to a Harlem performance Bessie gave the previous summer, and at some point may have corresponded with her.

Now Smith was appearing at Macon's Douglass Theatre, built by African-American entrepreneur Charles H. Douglass in 1921, and one of the most important movie theaters and vaudeville halls in the area. The lobby was lush and polished, with a chain-link motif stenciled on the walls, and Zora and Langston, who paid fifty cents for their tickets, likely had good seats in the gloriously ornate auditorium with its gold-and-red-painted walls. The opening act was a vocal quintet called Philips and Darling; then Bessie strutted on stage with her accompanists, hollering her saucy blues. However, "You didn't have to go near the theater to hear Bessie sing," as Langston wrote. "You could hear her blocks away."

After the show, the travelers and performers ended up staying at the same hotel together, and spent quite a bit of time hanging out. Among other things, Smith told them, "The trouble with white folks singing blues is that they can't get low down enough."

The hotel was almost certainly the Colonial, Macon's only hotel for black patrons, another Douglass building; it stood right next to the theater and advertised "25 Neatly Furnished Rooms with Hot and Cold Baths." (The theater has been beautifully restored; the hotel is no longer there.) With a population of 53,000 (two-thirds of them black), Macon was the fourth largest city in Georgia, and downtown was full of tall buildings; the Colonial was one.

Smith was accompanied by sixteen people on her Southern tent tour that summer, including Dinah Scott, a comedian who had directed a revue called *Harlem Frolics*; her brother and sister Clarence and Maud; and her husband and manager Jack Gee. She had just given tent shows in Athens and Atlanta, and would soon appear in Birmingham. She may not have brought her entire entourage with her to Macon, though, since this was a theater performance rather than a tent show.

In the day's journal entry—it was August 17—Langston also noted, "Hubbard drove in from Forsyth." Was this William Hubbard, then sixty-two years old, who had founded, in Forsyth, twenty-five years earlier, Georgia's first vocational school for African Americans? His son Samuel, who would soon become principal of that school? His son Maceo, who would wind up working for the US Department of Justice? His son Clifton, who would become an electrician in Philadelphia? Considering it was a twenty-four-mile trip, it was either someone who had met Langston before or who was rather anxious to do so. The Hubbards undoubtedly knew the Hunts well, and perhaps this Hubbard had visited the Hunts in Fort Valley at the same time as Langston and Zora, or perhaps the Hunts had told him about their visit and he wanted to meet them in person.

Zora and Langston were meeting a large number of African American educators; almost all of them were in what

W. E. B. DuBois had called the "talented tenth," the "best of this race," "its exceptional men" and women. They were staying not in the traditionally black areas of the cities they visited, but instead in the homes (and hotels) of the black elite, which were located in the center. Interestingly, these were decidedly *not* the kinds of people Zora and Langston were writing about. Langston's poems of the time focus on musicians, dancers, and low-wage workers, echoing blues lyrics about drunk women ("Ballad of Gin Mary") and gambling men ("Crap Game"); Zora's fiction and plays were mostly about relatively unsophisticated rural Southern black families and townspeople. There's hardly an educator in the lot. Being college-educated themselves, Zora and Langston doubtless had great respect for teachers, but didn't view them as suitable material for their creative efforts.

The next day, August 18, Zora and Langston went to "Southern railroad shops," probably the Norfolk Southern Railway's Brosnan Yard just outside Macon, accompanied by "Henry," probably Henry Hunt. Zora and Langston sat in the driver's seat of an old locomotive. But where they spent the next three days is a mystery. They spent seven dollars on car repairs; Langston heard a song that ran, in part, "Nobody wants me—I don't even want ma self"; and they visited a chain gang, giving three dollars to some prisoners. By the 22nd they were in Statesboro, and went from there to Savannah, meeting, en route, a 103-year-old root doctor, whom they paid a dollar for their fortune. Unfortunately, neither of them described the encounter.

Savannah was then Georgia's second largest city (after Atlanta), and boasted a thriving African American community not unlike Harlem's, with plenty of speakeasies, cabarets, and venues for jazz and blues performances (one was even called the Harlem Club). But the nightlife didn't interest our travelers as much as the folklife. When they arrived, they "met a little woman who was out shopping for a second-hand gun to 'sting her husband up a bit.' She told us where the turpentine workers and the dock workers hung out, and we got acquainted with some and had supper with them. We asked them to sing some songs, but the songs they sang we had heard before and they were not very good songs." (Turpentine workers hacked the bark off pine trees, collected the resin, and distilled it to make a product with many industrial uses; they would prove an important source for Zora twelve years later, when she interviewed, for the Works Progress Administration, a large group of them being held in virtual slavery in Florida. She wrote a brief unpublished essay, "Turpentine," about the experience.) They probably would have met these workers either on the eastern part of the riverbank or near Franklin Square, a green space dominated by First African Baptist Church, home of America's oldest black congregation.

One of the men they met was called Colonel Pinkney. He had been sent to a chain gang for nine years and seven months at the age of fifteen for striking his wife, was then "paroled" to a white planter (farm owners often took black inmates out of prison and enslaved them for the remainder of their term or longer, a practice called peonage), and finally ran away.

Zora and Langston's meetings with intellectuals and educators may have been supportive and convivial, but their encounters with blues singers, conjure men, turpentine workers, and chain-gang escapees were the ones that fed their imagination.

▾▾▾

After Savannah, Langston and Zora were intent on getting back to New York City, and spent little time exploring. They arrived in Charleston on August 24. Then, instead of going directly north to Cheraw, they went northwest to Columbia, where they had a puncture repaired on the 25th, and where, as Zora wrote to Van Vechten the next day, "Somehow all the back of my skirt got torn away, so that my little panties were panting right out in public. I suppose this accident will be classed as more tire trouble." She added that the bottle of "Chinese whiskey" that Langston had bought for Carl in Cuba was "no longer among the living." The reason for the detour was likely that they wanted to get on US 1 instead of navigating the smaller roads to Cheraw, which would have been rougher on the car. The US Highway System had been established in 1925 and the kinks ironed out in 1926: US 1 was less than a year old, though for almost all of its route it was simply the Atlantic Highway renamed. But since it was a major throughway, much of it paved, they trusted it. Almost as soon as they got on it, though, Zora got a five-dollar speeding ticket.

From Cheraw, they remained on Route 1 the rest of the way, rolling through the North Carolina towns of Rockingham, Southern Pines, and Raleigh, arriving in Richmond on the 27th, Baltimore on the 28th, Lincoln University and Philadelphia (where the car had some expensive brake work and where Langston bought a *Vanity Fair*) on the 29th, and New York (via ferry) on the 30th. Since leaving Tuskegee, they had put 1,128 miles on Sassy Susie, and spent over fifty dollars on gas, oil, repairs, parts, and speeding tickets.

▼▼▼

From the perspective of ninety years later, Zora and Langston's Southern road trip seems a halcyon journey of bonhomie, adventure, creativity, discovery, and intellectual challenge. It was certainly an eye-opening experience for Langston, who had learned of the South primarily through books and through talking to others who had been there. What surprised him most was the happiness of its inhabitants: "Most of the Negroes seemed to be having a grand time and one couldn't help but like them," he wrote in his characteristically naive manner. I doubt that Zora, on the other hand, saw anything very different from what she'd already seen on her journeys. And the trip had also "worn [her] down," as she later wrote: she only weighed 124 pounds by the end of it. For her, the grandest thing must have been cementing her friendship with Langston—and being "fed on the company of good things."

6

A Deep Well of the Spirit

Langston was anxious to return to Manhattan and see Godmother, who had written him a letter that read like a love letter. It began, "Can you guess, dear Langston, what a warm welcome waits [sic] the fresh young soul who left me early in June?" and ended, "Remember with what spirit I wait [sic] you Langston!" Since Mason's Park Avenue home wasn't quite ready after her months in her summer home in Connecticut, they met instead in a suite at the swanky Barclay Hotel at 48th and Lexington. There Langston not only gave Godmother a full report of his adventures, but also put in a very good word for Zora, urging Mason to get to know her.

Mason, though, had plans for Langston, taking up a suggestion Langston had made earlier. He was to turn his attention to a novel, making full use of his experiences in the South, and drawing on black folk art as much as he was able. The long form was foreign to Langston; he was a master of brevity. But Mason cared little. He should leave the distractions of Manhattan and let the power of Africa inspire him.

Characteristically, Langston did nothing of the kind. He and Zora remained in the city. On September 6, they dined with the great singer and actress Ethel Waters, the future novelist Nella Larsen and her husband physicist Elmer Imes, and Van Vechten and his lover Donald Angus at a party hosted by Eddie Wasserman. Zora brought her visiting husband, who played piano, and Van Vechten screeched out his impression of the congregants at a sanctified church.

Soon Zora and Langston were working on their "opera" again, which was more in the nature of a blues revue. Langston didn't return to Lincoln until registration started on September 19.

That week, Zora and Mason finally met—in Mason's Park Avenue penthouse. It was the precise fulfillment of the twelfth and last of Zora's childhood visions: "I would come to a big house. Two women waited there for me. I could not see their faces, but I knew one to be young and one to be old. One of them was arranging some queer-shaped flowers such as I had never seen [Cornelia Chapin was arranging a bowl of calla lilies]. When I had come to these women, then I would be at the end of my pilgrimage, but not the end of my life. Then I would know peace and love and what goes with those things, and not before."

Zora told Langston that she thought she and Mason had "got on famously." This turned out to be an understatement. Both felt that they had a psychic connection, that they could read each other's mind. "It was decreed in the beginning of things that I should meet Mrs. R. Osgood Mason," Zora wrote in the initial draft of her autobiography (in a section that was unpublished until 1995). "The moment I walked into the room, I knew that this was the end."

Zora spoke to Mason about the opera she and Langston were working on. She relayed to Langston that Mason told her, "We must do it with so much power that it will halt all these spurious efforts on the part of white writers. . . . She does not believe that any one but us could do it." Then Zora promised to take her to her church.

Zora's fawning letters to Mason are quite unlike any others she wrote, but perhaps that's because she really did view Mason as a kind of goddess, directing her work through invisible channels, enabling her to plumb the depths of the Negro soul and thus contribute to saving the world from the artificiality of white folks. Their relationship was complicated—pitting intellectual surrender against innate creativity, financial concerns against a spiritual bond—but it gave Zora a feeling of connection such as she had never before experienced.

Zora was fearless in defense of this connection. As late as 1941, in her autobiography, she could write, "My relations with God-mother were curious. Laugh if you will, but there was and is a psychic bond between us. She could read my mind, not only when I was in her presence, but thousands of miles away. . . . The thing that delighted her was the fact that I was her only Godchild who could read her thoughts at a distance." As evidence, Zora attested that Mason's letters would "lay me by the heels for what I was *thinking*." (Zora wrote that the black sculptor Richmond Barthé also believed in and experienced Mason's telepathic abilities, as did Max Eastman, the prominent white Manhattan intellectual whom Mason had hired to educate Katherine Chapin in 1911. According to Harlem Renaissance scholar Cheryl Wall, the African American composer Hall Johnson testified to them too, as did Alain Locke.) Moreover, Zora wrote, "She was just as pagan as I."

When Zora would go to Mason's Park Avenue apartment for dinner, Cornelia Chapin and Katherine Garrison Biddle would be there too. The three white women would admonish Zora—in her words, they would "hem me up and give me what for." Then "the sternness would vanish, and I would be wrapped in love. A present of money from Godmother, a coat from Miss Chapin, a dress from Mrs. Biddle." Sometimes Langston would be there too, sometimes one of Godmother's other godchildren—the artist Miguel Covarrubias, perhaps, or Paul Chapin (the young women's brother). On occasion, Godmother would open *The Indians' Book* and read passages from it for her appreciative audience.

As they all knew, Godmother could be fierce when she chose. If she detected insincerity or cunning, she would call out, "That is nothing! It has no soul in it. You have broken the law!" Perceived ingratitude prompted even worse tirades. Her comments could be withering; as Zora attested, "Her tongue was a knout, cutting off your outer pretenses, and bleeding your vanity like a rusty nail."

Despite the intensity of the relationship, Mason's immense wealth never receded into the background for Zora. "There she was sitting up there at the table over capon, caviar and gleaming silver, eager to hear every word on every phase of life on a sawmill 'job.'" The disparity between them perhaps increased Zora's worship of her patron. For truly, Charlotte Mason had all the attributes of a pagan goddess: she could read minds, she judged untruthfulness harshly, she was stern one moment and accepting the next, she had a whole group of disciples, and she lived on an altogether higher plane, perhaps spiritually, but most certainly materially.

A month after Langston had left New York, he came back to the city for a visit. According to his diary, he had dinner (lunch) at

Zora's on October 21 and spoke some French there with a French professor, Jean Adam, whom he'd met in Paris. (Barnard College required Zora to be fluent in either French or German, and she'd chosen the former; Locke had connected her with Adam, with whom he had traveled in North Africa.) In the evening Langston went backstage at a performance of the play *Porgy* to see Wallace Thurman and Bruce Nugent (both had minor roles in the cast). The next day he spent "seven hours that went like one" with Godmother, eating venison and doubtless talking to her about his and Zora's plans. It was at that point that Mason made him her great offer: to pay him a monthly stipend of $150 to free him to focus on his art. To Langston, it was a windfall, a sum that would take care of all his obligations. The only strings attached were that he must report his expenses and he must never tell anyone, except for a certain circle of intimates, where the money came from. He kept both promises faithfully.

If Zora's connection with Mason was strong, with Langston it turned into his great passion, and the feeling was reciprocated. Mason told Langston he was "a golden star in the Firmament of Primitive Peoples," and Langston later wrote, "I loved her. No one else had ever been so thoughtful of me, or as interested in the things I wanted to do, or so kind and generous to me. . . . Those months when I lived by and through her were the most fascinating and fantastic I have ever known."

As for her ideas, Langston and Zora embraced them with fervor. Langston's summary of them seems on the mark:

Concerning Negroes, she felt that they were America's great link with the primitive, and that they had something very precious to give to the Western World. She felt that there was mystery and mysticism and spontaneous har-

mony in their souls, but that many of them had let the white
world pollute and contaminate that mystery and harmony,
and make of it something cheap and ugly, commercial and,
as she said, "white." She felt that we had a deep well of the
spirit within us and that we should keep it pure and deep.

While this is not the phrasing Langston would have used about
his own thoughts, he expressed many of the same general sentiments in his writings of the era.

On November 5, Langston and Mason entered into a formal agreement; on December 8, Zora did the same. Zora was to
receive $200 a month, in addition to a car (a Ford in the contract,
a shiny gray Chevrolet in reality) and a movie camera. Making no secret of the difference, Zora asked Langston to let her
know if he were "strapped" and she'd send him some money. But
Langston would soon have a full-time secretary, monogrammed
stationery, and an open account with New York's best tailors,
all courtesy of Godmother; in addition, she would pay for the
schooling of Langston's foster brother Gwyn, anonymously, via
Alain Locke.

A more important difference in the contracts was that Langston's writing was to be his own property but Zora's would belong
to Godmother—and wasn't even to be shown to anyone else
without Mason's consent. This would prove a terrible burden
upon Zora, preventing her from working with scholars she highly
respected, and she would nervously find ways around it, request-
ing secrecy from Langston and Franz Boas when she showed
them her work without Godmother's permission. Zora was to
collect Negro folklore because Mrs. Mason was "unable" to do so
herself; she was to "collect all information possible, both written
and oral, concerning the music, poetry, folk-lore, literature, hoo-

doo, conjure, manifestations of art and kindred subjects relating to and existing among the North American negroes." While Langston was being paid to create, Zora was being paid to collect. Mason probably thought Zora's study of African American folklore would parallel Natalie Curtis's study of Native American folklore, and envisioned them as similar projects to support; it seems to have been tacitly understood that once Zora's collecting was over, the result would be published in book form. But in essence Mason was expropriating the black folklore of the South in the manner of a white colonizer (abetted by Alain Locke, with whom she consulted before drawing up the contracts, and who would oversee their implementation).

Both agreements stipulated that Mason would be consulted regularly about practically everything important and supplied with a monthly itemized account of expenses; both stipulated that the recipients were never to reveal the name of their benefactor. This latter promise, among others, Zora would signally fail to keep; she named Mason in her autobiography while Mason was still alive, and was the only one of Godmother's disciples to do so.

Suddenly both Langston and Zora were living in luxury. Their Harlemite neighbors, who paid higher rents and earned lower wages than any other ethnic group in the city, could not help but notice the sudden change in the spending habits of the formerly penniless writers, and soon other beneficiaries of Mason's generosity displayed the same extravagances. Zora obtained full support for expeditions to the South, though she tried to keep her expenses modest. For his part, Langston wore "new suits of dinner clothes from Fifth Avenue shops," ate fine food, wrote on "fine bond paper," and obtained the best seats for the theater; he went to and from Mason's Park Avenue apartment in Mason's private limousine, driven by her white chauffeur. He spent countless hours with Mason, accompanying her to shows, concerts, and lectures, driving with her through Central Park, or simply sitting on a stool in front of her throne-like ancestral chair, with her servants ready to attend to their every wish.

For both of Godmother's new devotees, a life very different from their formerly impecunious one had begun.

7

WINTER 1928–WINTER 1930

This Is Going to Be Big

For close to three years, Langston and Zora saw little of each other, though they kept up a constant and fond correspondence. Langston was working on his novel, *Not Without Laughter*, under Mason's close watch; Hurston was in the South and the Bahamas, collecting folklore, also under Mason's scrutiny. Zora entertained Langston with spicy tales of her adventures; in turn, Langston gave Zora invaluable advice on how to deal with Mason, telling her to write and send little gifts to Godmother more often, and to be more discreet with the "intellectually dishonest" (in Zora's words) Alain Locke, who was apt to betray her confidences to Mason.

For her part, Zora was anxious to continue to collaborate with Langston. In an October 1927 letter to Locke, she had written, "Why can't our triangle—Locke—Hughes—Hurston do something with you at the apex?"; and in March 1928 she wrote Langston concerning their folk opera, "I am truly dedicated to the work at hand. . . . We want to do this tremendous thing with all the fire that genius can bring. I need your hand." The "opera" was to be entitled *Jook*, and she ended up writing nine skits for it (copyrighted as *Cold Keener* in 1930). It would have been more in the nature of a musical revue than a unified opera—Zora envisioned it as a vehicle for "all of the songs and gags I have." Unfortunately, Mason's initial enthusiasm for the project quickly evaporated. At one point, Zora even proposed to Langston that the whole be done in his name since she knew Mason would never allow her to do it herself.

In that March letter, Zora told Langston that she was going to divorce Herbert, then said, "Langston, Langston, this is going to be *big*. Most gorgeous possibilities are showing themselves constantly." Langston suggested that they collect Negro love letters, and Zora quickly began to do so, obtaining some from people she met on trips to Mobile, Eatonville, and New Orleans. A few weeks later, she asked him, "Are you planning to join my vacation?" (She was being ironic—she was working hard.) "I hope so. I promise you one saw-mill and one phosphate mine as special added attractions." In the same letter she sketched the outline of her later essay "The Characteristics of Negro Expression," then laid bare her ideas for the "*real* Negro art theatre" she was planning, which would be a collaborative effort to dramatize short folktales with "the abrupt angularity and naivete of the primitive 'bama nigger."

The central question guiding both of their ideas, even if it wasn't made explicit, was how to best popularize African American folklore. "To create a Negro culture in America—a real, solid, sane, racial something growing out of the folk life, not copied from another, even though surrounding, race," reads the entirety of a journal entry Langston would pen on August 1, 1929.

Langston had made a valiant attempt to make the blues into a popular literature in *Fine Clothes to the Jew*, but he had now turned his back on poetry altogether. In September 1928, he wrote to Claude McKay, with whom he'd begun a scintillating correspondence, that after reading his poems to ladies' clubs and literary societies, "I began to hate my own stuff as much as I do Browning or Longfellow." The following June he added, "I've never felt so unpoetic in my life. I think I shall write no more poems"—he simply wasn't feeling miserable enough. Zora had been turning folktales into short stories, but she was prohibited, by contract, from publishing the tales she was now collecting, not to mention any fiction based on them. Both thus felt stymied, for very different reasons, in their primary mediums—poetry for Langston, storytelling for Zora.

However, both of them knew that a different medium presented a far better opportunity for realizing their shared goal. As Zora would later write, "It is almost useless to collect material to lie upon the shelves of scientific societies. It should be used for the purpose to which it is best suited. The Negro material is eminently suited to drama and music. In fact it *is* drama and music[,] and the world and America in particular needs what this folk material holds." Theatrical presentation was not just the ultimate solution to their frustration; it was what their material demanded. They *had to* write a play together.

Theater had long been a consuming passion for both of them. Zora listed it as her primary extracurricular interest when she began studying at Barnard, had been writing plays and theatrical sketches almost as long as she'd been writing stories, and apparently assisted W. E. B. Du Bois in his efforts to establish a black-focused theater in Harlem. Langston, whose mother had been an actress and who grew up worshipping the theater, dabbled in writing for the theater, and religiously attended New York the-

atrical productions. They had their differences, though. While
Zora dismissed white-authored and -produced spectacles like
Lew Leslie's 1924 *Dixie to Broadway*, which introduced Florence
Mills to the world, saying that the play might as well have been
written in pre-Soviet Russia, Langston enjoyed practically any
spectacle with black actors.

Zora wanted to make sure Langston thought she believed he
would helm the project. In May 1928, she wrote him, "Of *course*,
you know I didnt dream of that theatre as a one-man stunt. I had
you helping 50-50 from the start. In fact, I am perfectly willing
to be 40 to your 60 since you are always so much more practical
than I. But I *know* it is going to be *Glorious*! A really new departure in the drama." And in July, "Without flattery, Langston, you
are the brains of this argosy. All the ideas have come out of your
head."

If only Godmother didn't present such an obstacle. "She was
very anxious," Zora had written to Locke the previous December, "that I should say to you that the plans—rather the hazy
dreams of the theatre that I talked to you about[—]should never
be mentioned again. She trusts her three children [Zora, Langston, and Locke] to never let those words pass their lips again
until the gods decree that they shall materialize." The theater
was vulgar, commercial, and inevitably compromised, and thus
was not the format Godmother favored. In addition, Zora was
enjoined from showing anything she wrote to anyone but Locke
and Mason. She would soon apologize to Franz Boas: "I accepted
the money on the condition that I should write no one" (though
she promised to show him her material in secret nonetheless).
To use any of the folklore she had collected for a play would
not only defy her employer's proscriptions against theater but
would violate her contract with her. She was even forbidden to

contribute to Wallace Thurman's successor to *Fire!!*, a magazine called *Harlem*: "I'm heartbroken over being bound to silence," she confessed to her housemate and literary companion, the future novelist Dorothy West.

Meanwhile, perhaps to assuage her disappointment that Langston hadn't joined her "vacation," Zora had been showing his book *Fine Clothes to the Jew* to black workers all over the South. "*They got the point* and enjoyed it *immensely*," she wrote him, and called it the "party book." One weekend, she wrote, "Two men came over with guitars and sang the whole book. Everybody joined in. It was the strangest & most *thrilling* thing." (When Zora told Godmother about this, the latter wrote to Langston, "How gloriously primitive!") "Oh, honey," Zora wrote him in November 1928, "you ought to make a loafing tour of the South like the blind Homer, singing your songs. Not in auditoriums, but in camps, on water-fronts and the like. You are the poet of the people and your subjects are crazy about you. Why not? There never has been a poet who has been acceptable to His Majesty, the man in the gutter before, and laugh if you will, but that man in the gutter is the god-maker, the creator of everything that lasts." Zora would later read the entire book at a talk on poetry she gave to students at the University of New Orleans. "My they liked it," she wrote Langston in April 1929. "The boys et it up."

Zora's appreciation for Langston's art is perfectly encapsulated in an observation Bruce Nugent made to Robert Hemenway. Speaking about Countee Cullen, he remarked, Zora "could admire his ability and talent, and his ability to use his tools, but I don't think she had great respect for the tools. And I think perhaps one of the things that she loved about Langston was that he didn't have to use these tools. He made his own tools like any other good African."

In the meantime, Langston had been sharpening those tools. He was listening to Charlotte Mason's wonderful collection of blues records and reading Claude McKay's bestseller *Home to Harlem*; Edward Adams's *Congaree Sketches*, a collection of Negro folktales and scenes from the South Carolina swamps; and books on Africa. Of the latter, he wrote to Locke, "I discover therein that one had almost as well be civilized,—since primitiveness is nearly as complex." In the same letter, he called *Home to Harlem* "the best low-life novel I've ever read," implying that it was better than *Nigger Heaven*. *Home to Harlem* had been partly inspired by McKay's hearing about Van Vechten's forthcoming novel—he confessed to Langston that he had wanted to beat Van Vechten to the punch. And though he failed to do so, it was a singular work, vivid and complex, the best novel about Harlem yet. Unfortunately, the black press vilified it.

Zora was also sharpening *her* tools. Her adventures were both bringing her more success in gathering folklore and providing her with rich new stories to tell about her experiences. Having received her undergraduate degree from Barnard, she was no longer under the compulsion to produce the kind of academic presentations that Boas and Woodson would have required, which were unsuited for a mainstream audience. She was free to immerse herself in the social life of her subjects with the aim of gathering stories rather than studying lore. She knew that those stories would soon disappear if they were not harvested, and she went about doing so with tremendous enthusiasm—and considerable bravery.

Especially important was a sojourn at a lumber camp in Polk County, Florida, where she persuaded the laborers that she was a bootlegger wanted by the Jacksonville and Miami police, so she was hiding out there. "That sounded reasonable," she wrote.

"Bootleggers always have cars." She swapped verses of "John Henry" at a juke joint, organized a lying (tall-tale) contest, and harvested a rich trove of stories, songs, and "dozens" (insults). But it all came to an end one Saturday night. She went to a wedding celebration at a pine mill when her sworn enemy Lucy (who was jealous of the time Zora was spending with Slim, an excellent storyteller) came after her with a knife; fortunately, her formidable friend "Big Sweet" stepped in and she escaped during the ensuing brawl.

Everything changed once she arrived in New Orleans in August 1928 and made contact with the voodoo practitioners whom Langston had met the previous summer. Soon she was undergoing an initiation into hoodoo that was unlike anything she—or anyone she knew—had undergone. She knew well that she was departing in a radical way not only from her previous folklore collecting, but also from the practice of any previous researcher, and though she'd had some experiences with hoodoo before, they could not have prepared her for what she went through.

The initiation ceremonies could be mind-numbingly complex. In one, she was required to bathe in a mix of scented liquids, utter various prayers, light special candles, cut her finger, wear new underwear, read the third chapter of Job at specified hours eighteen times, and talk to spirits with names like Great Moccasin and Kangaroo through candle flames. In the most terrifying ceremony, she had to catch a black cat, throw it in a pot of boiling water, take its bones out, and find the bitterest-tasting one. But her sojourn's most arduous interval was when, under the tutelage of a hoodoo doctor named Samuel Thompson (called Luke Turner in *Mules and Men*), she lay face down on a sofa with her navel touching a snakeskin, in the nude, without food, for sixty-nine hours straight. Nothing could have been further from Zora's life in Harlem than this, and it is impossible to imagine anyone else she knew—including Langston—taking part in such a ritual. This was not just a challenge, an adventure, a lark—it was a deadly serious religious rite, requiring Zora's total immersion in practices of extraordinary strangeness and power.

She never spoke about the experience except for the sober sentence in her 1931 report on New Orleans hoodoo, repeated in *Mules and Men*—"I had five psychic experiences and awoke at last with no feeling of hunger, only one of exaltation"—and the comment in her autobiography, *Dust Tracks on a Road*—"On the third night, I had dreams that seemed real for weeks. In one, I strode across the heavens with lightning flashing from under my feet, and grumbling thunder following in my wake." Then she described what happened next: lightning symbols were painted on her back, a pair of eyes on her cheeks, a sun on her forehead; she drank her own blood mixed with wine, and a black sheep was sacrificed.

The five months Zora spent in New Orleans (she stayed until December), as Hemenway wrote, "transform[ed] her from an enthusiastic artist-folklorist into a mature, thoughtful scholar.... The quality of her enthusiasm changed; she began to see more serious implications in her research.... The New Orleans ceremonies marked her for the rest of her life."

In 1929, Langston read a good deal of the material that Hurston had been collecting. She asked him to "make plenty of suggestions. You know I depend on you so much." He wrote her that he liked her material a great deal. But he warned her against sharing too much of it with Locke, and cautioned her about Godmother's jealousy. The material, according to their contract, was Mason's, not Zora's, and even in showing it to Langston first, Zora was going against her patron's wishes. Showing it to Locke, on the other hand, seemed to be part of the deal—the man Godmother called her "precious Brown Boy" (echoing Cullen's poem "To a Brown Boy") was acting as a kind of go-between, and Godmother had told Zora quite clearly to consult with him often. Locke read each manuscript that Zora sent to New York; he made copious notes on them too, which both Zora and Langston saw. After Langston's warning, though, Zora promised, "I'll be even more reticent from now on. I'll keep my big mouf shut." She added in a postscript, "The trouble with Locke is that he is intellectually dishonest. He is too eager to be with the winner." Not only that, but he continually addressed her in the condescending tones a teacher uses to his students, as if *he* were the expert in Southern folklore. Mason later recognized this, writing to him about his superior attitude to Zora, "Such a pity your tongue couldn't be hung front to back so you could preach to yourself and not to the world!" In the end, all three of them were quite right to distrust the mercurial professor.

Zora's folktales were not the only thing she sent Mason from her travels. Langston let her know that Godmother particularly liked a woodcarving Zora had sent her; more carvings followed. She sent orange blossoms from Florida, a piece of the ship *Clotilda* from Mobile, melons from New Orleans, and her transcriptions of humorous tales and sayings from all over the South.

And all the time, Zora continued to write sweetly to Langston, who responded in kind. She disclosed to him that she had discovered one of the last living African slaves, a woman even older than Cudjo Lewis, who was the oldest known at the time; but she had decided to keep her existence a secret from everyone but Langston. At another point, she envisioned Langston, herself, Thurman, Nugent, Aaron Douglas, other Niggerati, and even A'Lelia Walker all working together in "a neat little colony of kindred souls" near Eau Gallie, Florida. Her plan for creating this artists' colony was very specific, from the location (between a river and the ocean) to the price of the land ($4,000, or $57,000 in today's dollars); she even suggested that they have their own railroad station there and start their own town, "a lovely place to retire and write on occasion."

She also flattered him about his poems, perhaps unaware that he had stopped writing them:

> Langston, really, MULATTO is superb. I have read it about the hundredth time and it is so good. So truly negroid. Little bits of drama thrust in without notice. Pictures. I don't want to be sloppy, but the tears come every time I read "MOTHER TO SON". You are a great poet. May I dedicate one of my volumes to you? I hope they will rate it.
>
> Give me a picture, old thing. I'd like to gaze upon thy pan.

By October 1929, Zora's collection of folktales was complete and in Godmother's hands. She was now working on volumes about religion, from evangelical preachers to hoodoo spiritualists, and a book of folksongs, blues, and work songs, from "John Henry" to "Don't Let the Deal Go Down." Zora seemed to be everywhere during the second half of 1929: St. Augustine and Miami, Nassau and New Orleans. She was avidly collecting as much material as possible, convinced that she could further link African American with Afro-Caribbean folklore, amassing over 100,000 words of stories, games, and spiritual material, all the while barely scraping by on Godmother's stipend.

Godmother, however, decided that the book of folktales needed more work. The news was a blow. Zora wrote Langston that month, "Gee, I felt forlorn. Too tired. Been working two years without rest, & behind all that my school life with no rest, no peace of mind." But Langston helped keep her courage up. "Well, honey, your wire did me *so much* good.... No flattery, though. You are my mainstay in all crises. No matter what may happen, I feel you can fix it. Let me hear soon, honey." Then, in December, "Your last letter comforted my soul like dreamless sleep.... Well, I tell you, Langston, I am nothing without you. That's no flattery either." She concluded with "Love and everything deep and fine, Honey." (Langston was the only correspondent she addressed as "Honey" until much later in her life.)

▼▼▼

Langston, meanwhile, was expressing the same sorts of sentiments toward Godmother. None of his letters to her survive in their final form, but he kept a number of drafts, including two dated February 23, 1929. The first begins,

Dearest Godmother,

All the week I have been thinking intensely of you and of what you have done for me. And I have written you several letters but I have not sent them because none of them were true enough. There were too many words in them, I guess. But all of them contained in some form or other these simple sentiments:

I love you.

I need you very much.

I cannot bear to hurt you.

Those are the only meanings in all that I say here. You have been kinder to me than any other person in the world. I could not help but love you. You have made me dream greater dreams than I have ever dreamed before. And without you it will not be possible to carry out those dreams. But I cannot stand to disappoint you either. The memory of your face when I went away on Monday is more than I am able to bear. I must have been terribly stupid to have hurt you so, terribly lacking in understanding, terribly blind to what you have wanted me to see. You must not let me hurt you again. I know very well that I am dull and slow, but I do not want to remain that way.

And the second ends,

Because I love you, I must try to tell the truth. We agreed upon that, didn't we? Do not misunderstand me, dear Godmother. Of course I need you terribly,—but you must be free to live for all the others who love you too. If I am too much for you, you must not have me.

Nowhere in Langston's extensive correspondence is there language like this. These drafts of letters to Godmother uniquely reveal a depth of feeling he kept hidden from practically everyone else.

We do not know what set Godmother off. They seem to have patched up their differences, for Mason's correspondence continued as before, though her effusiveness seems to have been toned down a little in favor of more practical discussions. For instance, she gave him twenty-eight pages—Cornelia Chapin's handwritten transcription of Godmother's dictation—of chapter-by-chapter comments on his novel, which Langston relied on heavily when revising it.

Godmother believed herself to be a "better Negro," as she told Claude McKay, than most of the African Americans she knew;

Winold Reiss, *Miss Hurston (Zora Neale Hurston)*, 1925, pastel on Whatman board. Gift of the artist. Fisk University Galleries, Nashville, Tennessee. (Photo: Jerry Atnip.)

© Estate of Winold Reiss. Used by permission of Fisk University Galleries.

Winold Reiss, *Langston Hughes*, c. 1925, pastel on illustration board. National Portrait Gallery, Smithsonian Institution; gift of W. Tjark Reiss, in memory of his father, Winold Reiss.

© Estate of Winold Reiss. Used by permission of the National Portrait Gallery.

Carl Van Vechten (undated). Photograph by Nickolas Muray. *Beinecke Rare Book and Manuscript Library, Yale University. © Nickolas Muray Photo Archives. Used by permission of the Nickolas Muray Photo Archives.*

Fannie Hurst, 1932. Photograph by Carl Van Vechten. *Beinecke Rare Book and Manuscript Library, Yale University. © Van Vechten Trust. Used by permission of the Van Vechten Trust.*

The only issue of *Fire!!*, published in October 1926.
Beinecke Rare Book and Manuscript Library, Yale University.

Zora in 1927. Photographer unknown.
Beinecke Rare Book and Manuscript Library, Yale University.

Langston in 1927.
Photographer unknown.
*Beinecke Rare Book and Manuscript
Library, Yale University.*

Jessie Fauset, Langston, and
Zora, Tuskegee, Alabama, July
1927. Photographer unknown.
*Beinecke Rare Book and Manuscript Library,
Yale University.*

Zora and Langston outside the Veterans Administration Hospital at Tuskegee, Alabama, July 1927. In the top picture is Sadie Delaney, the hospital's librarian. The man on the left in the bottom picture is Colonel Joseph Henry Ward, who ran the hospital. One of the men in these two photos is likely Dr. Jesse Jerome Peters; the others have not been identified. Photographer unknown.

Beinecke Rare Book and Manuscript Library, Yale University.

Charlotte Mason.
Photographer unknown.
*Beinecke Rare Book and Manuscript
Library, Yale University.*

Alain Locke, 1926.
Photographer unknown.
*Beinecke Rare Book and Manuscript
Library, Yale University.*

Louise Thompson,
likely late 1920s.
Photograph by James
Latimer Allen.
*Beinecke Rare Book and
Manuscript Library, Yale
University.*

Langston in 1930,
likely after his
breakup with
Charlotte Mason.
Photographer
unknown.
*Beinecke Rare Book and
Manuscript Library, Yale
University.*

Langston and Louise on the boat to Russia, May 1932. Photographer unknown.
Beinecke Rare Book and Manuscript Library, Yale University.

Zora Neale Hurston, November 1934. Photograph by Carl Van Vechten.
Beinecke Rare Book and Manuscript Library, Yale University. © Van Vechten Trust. Used by permission of the Van Vechten Trust.

she went even further in a letter to Locke, writing, "I am a Black God in African art compared to you in the nourishment I give the Negroes, from the root of their primitive ancestry." Her arrogance now seems absurd, but her correspondents seemed to have taken it in stride. After all, there *was*, by common agreement, something superhuman about Charlotte Mason.

Still, her godchildren might find themselves perturbed by her behavior. Zora could confide only in Langston about her troubles with Godmother. When Zora needed a new car and mentioned this to Mason, the latter "simply exploded." Mason "wrote me a letter that hurt me thru and thru," Zora told Langston, and with good reason: Godmother had asked her, "Why couldn't Negroes be trusted?" "I just feel that she ought not to exert herself to supervise every little detail," Zora complained. At the same time, when Zora sent Mason her critique of a book, *The Negro and His Songs*, by two white folklorists, Mason misread Zora's comment "that white people could not be trusted to collect the lore of others"—a sentiment Mason had expressed herself—as applying *to herself.* When Zora's essay "How It Feels to Be Colored Me" was published, Godmother was angry, feeling that in publishing something without submitting it to her, Zora was violating the terms of her agreement. Zora wriggled out of this by telling Godmother that she had submitted the essay to *The World Tomorrow* prior to signing the agreement; she did not point out that the essay had nothing to do with her collecting work. Mason also got angry at Zora when she found out that Zora wanted to do some work for Franz Boas, and Zora was forced to write him that her hands were tied. Godmother constantly worried she was being taken advantage of, kept insinuating that Zora was being extravagant, and continually reminded her of the terms of her contract. Mason acted in just as controlling and accusatory a manner with some of her other protégés (though less so with Langston, whom she petted and indulged). Aaron Douglas, for example, had to turn down some important commissions because Godmother deemed them too white-leaning, and he eventually disentangled himself from her patronage. The constant supervision Mason imposed "destroys my self-respect," Zora wrote to Langston, "and utterly demoralizes me for weeks. I know you can appreciate what I mean. I do care for her deeply, don't forget that. That is why I can't endure to get at odds with her." Zora was so nervous about the relationship that she went out of her way to "conjure" Godmother when visiting Louisiana, making a wish at a fortune teller's establishment in Marrero "that a certain influential white woman would help me." The conjure woman told Zora that this woman would look after her for the rest of her life. Sure enough, the next morning, or so Zora later wrote, she received a telegram from Mason "stating that she would stand by me as long as she lived." As indeed she would.

Zora undoubtedly felt that Langston would too. By this time, however, a different woman had entered his life.

▼▼▼

Louise Thompson grew up poor, an only child, in small towns in Nevada, California, Utah, Idaho, Washington, and Oregon, attending all-white schools and, though light-complexioned, ostracized for being black. She graduated with honors from the University of California at Berkeley in 1923, but as a black woman was unable to find work in the Bay Area and had to pass for Mexican in order to get a menial job. She and her mother soon moved to Chicago; inspired by a talk she had with W. E. B. Du Bois at the NAACP convention there, she longed to go to New York City, but the amount of money she'd saved would have gotten the two women only as far east as the Chicago suburb of Evanston.

On a whim, she decided to take a teaching job at the all-black Agricultural, Mechanical and Normal School of Pine Bluff, Arkansas, traveling to the Jim Crow South for the first time.

She vividly described her disheartening experiences there in her unfinished and unpublished memoir; it's a fascinating account of Southern racism and its effects during the 1920s. After one year, she took a position at the Hampton Institute in Virginia, another school for black youth, this one run mostly by whites. There she witnessed a groundbreaking student strike in 1927, an example of dignified nonviolent resistance to top administrators' dismissal of radical students and professors, demeaning remarks, and segregationist policies. The strike greatly impressed her, despite its failure.

Thompson first met Langston at a reading he gave at Hampton that March, near the beginning of the Southern tour during which he would encounter Zora in Mobile. Langston encouraged Louise's move to Harlem; as soon as she arrived in 1928, Wallace Thurman hired her as a typist for his novel *The Blacker the Berry*, and then promptly married her. She was beautiful, intelligent, and twenty-six years old. The marriage was a great surprise to everyone who knew Thurman; he would never admit to being homosexual but his secret was known to—and accepted by—all. The marriage only lasted a few weeks before it fell apart.

The Urban League had awarded Thompson a fellowship so that she could earn a master's degree in social work at the New School for Social Research, but she soon realized that she wasn't inclined toward that vocation, and left the program. She continued to work as a typist for Arna Bontemps and others while trying to get a favorable settlement from Thurman. In the summer, she went to Reno to finalize her divorce and was planning to stay there for the requisite three months, but her mother was diagnosed with cancer so she returned to Harlem.

On October 2, 1929, as Louise later wrote,

> Suddenly, just like manna from heaven, Alain Locke appeared at my door and told me he wanted to take me down to meet someone. That someone was 'Godmother.' . . . She wanted to hire me to be secretary for Langston and Zora. I could work at home. Alain and she had discussed the arrangement before I met her. So she gave me $150 to buy a typewriter and desk to have at home. I was to be at her and their beck and call. . . . Before I left Mrs. Mason, it was all agreed and arranged. . . .
>
> Meeting her was like coming into the company of royalty. . . . I was awed, to be quite frank. She was quite different from the other types, the ones who went slumming and seeking new outlets for their jaded tastes. Mrs. Mason was a woman who had been wealthy probably all of her life. Her house was very formal. She had all English servants, and she was very kindly. In the beginning, I did not see her as condescending. She was very soft in her manner and questioned me about my background and circumstances very skillfully. . . . And she was very nice and very kindly to me. I was very, very happy with the arrangement.

In fact, Louise "was so taken with her" that she wrote an ode to her. It's too long and effusive to reprint in full here, but it's structured as the obverse of Little Red Riding Hood, in which Louise plays the title part and Godmother plays the grandmother, who seems to have defeated the Big Bad Wolf:

She has walked with God. . . .

"Ah, Godmother—what beautiful eyes you have."

"The better to see you with my child." And she does see as only one who has stood apart from the world, on the edge of the world[,] looked down upon it, was troubled by it, loved it, and came from the high places to succour it. . . .

"Ah, Godmother, how tiny you are."

"The better to fit into the nooks and crannies of my dear children's lives." Legion are her children and always she must hide away behind them. . . . And with this she reaches into her magic bag and brings the necessary potion of material of spiritual encouragement. What fascinating little hidden pockets she has in her full soft skirt—she pulls out crackly paper bills from a soft leather purse and presses them gently into the empty hand. . . .

This may strike us now as parodic, but it was quite heartfelt. Once again, Godmother was giving the impression of being a minor goddess.

Godmother proceeded to read a Native American myth to Louise, prefacing it with the observation, "There is a spontaneity and beautiful emotional freedom and communion with the life of earth and sky in these peoples which civilization has had not yet time to destroy, thank God."

Godmother would send for Louise every once in a while and talk to her, Louise sitting on a stool at her feet. She related her experiences with American Indians; she introduced Louise to her vicious anti-Semitism, which she espoused openly; she told her how much she looked down on the vulgarity of the nouveaux riches like the Astors and the Vanderbilts; she told her not to polish her nails, as it was vulgar; she would probe into the intimate details of Louise's personal life, including her diet and bowel movements; she would give her nutritional advice. "When she talked about blacks," Louise wrote, "the thing that interested her was their nearness to nature and the idea that they had not been corrupted by modern society.... Her model was Zora. She would tell me how Zora was so close to the earth and so forth." Mason was so "ecstatic" when talking about Zora that Louise couldn't wait to meet her. Mason was also clearly very fond of Langston, but had reservations about Locke, who "apes white people too much." She was "solicitious" about Louise's mother's health, and would usually give her money to "get something for your mother." And she took a keen interest in Louise's own career—she didn't view Louise as simply a stenographer, but as a future writer.

Louise, however, also saw another side to Godmother, one that wasn't quite so kind. Once, during lunch, an English servant girl "dropped a spoon or something and got fired on the spot."

Another time, Louise, feeling uncomfortable and at a loss for words, commented to Godmother during one of their formal luncheons (she felt as though she were eating at Buckingham Palace), "This is a lovely table arrangement of flowers, Mrs. Mason" (Louise never called her "Godmother" to her face, despite Mason's desire for her to do so; "she was my employer," she later explained, "not my godmother").

"Oh, you like it, my child?"

"Yes it's beautiful. Very nice."

"Which color do you like?" Godmother asked.

"I think the red ones are lovely. They're all lovely, but I think the red ones are very pretty."

Godmother replied, "You would say that, my dear little primitive child."

Louise, chagrined, did not respond.

▼▼▼

For his senior project in sociology at Lincoln, Langston had studied the student culture there, and the resulting survey, condemning the all-white faculty and the students' apathy about it, had caused a furor. Locke, who visited him, commented to Mason, "The quiet informal way he is doing it is masterly," and told Langston, "Instead of going out of Lincoln by the front door, it seems to me you are coming out through the roof and taking it off with you."

Langston appended a brief foreword to the survey, which read in its entirety,

> In the primitive world, where people live closer to the earth and much nearer to the stars, every inner and outer act combines to form the single harmony, life. Not just the tribal lore then, but every movement of life becomes a part of their education. They do not, as many civilized people do, neglect the truth of the physical for the sake of the mind. Nor do they teach with speech alone, but rather with all the acts of life. There are no books, so the barrier between words and reality is not so great as with us. The earth is right under their feet. The stars are never far away. The strength of the surest dream is the strength of the primitive world.

Perhaps nowhere is the primitivist philosophy that Charlotte Mason, Langston, and Zora shared so clearly and succinctly expressed. As Carla Kaplan points out, it reads as if Mason had written it herself.

After graduating, Langston visited Manhattan for two weeks

before returning to Lincoln to spend the summer revising his novel. He found Harlem completely changed: many of the nightclubs had started to cater exclusively to whites. Langston complained to Claude McKay about the "awfully bad" and "unbearably vulgar" shows and music now being produced by African Americans in Manhattan. And the better work, like Wallace Thurman's literary magazine *Harlem*, couldn't survive—it folded after only one issue.

▼▼▼

In September 1929 Langston moved from Lincoln to 514 Downer Street, Westfield, New Jersey, about an hour from Manhattan, since Godmother felt that in New York he would be subject to too many distractions. He stayed in a tiny clapboard-paneled attic room in the front of the late-Victorian house, which was occupied by an elderly black couple, the Peeples (the room is still there, looking much as it did then). Louise now started working as a stenographer for him, traveling to New Jersey, as well as for Mason herself, assisting Katherine Biddle and Cornelia Chapin. A few weeks later came Black Thursday, October 24, 1929, the Wall Street crash that would plunge the nation into the Great Depression. Mason lost half her money, but continued to fully support her beneficiaries, and Langston and Louise were unaffected.

Louise, her mother, and her friend Sue Bailey lived in a Harlem apartment at 425 Convent Avenue, just north of 148th Street, not far from City College. Although Louise had many suitors, a reporter for a black gossip magazine, the *Inter-State Tattler*, mentioned seeing her holding hands with Langston on Seventh Avenue. Her boyfriend at the time grew so jealous that he moved to Africa. Louise and Langston frequented the Savoy Ballroom, where she tried in vain to get him to learn the Lindy hop; they watched football games at the Polo Grounds (home of the New York Giants); and they went out on the town with Aaron Douglas and his wife Alta.

A year earlier, in November 1928, Langston had fallen in love with a young woman named Laudee Williams, of whom little is known; they had exchanged rings, but he seems to have lost interest rather quickly, and she had left him "broken hearted— not even in love anymore," as he wrote to Wallace Thurman in a joking tone the following summer. In contrast, Langston never gave anyone any indication that he was "in love" with Louise. Louise, however, was clearly in love with Langston.

Langston was seeing plenty of Mason as well. And under her guidance (she sent him copious notes and tendered valuable advice) and with help from Louise ("who must have done certain pages over for me so often she could have recited by heart their varying versions"), he finished his novel, which Knopf accepted for publication.

A medical report from early November states that Langston was working eight to twelve hours a day; devoted an hour a day to walking and running; did twenty or thirty minutes of calisthenics; refrained from coffee, alcohol, and tobacco; and suffered from nervousness and some insomnia, "probably due to overwork." At five foot five, he weighed 124 pounds, and his musculature was "moderately firm."

Langston, however, felt uneasy about being so well taken care of when masses were going hungry. He was sick of his novel, and he had written almost no poetry of note during the last few years. As usual, he found relief by traveling, and spent ten days in Cuba looking for a musician to collaborate with him on a "singing play." There, to his surprise, he found himself the toast of Havana: "Everyone," writes his biographer Arnold Rampersad, "wanted to be introduced to the greatest Negro poet of the United States of America—indeed, the greatest Negro poet in the world." Never before had he felt so *important*.

By the time he returned to Westfield, he had company there. Zora had moved into a one-room rental unit at 405 West Broad Street, another late-Victorian house not much bigger than the one Langston occupied, only two blocks away.

8

The Bone of Contention

Charlotte Mason had orchestrated it all. Upon Zora's return to New York in March (she had been in the Bahamas for the last two months, writing an article entitled "Dance Songs and Tales from the Bahamas"), Godmother had summoned her to come to her Park Avenue apartment, where she asked Zora to tell the stories, sing the songs, do the dances, and show the film footage she'd gathered in the South.

We can imagine the performance. There are recordings from a few years later of Zora singing the songs she collected in a beautiful contralto; her distinctive voice radiates joy. There are three photographs of her doing the crow dance in 1935, and she looks lithe and nimble. The footage she filmed in the South survives. One sequence shows a boy performing a dance with cartwheels and splits surrounded by clapping children, next pans the faces of these children, going around the circle, and then focuses on their stomping feet.

Following this performance, and echoing the logic she'd

used with Langston, Mason informed Zora about her new digs. The two writers would share Louise Thompson as a secretary; Mason had even briefed Louise on what to expect: "She used to talk about Zora," Louise later said, "about this wonderful child of nature who was so unspoiled, and what a marvellous person she was. And Zora did not disappoint me. She was a grand storyteller." The moment the two women first met "was quite a moment. Here came in this 'professor,' a woman full of energy and vitality and laughter and stories. And I just thought she was wonderful, as Mrs. Mason had said."

Naturally, Zora and Langston were overjoyed to be together again. They talked nonstop and, faced with Zora's task of editing down her piles of folklore, Langston gladly pitched in. Louise started typing for Zora too, often spending half the night preparing the folktale manuscript for Godmother, occasionally spending the entire night in Zora's room, typing until her arm hurt from throwing the typewriter's carriage so often.

"How do you like that one?" Zora would ask Louise about one of her folktales. "Fine," Louise would answer. "I made that one up," Zora would inform her. Mason would send Zora exotic dresses to wear and Zora would call her to tell her how stunning they looked. After hanging up she would tell Louise, laughingly, that she wouldn't dream of wearing such a thing. One day Zora telephoned Godmother and said, "Godmother, were you at the window sending me signs at 5:00 a.m.? I got the vibrations." Of course, Zora had been in bed asleep at the time, for she would habitually stay up half the night telling hoodoo stories.

And one night, while they were both in the only bed in Zora's room, Zora asked Louise if she was interested in homosexuality. Louise didn't sleep the entire night.

Is it possible that Zora fell in love with Louise during those long days and nights working, talking, and sleeping together? The outsize role that Louise would come to play in the breakup of Zora and Langston's friendship might indicate that Zora's jealousy may not have been caused as much by Langston favoring Louise as by Louise favoring Langston. Whether Zora had homosexual desires is a complicated question. In the 1930s she was close friends with the bisexual singer and actor Ethel Waters, and later wrote, "I am her friend, and her tongue is in my mouth. . . . She is shy and you must convince her that she is really wanted before she will open up her tender parts and show you." Reading this literally, as some have done, as evidence of homosexual desires strikes me, however, as specious—the context of these words in *Dust Tracks on a Road* is not the least bit suggestive. More seriously, in 1940 she "fell in love with" the thirty-six-year-old white anthropologist Jane Belo—those are the words she used in the initial draft of her autobiography—and some of her letters to Belo are effusive love letters. Yet being "in love," for Zora, did not necessarily imply sexual desire. When Belo fell in love with the man who would become her third husband, Zora told her that it didn't change the way she felt, that she was happy for her, and that she had fallen in love with a man herself. Zora married three times but never lived with any of her husbands for more than a few weeks; like Langston, she had few long-term physical relationships. Unlike Langston, though, she did admit to a strong appetite for the opposite sex.

At any rate, Zora, Louise, and Langston spent many hours together, not only in Westfield, but at Louise's Harlem apartment. They went to parties together, where Zora liked to "perform," sometimes wearing a different shoe on each foot, and where Langston would tell shaggy-dog stories, fooling people with a long tale with no punch line.

But soon Godmother learned, probably from Locke, that the three were spending too much time having fun and not enough time working, even though, as Langston later wrote, Zora was arranging her "folk material, stacks and stacks of it," and was planning to dedicate it all to Mason. (After all, it was Mason's property, even if Zora would be allowed to publish it under her own name. The dedication ran, "This breath from the spiritual life of my people is dedicated to the Mother of the Primitives who, each morning at the coming of the yellow line, takes my people with her to meet the high gods in space.")

Mason was angry about what Locke told her. She scolded Zora and, in response to a phone call from Langston, sent him a simple note that read, "Dear Boy, What is the Matter? Love, 'Godmother.'"

Langston replied with a long letter that began, "It was immensely cheering to have your little note—and very kind of you to write me—especially when I know how difficult it is physically for you to write." (Langston seems to be referring to a longer note than the eight-word one just quoted, but no such note from early 1930 is in Langston's papers, and he was assiduous about keeping her correspondence.) It was clear, however, that despite his profuse apologies he wasn't quite sure what he was apologizing for.

> I had been terribly worried because Zora and I both felt that you had been displeased, or hurt in some way about her work. . . . I do care for you, and when I hurt you through stupidity or error, I cannot bear it. . . . Whatever happened last week to make you unhappy must have been my fault— not Zora's—because it was I who called you by phone. But maybe I'm all wrong—all tangled up. You will forgive me

if I do not understand. Perhaps it is all "nerves" on my part. "Emotional instability" or whatever they call it. But now I feel physically better, a little rested, and it was good to have your dear letter. . . . But, for a week, I had never been more miserable in my life—except after that unfortunate Christmas when you gave me the bag—and I didn't know how to say thanks—and you were unhappy. That's why it makes me afraid when you are displeased, because I couldn't bear for anything like that to happen to you again. I'd rather go back to the hotel kitchens or the freight steamers—and let go of my dreams. But I am not always wise—too often wrong—and I am sorry.

Considering his hurt, it's not surprising that Langston told neither Mason nor Locke when, in April, a month after he had come back from Cuba, he began to work in earnest with Zora on a play. Indeed, Locke wrote Zora at the end of that month that he was looking forward to working with her to wrap up her folklore manuscript, advising her that Mason "thinks it would be a mistake even to have a scientific tone to the book, so soft pedal all notion of too specific documentation and let loose on the things that you are really best equipped to give—a vivid dramatizing of your material and the personalities back of it." Zora was also writing to Franz Boas how hard she was working to finish the folklore project. Nobody but Langston expected that at this point, so close to completion, she would turn her attention to the theater.

One impetus for the Hurston-Hughes collaboration was a conversation Langston had had in February with Theresa Helburn, executive director of the Theatre Guild, who complained to him that most of the plays about black people were serious problem dramas, and what was needed was a comedy (but not, of course, of the minstrel-show variety). This echoed a lament common among the black and white literati of the era, from W. E. B. Du Bois to Eugene O'Neill: whites were writing most of the good dramas with African Americans in them because black playwrights were afraid that black audiences wouldn't appreciate nonminstrelish theater. So Langston and Zora decided to write a folk comedy based on Zora's story "The Bone of Contention," written late in 1925 but unpublished until after her death, which was based in turn on a tale she had heard in Eatonville and had often retold during her Harlem days. Mason would later attest that "it was the regular thing for people to ask her for that story."

A full-length African American nonmusical nonminstrel comedy was not unprecedented: the actor Frank Wilson had written two, *Pa Williams' Gal* and *Meek Mose*, the first having a successful run at the Lafayette Theater on 132nd Street, one of the largest theaters in Harlem, in 1923, and the second having a short run at the Princess Theater on Broadway in 1928. In addition, there was a tradition of "folk plays" performed at churches and small theaters like the Harlem Experimental Theatre, which featured another full-length black-authored comedy in 1929 or 1930, Andrew M. Burris's *You Mus' Be Bo'n Ag'in.* But Zora and Langston felt that the commercial potential for their venture was large in comparison. Theirs was not to be a folk play to be performed on a basement stage or for a short run at the Lafayette, but was aimed squarely at Broadway, where African American musicals had enjoyed huge success, where at least five black-authored nonmusical dramas (not comedies) had already been performed (including the wildly successful *Appearances* in 1925, the first Broadway play with a mixed-race cast), and where the white playwright Marc Connelly's all-black drama *The Green Pastures* was the biggest hit of the era, winning the 1930 Pulitzer Prize.

During their work together, Langston and Louise would be convulsed with laughter as Zora acted out the scenes, using different voices for each character. Louise transcribed, Zora and Langston invented, and the pages flowed—Louise typed around the clock and got so tired she couldn't lift her arms.

Whether intentionally or not, Zora and Langston ignored Helburn's advice about steering clear of minstrel tropes. At the center of "The Bone of Contention" was a courtroom scene that could have come straight out of a minstrel-show afterpiece: Jim is accused of stealing a turkey and hitting Dave over the head with a mule bone, and the Baptist and Methodist reverends (acting the part of lawyers) get into a ridiculous argument about whether or not a mule bone is a weapon, invoking the story of Samson using the jawbone of an ass to slaughter the Philistines. Four of the all-black musicals of the 1920s—*Darktown Jubilee, Africana, His Honery,* and *The Judge*—had also featured comic courtroom scenes with malaprop-spouting judges like Hurston's Eatonville mayor Joe Clarke.

The play, at first entitled *The Mule-Bone,* added several more scenes that did not appear in the story, with less of a minstrel flavor. But with nineteen "principal characters" and another thirty or so "minor characters," there was little opportunity for an exploration of any of them in depth. While it succeeded in breaking from many of the stereotypes that urban black drama had indulged in for the past few decades, it replaced them with equally hoary stereotypes of Southern folk: Jim and Dave are too lazy to lift anything heavier than a guitar; the women are all either arguing shrews or coquettes; the mayor-cum-judge is a pompous fool and his deputy incompetent and clumsy.

By this point Zora had written at least five other plays, three of which had been published, as well as a number of theatrical sketches; she had seen her work staged on several occasions. She had been a member of W. E. B. Du Bois's theater company, the Crigwa Players (Crigwa stood for *Crisis* Guild of Writers and Artists; its spelling was later changed to *Krigwa*), and apparently helped establish its Little Negro Theatre in Harlem (which was where the Harlem Experimental Theatre, a successor to the Krigwa Players, would stage its plays). Langston had had little experience writing for the theater: he had written only a three-page drama for children called "The Gold Piece" and the beginning of a musical play called *The Emperor of Haiti*. Zora had long considered herself a playwright, and her output in the genre almost equaled that of her fiction. By this point in his career, Langston, despite his lifelong adoration of the theater, had preferred, in his writing, the solitude of poetry and fiction.

The play itself seemed to draw on all of Zora's strengths and few of Langston's. The setting was one she had been immersed in and had written about extensively: an all-black community in the backwoods South; the scenes were full of the kinds of "lies" (tall tales) that fill the pages of her work; the comedy in it is completely characteristic of her writing at the time. Langston would later describe to his lawyer the composition of the play as follows: "I would do the construction, plot, whatever characterization I could, and guide the dialog. Miss Hurston was to put in the authentic Florida color, give the dialog a true Southern flavor, and insert many excellent turns of phrase and 'wisecracks' which she had in her mind and among her collections." Given that the plot and dramatis personae are almost completely derived from Zora's stories—not only "The Bone of Contention," but also the 1926 "Eatonville Anthology," a group of very brief sketches whose characters included Joe Clarke, the mayor and store owner; Daisy Taylor, the town vamp; Mrs. Roberts, the "pleading woman"; Lum Boger, the marshall; Elijah Mosely and Walter Thomas, two "village wags"; and a few others, all of them real Eatonville residents—the first part of Langston's description seems disingenuous at best. Langston claimed to have suggested, over Hurston's objections, changing the main cause of the dispute between Dave and Jim from an argument over who shot a turkey to a fight over Daisy, thus providing the occasion for the third act, in which Dave, Jim, and Daisy are the only characters on stage. But even if that were the case, Daisy herself was a real person Zora had known in Eatonville, whose persona she had already established in "Eatonville Anthology." The dialogue, all in dialect, is completely characteristic of Zora: while in Langston's novel *Not Without Laughter* and his play *Mulatto* (written a few months later), the characters speak in minstrel-derived dialect like "I's gwine," in *The Mule-Bone* they say "I'm goin'." Zora admitted that Langston had come up with the idea of setting the third act on a railroad track. It's also easy to believe his assertion that he suggested making Dave and Jim best friends, Dave a dancer and Jim a guitarist, and eliminating the turkey from the plot. But what else he contributed is an open question. The early notes for the play are in Langston's handwriting, but many of his ideas (such as having Daisy Taylor be a new woman in town) were not used in later drafts. (In one draft, Daisy has been to Harlem and comes back to Eatonville to a warm welcome, thus linking her experience with Zora's; but subsequent drafts bring her back to the original portrayal in "Eatonville Anthology.") In *The Big Sea*, Langston stated, "I plotted out and typed the play based on her story, while she authenticated and flavored the dialogue and added highly humorous details." Zora's recollection would turn out to be quite different.

Much later, Langston remembered, "Zora, a very gay and lively girl [she was hardly a *girl*, even if Langston believed she was only thirty], was seriously hemmed in in village-like Westfield. . . . She was restless and moody, working in a nervous manner. And we were both distressed at the growing depression—hearing of more and more friends and relatives losing jobs and becoming desperate for lack of work." Indeed, when Zora finally visited her old haunts in Harlem at the end of May, she wrote her old friend Larry Jordan, "Some of my friends are all tired and worn out— looking like death eating crackers."

Langston, Zora, and Louise were much better off than most, with stipends from Mason continuing to flow at $150 per month for Langston and Louise and $200 for Zora. They often bor- rowed money from each other: on May 4, Langston lent fifteen dollars to Zora, who paid it back five days later, and on May 20, Zora bought Louise dinner, typing paper, and a new typewriter ribbon.

Louise was being paid by Mason for typing Zora's folklore manuscript, not for typing a play, so Langston felt that she should get some additional recompense for her stenographic contribu- tions and proposed that they split the royalties three ways. Zora objected, and the next day offered to pay Louise five dollars a day—a generous amount for the era. According to Zora, Lou- ise responded to Langston, as if the suggestion was his, "Pay *me*, Langston! No, I don't want a thing now, but when it goes over, then you all can take care of me then"; Louise later confirmed that she had indeed offered to wait for payment until the play should be produced. Perhaps this was merely a way for Louise to pleasantly delay compensation, but Zora took it as a clear sign that Langston and Louise had come to an agreement that, in principle, Louise should be financially rewarded for her work if the play took off. Zora could not wrap her head around this principle. After all, she reasoned, has a *typist* ever shared in the proceeds of a creative work? Zora had already signed away her authorial rights to Godmother; now Langston was proposing to sign some more away to Louise. Langston then came up with the idea of having Louise act as their business manager. "That struck me as merely funny," Zora would write to Langston the following January. "With all the experienced and capable agents on Broadway, *I* should put my business in the hands of some one who knows less about the subject than I."

The matter was soon settled, however. Zora and Langston phoned Godmother and told her about the play in order to clear up the question of Louise's compensation. She asked them, as she later wrote in her notebook, "not to go on with the play[,] to put it aside as it would conflict and interfere with Zora's completing the real work she was doing[,] that her book must get ahead." They could have expected such a reply, given Mason's objections to their earlier plan to write an opera.

Somehow that phone conversation with Godmother solved the problem of compensating Louise—most likely, Godmother increased Louise's allowance. As a result, Louise would no longer have anything to do with handling the play's production. That would be left up to its authors, who were anxious to make of it a grand success.

▼▼▼

Shortly afterwards, in late May 1930, Langston visited Godmother. He wrote in *The Big Sea*, "I knew that my friend and benefactor was not happy because, for months now, I had written nothing beautiful." In fact, with the exception of his contributions to *The Mule-Bone*, he had written nothing since he'd completed *Not Without Laughter* in February, and during the years he'd been working on the novel, he had written very little poetry. "So I asked kindly to be released from any further obligations to her, and that she give me no more money, but simply let me retain her friendship and good will that had been so dear to me. That I asked to keep. But there must have been only the one thread binding us together. When that thread broke, it was the end."

If there was one thing Mason could not abide, it was ingratitude, and that was exactly what she considered Langston's offer to wean himself from her support. Like the Old Testament God, she needed to be thanked effusively for everything. Langston's proposal—to end his contract but to retain her friendship—must have felt like a slap in the face to Mason, especially after he had betrayed her trust by delaying Zora's work with the crazy theater idea. Langston had misjudged her, expecting that she would be happy to be freed of her financial obligations to him, especially since he did not feel he was making good on her expectations. But on hearing that her "precious brown boy" no longer needed her, she exploded in fury.

Langston told Louise all about it. "The way she talked to Langston," Louise recalled, "is the way a woman talks when she's keeping a pimp. 'I bought those clothes you are wearing! I took care of you! I gave you this! I gave you that!'" Mason enumerated precisely how much she had spent on Langston, including what she had paid Louise, and asked, rhetorically, what she had gotten in return. Langston dramatized the scene in his autobiography:

That beautiful room, that had been so full of light and help and understanding for me, suddenly became like a trap closing in, faster and faster, the room darker and darker, until the light went out with a sudden crash in the dark. . . . Physically, my stomach began to turn over and over—and then over again. I fought against bewilderment and anger, fought hard, and didn't say anything. I just sat there in the high Park Avenue drawing-room and didn't say anything. I sat there and listened to all she told me, closed my mouth hard and didn't say anything.

I do not remember clearly what it was she said to me at the end, nor her face as the door closed, nor the elevator dropping down to the street level, nor my final crossing of the lobby through a lane of uniformed attendants.

But I do remember the winter sunshine on Park Avenue and the wind in my face as I went toward the subway to Harlem.

The shock was terrible. That evening, Langston went to dinner at Louise's house. "There were other guests," he later remembered, "and her mother had prepared a wonderful meal." But Langston couldn't eat, and felt as if he were going to die. He "cried like a baby," Louise testified. He began to experience the signs of a breakdown—"My voice seemed far away and the whole thought lost in such a void that I couldn't correct myself." It was eight in the evening. He went straight to his doctor's office and "said I felt as if I had gone to the other world." He felt violently ill, but the doctor told him there was nothing wrong with him. He couldn't eat for a week. He saw three other doctors, had some X-rays taken, gave samples of his urine and blood, and, of course, remained undiagnosed.

Langston thought that one immediate cause of the fracas was his decision to go to Washington, D.C., to keep a commitment he had made, rather than stay in New Jersey and write. But Langston never understood exactly why Mason erupted as she did. Scholars have offered a multitude of explanations for Mason's conduct. Arnold Rampersad believes that she was upset about the lack of work Langston had done since finishing his novel. And indeed it is quite clear from their correspondence that Langston's idleness upset Mason, even if she often advised her beneficiaries to rest and revive. Faith Berry, another Hughes biographer, thinks it was Langston's overtly political poems and essays that caused the breakup, but Langston didn't begin writing those until later that year. In *The Big Sea*, Langston misleadingly places the composition of his poem "Advertisement for the Waldorf-Astoria" prior to the breakup and intimates that because Mason didn't like it the relationship turned sour. (It included the line "Dine with some of the men and women who got rich off your labor, who clip coupons [something that Mason did habitually] with clean white fingers because your hands dug coal, drilled stone, sewed garments, poured steel to let other people draw dividends and live easy.") However, the poem could not have been written prior to 1931, since the hotel didn't open until that October. Carla Kaplan suggests that "the cause was an escalating conflict between Hughes and Hurston over their play," but there is scant evidence of any conflict at this point. At the end of May, after Langston's breakup with Godmother, Zora casually mentioned Louise favorably in a letter she wrote Larry Jordan, and she and Langston visited Carl Van Vechten together on June 10 to wish him farewell (he was going to Europe for the summer). Kaplan also suggests that the cause was Langston publishing "Afro-American Fragment," a poem that questioned Mason's belief in the direct linkage between Africa and African Americans. But once again, the break preceded the publication of the poem in July 1930, and probably its composition. (Neither Langston nor Mason mentioned the poem in their correspondence, making it unlikely that Mason had seen it by May.)

As I mention above, *The Big Sea* and Langston's correspondence with Mason indicate that the immediate cause was Langston's desire to increase his financial independence, which was in part motivated by guilt over being driven around New York by a white chauffeur when his peers were sleeping in subways and going hungry (the unemployment rate in Harlem was five times that of the rest of the city). Mason interpreted this desire as the basest ingratitude.

But I believe another major cause was his collaboration with Zora. Mason's fondest hope was to make a difference to the world through a mystical connection to the primitive, which would overwhelm the malign forces of civilization. There were many linked routes to that connection, but by this time her energy was focused on Zora's work. Langston's novel was finished; Locke had become, as Kaplan points out, "disenchanted with [Mason's] 'vision' of the Harlem Museum of African Art." Mason "could no longer invest in those who could not—or would not—produce according to her lights"; her "last hope" rested on Zora's unfinished manuscript. It had become, for her, an obsession.

The phone call from Langston and Zora about their play had to have been a major disappointment. Mason had never had a kind word to say about the theater. And the call made her believe that the play had been instigated by Langston. It was taking Zora away from her most valuable work. As Kaplan writes, Mason "did not want Hurston distracted by Hughes, who she now claimed made her 'earth path even harder.'" Zora was at this point indispensable for Mason's plans; Langston was simply getting in Zora's way while failing to produce anything of value himself. And then he had the audacity to insult Mason, as she thought, by claiming his independence from her.

Langston borrowed some money from Van Vechten on May 26, now that his monthly stipend was gone. He wrote a series of pleading letters to Mason. Again, we have only drafts—we don't know whether they were actually sent. And they were likely interspersed with telephone conversations, since in the June 6 letter, Langston mentions Godmother's "kind and sincere talks with me the last few weeks."

The first of these letters was dated May 28. "You have been more beautiful to me than anybody in the world, and my own failure is miserable beyond speech, so I will say no more about it. . . . I did not want to hurt you. I wanted only to be true to your love for me, but human words have too many meanings other than the single meaning of the heart. . . . I want to be your spirit-child forever."

The second and third letters (one an impassioned plea for forgiveness, the other about financial matters) are far longer, and were written a few days later in Washington, where Langston had met with Locke, who in turn had introduced him to a young Cuban who was helping Langston with translations of Cuban poetry. "Washington is lovely," Langston wrote.

> Companionship and sleep have done wonders for my nerves. I had just about gone to pieces when I came down here. I could not control the musles [*sic*] in my body—and I was terribly worried. . . .
>
> Now that I am quite unworthy of your goodness, I beg of you to release me—or rather to release yourself from the burdens of my own lack of wisdom. Let us be as we were three years ago when I first knew you and loved you for the beauty of your soul—before my own selfishness came between us and the flaming gifts of your spirit. ~~Now I am shut out and must find my way back alone.~~ The fault is mine. The darkness is mine. The search is mine. The gods

have given me the light of your kindness and I do not know how to follow. Forgive me. I am sorry.

The physical truth of what is happening now, as nearly as I can arrive at, is this—that I have not the capacity to do the things which you think wise. A full year of living by myself, working by myself, has caused my natural isolation to grow into a loneliness that is unbearable. And your insistence on gratitude has made me feel that I have not been any where near able to give you the thanks which you deserve—and that therefore I must not receive any more help from you since I do not know how to thank you— especially since I can not write—and I feel my nerves going to pieces. I love your friendship, dear Godmother, and I need your monetary help badly, but I can have neither now, unless I have your permission to live and move again as it satisfies my own understanding—and unless I may spend the money as wisely as I know how without accounts or pressure. I cannot keep another account. . . .

But I cannot write at all when everything is planned in advance because I must feel, however mistakenly, that I owe an unpayable debt to you—or any other person. The pressure is too great. It is greater than the pressure of hunger. I can only write when I write for myself. Anything else is terrible. And it is not ingratitude which makes me say this—it is that I cannot live as you would have me.

On June 3, Mason sent Langston a list of foods in two columns, classified into "top vegetables" and "root vegetables." She followed this with a note on June 6: "Your letter stating your desires, describing your feeling of restraint has come to me. Dear child, what a hideous spectre you have made for yourself of the dead thing Money!" She enclosed a check for $250.

Langston wrote her again that same day; perhaps the letters crossed.

> In all my life I have never been free. I have never been able to do anything with freedom, except in the field of my writing. With my parents, with my employers in my struggle for food, in all the material circumstances of life, I have been forced to move this way and that—only when I sat down for a moment to write have I been able to put down what I wanted to put down, to say what I've wanted to say, when and where I choose. . . . [W]hen you told me I should have begun my writing again the week after I returned from Cuba—I must disagree with you. I must never write when I do not want to write. That is my last freedom and I must keep it for myself. . . . [ellipses in original] Then when you tell me that you give me more than anybody ever gave me before—($225⁰⁰ a month—my allowance and half of Louise)—and that I have been living in idleness since the first of March—I must feel miserably ashamed. . . . I cannot write on any sort of pre-arranged schedule. The nervous strain of finishing the novel by a certain time has shown me that.

There is no evidence that Mason replied.

▼▼▼

Sometime in June, rather suddenly, with the first and third acts and the brief first scene of the second of *The Mule-Bone* mostly finished, Zora left Westfield. There was no drama about it—she did not "break up" with Langston, who remained there. That was still to come. She simply moved back to Manhattan. Langston claimed to have no idea why, but guessed (correctly) that she needed to get her folklore collection ready for publication. Of course, that wasn't the only reason, as ensuing events would make clear. Zora promised to work on the play some more, and made at least one trip to Florida to collect folklore that summer.

Louise was puzzled. Word got back to her that Zora wanted to beat her up and had said that Louise and Langston had "done her in." Sue Bailey, her roommate and close friend, warned her, "Louise, you're so fond of Zora; you think she's your friend. I'll bet you she's not. She's cutting your throat as high as she can, right now." Another of Louise's friends told her that Zora had accused her and Langston of trying to steal her play.

One night at the Savoy, Louise saw Zora on the dance floor. She turned to the man she was dancing with and told him, "Zora Neale Hurston's here tonight, and she's threatened that if she ever sees me, she's going to wipe up the floor with me. So don't be surprised at what happens, if anything happens here tonight."

To Louise's surprise, Zora walked up to her, threw her arms around her, and kissed her. It was the last time Louise would ever see her.

Even decades later, Louise still didn't know what to think. "Arna Bontemps always believed," she wrote in her memoir, "that Zora was jealous of me. It was not over Langston because we were just good friends." Indeed, Bontemps wrote, much later, that Zora had told him herself how jealous she'd been of Louise; Zora confessed the same thing to Langston himself in 1931. Louise wondered, though, if Zora might have been jealous of her relationship with Godmother. She never understood how strongly Zora felt about her relationship with Langston.

Zora was justifiably proud of her play and felt that Langston had wanted to give Louise too much credit for it. But in addition,

Zora may have discovered that her feelings for Langston were deeper than she'd ever admitted, even to herself.

After all, Langston was not just Zora's best friend, but one of the few people with whom she felt a deep kinship. Her affection for him is obvious from her letters to him. One could easily make the case that she was in love with him, even if it was Platonic: her letters are full of endearments like "honey" and "darling," not to mention her "lovingly yours" signatures and her request for a picture of him. He was, she would soon confess, not just her best friend for years, but "the nearest person on earth to me." He was the only person she really wanted to show her work to, probably the one who understood it best, and whose reaction she most desired. He was one of the very few who fully shared her ideas about folklore and black language—possibly the only one. She thought highly of his poems, and he thought highly of her writing. He had introduced her to her benefactor, and was the only person she could consult when she was in trouble with Godmother. Langston and Zora had collaborated not just on an aborted opera, a magazine, and a play, but on a shared vision of what Negro literature could be. So when Louise replaced Zora as the main object of Langston's affections, who could blame Zora for feeling jealous?

And indeed, Langston's affection for Louise, even if it was also Platonic, went deep. His mother wanted him to marry her. Louise later said that if he had asked her, she would have said yes, despite the fact that she was not yet divorced. Was she in love with him, even if she never said so in so many words? It certainly appears so. In any case, Zora could have felt supplanted, especially when Langston turned to Louise for comfort after his breakup with Godmother.

Langston may have sought out Louise's company but he would never talk to her about his relationship with Godmother—or to anyone else. (Even in 1967, a few weeks before he died, Langston insisted on not revealing Mason's name to an interviewer.) But, for that matter, Langston wouldn't talk to Louise about relationships at all. "Langston was not one to go very much into things like this," Louise explained. "He'd make jokes and laugh. But sit down and have a serious discussion about something?" That he wouldn't do. He probably didn't even talk to Zora about these things.

It's difficult these days, when love and sex are so intertwined, to imagine a world like the one in which the protagonists of this book lived. Langston, Louise, Zora, Locke, and Godmother were each "in love" with at least one of the others to varying degrees, yet sexual desire was rarely part of the equation. (In fact, there was so little heterosexual activity among the leading lights of the Harlem Renaissance that almost none of them ended up having children—as Arnold Rampersad points out, besides Langston and Zora, Countee Cullen, Wallace Thurman, Alain Locke, Jessie Fauset, Harold Jackman, Bruce Nugent, Rudolph Fisher, Nella Larsen, and Aaron and Alta Douglas were all childless.) On the other hand, what I mean by "in love" is more than just a strong friendship. It requires intimacy and passion: the kind of intense feeling that unbalances one's emotions and that, when brought to an end, can produce anxiety and depression. That's what Langston and Godmother felt for each other; what Zora, Louise, and Locke all felt for Langston; what Zora would later feel for Jane Belo. Physical desire has little or nothing to do with these passionate attachments: Locke had never met Langston when he fell in love with him, and Langston never seemed to show any physical desire for anyone.

But relationship experts recognize that emotional attachments are usually stronger than physical ones. In a recent study, two-thirds of women surveyed said that a partner's emotional

affair would be more hurtful than a sexual one. Zora's emotional attachment to Langston had lasted at least three years
by this point and was the strongest bond in her life. It's small
wonder that when Louise and Langston "clicked" so well, Zora
became jealous.

Zora's jealousy, though, was not the kind of all-consuming rage
associated with sexual infidelity. It was, instead, a deep, cutting
sorrow that she wanted to keep hidden. She kept imagining the
things she wanted to say to him, and couldn't bear the thought of
doing so. As she later put it to Langston, "I felt that I was among
strangers, and the only thing to do was to go on away from there."

And then, of course, Zora knew about Langston's break with
Mason, and could easily guess that her own inability to finish
her folklore work and her collaboration with Langston on the
play had helped cause it. It was quite clearly in her best interest
to distance herself from Langston at this point if she wanted to
remain in Mason's graces.

▾▾▾

These very close friendships followed by sudden breaks had
become endemic to Langston. First Alain Locke in Venice
in 1924; then Countee Cullen later that same year; now both
Godmother and Zora. The people who loved him the most all
expected more than he could give.

On June 15, Langston wrote Godmother again, still trying to
appease her.

I love you, Godmother. I need you. You can help me more
than anyone on earth. Forgive me for the things I do not
know, the things I cannot fight alone, the things I haven't
understood. You know better than anyone else how stupid
and unwise I am, how I must battle the darkness within

myself. No one else would help me. No one else would care as you care. No one else would even try to understand. The door is never closed between us, Godmother. Only the shadow of my self stands in the way now. May the sea, the summer, the sun, and my new realization of what goodness means (through your ever generous kindness and your dear letters) sweep the path clean again.

I shall save twenty-five dollars a month from what you have given me for the summer. The remainder I shall use as wisely as I know how. It will last me until October. Forgive me, but I cannot keep any more accounts. The harder I try, the less I can bear it. I can't get rid of the feeling of my father and his eternal bookkeeping—for he had nothing that anybody would want except money and land—nothing else at all to make him happy—and nothing worth giving to those he wanted to love.

But the door *was* closed between them. Mason refused to see him. She sent him a telegram that month: "UNDER PRESENT CONDITIONS IT IS USELESS FOR ME TO UNDERTAKE ANY MORE THAN I HAVE PROMISED."

Langston tried yet again. He sent her the first copy of *Not Without Laughter* with a note that read, "For the beauty of your eyes that first night at Carnegie Hall when I looked down on you; for the love of your hands on my own; for the strength of your voice; for the truth of soul, and the great freedom of your heart—I send you today my love to greet you."

Godmother's response was equally emotional, but dark (referring to herself in the third person was typical of her letters). "As the sun sets on the western slopes of Godmother's life her spirit holds in its eternal belief the morning star that Sandy [the protagonist of *Not Without Laughter*, based on Langston as a child] was destined to carry into the hearts of his people." A long metaphorical passage ensues in which Godmother urges "Sandy" to "cling close to the parapet and watch day and night for Alamari's spear to catch the light of the Great Spirit" (Godmother often called Langston "Alamari"—the name of a Guinean war drum and also of the dance around it—in her letters) and to "call him higher and higher until he hears your whole race and feels them standing in that mountain of Transfiguration." And then she adds, "Dear Little Sandy, I feel so badly that you should be hampered in any way through the lack of vision of those who have the privilege of opening the door of your material appearance in this world. I can not bear the disfigurement of your 'new suit of clothes.'"

David Levering Lewis has written of *Not Without Laughter*, "Since Toomer, no Harlem writer had written as beautifully about the vices and virtues of ordinary Afro-Americans and the truths governing their lives; (except for [Nella Larsen's] *Quicksand*) it would not be equalled or surpassed until Zora Hurston's *Jonah's Gourd Vine* four years later." Yet neither Langston nor contemporaneous critics (with a few exceptions) held it in high regard—as he later wrote in *The Big Sea*, "I had wanted [my characters'] novel to be better than the published one I had given them; I hated to let them down." And indeed, the novel seems to lack an emotional core, a driving spirit. It reads almost as if it were written out of obligation. Novelist Angela Flournoy hints at this when she writes that *Not Without Laughter* was "the novel both Hughes and his readers knew he had to write, coming as it did on the heels of Hughes's two well-received poetry collections" and that "Hughes takes an anthropological approach to setting and character development."

Meanwhile, Langston had heard that Mason had been spending time with Zora and Alain Locke. What he didn't hear was how they had been talking about him—in no flattering terms.

Langston continued going through withdrawal. He wrote to Mason on August 15:

> I ask you to help the gods to make me good, to make me clean, to make me strong and fine that I might stand aflame before my people, powerful and wise, with eyes that can discern the ways of truth. I am nothing now—no more than a body of dust without wisdom, having no right to see. Physically and spiritually I pass through the dark valley, a dryness in my throat, a weariness in my eyes, fingers twisted into strange numb shapes when I wake up at night, the mind troubled in the face of things it does not understand, the mouth silent because there is no one to talk to, the sweet air burning the lungs, the hot sun cold to the body. Too far away the spear of Alamari. Too far away the gentle hands of Sandy's faith. If you understand, perhaps it will not be so hard to climb toward the hills again. . . . You have been continually in my thoughts this summer, and continually I've been trying to puzzle out what happened between us, and what I must do to keep it from ever happening again. We could not bear it. Love has no armor against itself.

Mason did not reply.

▼▼▼

The breakup with Mason was likely the instigation for Langston's burst of poetry in the second half of 1930. He had not published a single poem since November 1928; suddenly, starting in June and continuing through December, he published thirteen new poems, including some of his best yet. "Dear Lovely Death" and its sister poem "Tower" were perhaps the darkest poems of his career, treating death in one instance as an agent of change and in the other as a triumphant pause, and using elevated, archaic diction in doing so—it was as if Langston were condensing Shelley's "Adonais" into just a few shattered phrases. "Afro-American Fragment" beautifully mourned his now discarded primitivism; it ends:

> Subdued and time-lost
> Are the drums—and yet
> Through some vast mist of race
> There comes this song
> I do not understand
> This song of atavistic land,
> Of bitter yearnings lost
> Without a place—
> So long,
> So far away
> Is Africa's
> Dark face.

His first poetic foray into world politics, the radically scabrous "Merry Christmas," followed soon thereafter, each tightly rhymed verse imparting ironic holiday cheer to a different locus of oppression, corruption, or war.

For over two months, from early July to late September, Langston did not hear from Mason. He worked on a tragedy, *Cross* (later called *Mulatto*), but he was miserable.

In 1929, the Communist Party had decided to prioritize the struggles of black Americans, and white organizers began to appear in Harlem and other black communities. As the activist Nancy Cunard put it in the early 1930s, "The Communists are the most militant defenders and organizers that the Negro race has ever had"; while that might be an overstatement considering the history of the abolitionist movement, it was certainly true of the era in which she wrote. The Party would be vigorous not just in defending the Scottsboro Boys (nine black teenagers from Alabama falsely accused of raping two white women on a train in 1931) but on all fronts: it organized workers, dealt with employment problems, prevented lynchings, and took Jim Crow laws to court. By comparison, the NAACP and the Urban League were diffident and/or ineffectual.

So it should not have surprised anyone when, late in 1930, Langston turned—perhaps for solace, perhaps out of pure anger not just at his fate but at that of his fellow workingmen—to Communism. In March and April 1925 he had published some poems about the plight of the black proletariat in the Communist publication *Workers Monthly*, but he had never before been affiliated with a Communist organization; now he joined the John Reed Club (a Communist Party–backed group of leftist artists, writers, and intellectuals) and, in September, the masthead (as one of many contributing editors) of *New Masses*, a CP-backed Marxist magazine. In December, *New Masses* published, along with his "Merry Christmas," an open letter from Langston, "Greetings to Soviet Workers": "I send my greetings to the great Soviet ideal, to its true realization in your own land, and to its sunrise hope for the downtrodden and oppressed everywhere on earth."

▾▾▾

In August, Zora had sent Langston a postcard from Alabama that read, in part, "Dreamed last night that you were working on the play" (*The Mule-Bone*). She had kept to herself any reaction she might have had to his break with Mason, and this was her first note to him since then. Clearly she was having some mixed feelings about having left him two months before. But Langston wasn't working on the play at all. Instead, he was trying to procure a production of it.

He had, in June, visited Theresa Helburn of the Theatre Guild, the woman who had first suggested that he write an African American comedy. He told her that as soon as the play was ready he'd send it to her.

Then, in September, he visited Moylan, Pennsylvania, about twenty miles from Philadelphia, where a former actor and theatrical impresario named Jasper Deeter had invited him to be a playwright in residence for his troupe, the Hedgerow Players. Deeter, a white man, had played Smithers in the original production of Eugene O'Neill's *The Emperor Jones* in Provincetown, and it was he who had convinced O'Neill to cast a black actor in the title role rather than a white actor wearing blackface. He formed the Hedgerow Theater Company, America's first repertory theater, in 1923. Langston showed act one of *The Mule-Bone* to Deeter, who "seemed to think it would be a grand play, and gave me a little advice on some bits of dialog, etc." Langston then contacted Zora by telephone to share the good news and to ask about act two. According to an account that Zora gave Godmother at the end of January, it was at this point that she told Langston that the play was hers now, that he had contributed no dialogue to it, that she had thrown out the one suggestion he had made—that of setting act three on a railroad track—had finished the play herself, and would not be sending him any of it (in fact, at this point the third act was still set on a railroad track). Again according to Zora, Langston replied that his friend Mr. Spingarn was a lawyer, and a good one. Given Langston's apparent bafflement over subsequent events, though, I seriously doubt that Zora staked out her claim to the play at this point; more likely, she kept her feelings about Langston's initiative to herself and evaded his request.

Ever since she'd left Westfield in June, Langston had been trying to talk with Zora about the play, but to no avail. In October,
he asked Louise to try to get in touch with her, but Zora's line
was disconnected. In November, Zora told Godmother that she
would be returning to Manhattan to "see what a certain person
has to say to me," and finally consented to meet him. But she
failed to show up—more than once. Langston may have been
exaggerating when he related his frustration to his lawyer Arthur
Spingarn in January, but these are the (self-serving) details he
offered, which were almost the same as those he offered Van
Vechten around the same time:

> When I came back to New York in November and attempted
> to work with Miss Hurston, saying that we should put the
> play together and type out the final version, she gave me an
> appointment for work, but when I came, was not at home.
> Other appointments followed, but always she either was not
> home or had to go out at once as soon as I arrived; had no
> copies of the play in the house to work on; said she was ter-
> ribly busy and terribly nervous and couldn't work anyway;
> said she thought we ought to put the turkey back in the story
> and cut down on the girl-interest; finally gave me a copy
> of what she had done in the South, but demanded it back
> almost at once before I could make a copy of it for myself;
> said she had to go back South again almost at once; was not
> home for the last appointment that she gave me—and I have
> not seen her since. (That I believe was early December.)

Langston professed to be baffled by her coldness, though it's
hard to believe he had no inkling of the reason. He did not tell
Spingarn that he'd shown the play to Deeter without first asking for her permission to do so, which was likely one reason for

Zora's evasiveness. She may have decided that he had tried to steal her play. Nor did he reveal that the copy of the play that Zora showed him had her name on it alone, which prompted him to sheepishly ask her why there couldn't be two versions of it.

When Zora decided to deny Langston's authorship, sometime in September or early October, she may have been mulling it over for months. Perhaps it had occurred to her as early as May, when Langston had suggested that Louise should be entitled to some of the proceeds. Or it may have been the Hedgerow offer, which has been downplayed in subsequent accounts of the *Mule-Bone* affair, that inspired her.

For some time now, Zora had, with the support of Langston and Carl Van Vechten, envisioned *The Mule-Bone* as her big act, her first grand work of real consequence. Until that point, her work had been published mainly in black newspapers and magazines, and her contract with Mason prevented her from publishing any of the folklore research she'd been collecting the last few years. Since her theatrical work had never been produced, a staging could be her opportunity to make a real name for herself. For Langston to have shown this work with so much commercial potential to a small troupe in Moylan, Pennsylvania, without even asking her may have seemed like a slap in the face—or worse, an attempt at sabotage.

▼▼▼

Meanwhile Louise, despite doing no work for Mason, Langston, or Zora, kept getting her monthly $150 checks. Finally she found a job with the Congregational Education Society, handling race and labor relations for the Congregational Church. She wrote to Godmother, remarking that her contracted year was almost over and that she had another job, and wanted to know what Godmother had in mind for her.

She received a "curt note" from Godmother in reply, who was in a "very secluded" posh Lexington Avenue hotel. She went to see her there on September 22. Cornelia Chapin answered the door and showed her in. "I went into the room where Mrs. Mason was sitting in the corner like Queen Victoria. She even had on purple velvet. She beckoned to me, and I went over and said, 'How do you do, Mrs. Mason,' and I reached over, and took her hand—and this infuriated her. She didn't even ask me to sit down. As I stood there before her, she went into a tirade. She called me everything but a child of God. She didn't swear, but her words were even more insulting. She said I wasn't a 'true Negro' and that I had betrayed her."

Louise offered additional details about this "short but excruciating" meeting in a letter she wrote Langston a week later. As Mason told her, "I had failed utterly, all Negroes had failed utterly and she was through with us.... Miss Chapin threw in her rather nasty amens to everything Mrs. Mason said."

When Godmother stopped for breath, Louise asked her, "Well, what do you want me to do with the typewriter and desk, Mrs. Mason?"

Mason responded, "You don't mean that. You have no intention of giving that back to me." Then she seemed to get a second wind, and lit into her again.

Louise answered, "Is that what you really think of me? If you have nothing further to say, I'll bid you good afternoon."

"I had never had such a humiliating experience," Louise wrote. "All of the name-calling in my childhood had not prepared me for this debasing moment. I walked around the block; I didn't know where I was."

Louise had no idea why Godmother had disparaged her, though she suspected Zora was somehow involved. She probably

did not know, either, that Alain Locke had recently scuttled an
appointment for her as a secretary to a new Howard University
research council on the grounds of her supposed "disloyalty" to
Mason, "especially about the acceptance of four months' checks
without even offering to do any work." She would later charac-
terize Mason as racist, "indulging her fantasies of Negroes," and
lashing out at anyone who acted "white." (Aaron Douglas would
report similar experiences.)

▼▼▼

Mason, who was now seventy-six years old, was on the verge of
giving up not just on Langston and Louise but on her entire Negro
project. She had written to Locke in August, "I am helping myself
forget the discouraging things that have fallen on me from the
Negroes by talking about my Indian days." Even though she had
read Zora's latest draft of her folklore manuscript and called it
"excellent," she soon started talking with her about reducing her
monthly salary from $200 to $100, and told Zora to sell her car. And
she was not at all pleased with Langston's latest political poems.

On November 11, Zora wrote to Godmother, "I am beginning
to feel fagged. The weariness is beginning to break thru my sub-
consciousness & call itself to my attention." She sent the latest
version of *The Mule-Bone* to Carl Van Vechten on November 14,
calling it her "first serious whack at the play business," and telling him that she had discarded Langston's work on it and that it
was now her work alone. Even after sending it to Van Vechten,
she worked on it some more; in late November she rewrote and
polished the first act. She also finally showed the play to Godmother, who commented that "the play has great wit and great
possibilities of local color.... Perfect Negro!"

Low on funds because of the reduction of her stipend, Zora was
now living in her sister Sarah's home in Asbury Park, New Jer-

sey, where she continued to write: besides her new version of *The Mule-Bone*, she would work over the next two years on a collection of Caribbean folktales, *Barracoon* (her book about Cudjo Lewis, which would not be published until 2018), and *Mules and Men*, her folklore manuscript. Godmother was gradually loosening her grip on Zora's writing, and Knopf editor Harry Block wanted to see something more creative than simply transcribed folktales.

Mason's generosity increased around Christmas, when she raised Zora's stipend to $150, but the two of them continued to exchange complaints and hurt feelings mingled with Zora's sycophancy and Mason's mean-spiritedness. Mason even asked Zora if she'd spent Christmas with Langston; it's unlikely that she was being sarcastic.

Mason wrote to Langston several times in December, warm and friendly letters, as if nothing had happened between them; perhaps she missed his company. But Langston then left the New York area and settled with his mother in Cleveland without telling Godmother, which she of course regarded as another slap in the face. She wrote him on January 10:

> It was my hope that the New Year would open for you with Alamari in the lead. No weakness making shadows on your life and activities.
>
> Of course you have realized why I did not send the check as by mere accident it came to me that you had gone and where you were.
>
> Dear child, what am I to believe, what am I to think under these circumstances?

By now, though, Langston was resigned to his fate. His friendship with Godmother appeared to be over.

His friendship with Zora, though, was about to take center stage in a remarkably dramatic turn.

9

WINTER 1931

A Miasma of Untruth

Henry Louis Gates Jr. has described the contretemps that occurred over the course of nineteen days in late January and early February 1931 as "the most notorious literary quarrel in African-American cultural history." But part of its notoriety may be due to how baffling the sequence of events can appear. The "quarrel" ended up involving literary agents and lawyers and theater impresarios; Louise Thompson, Alain Locke, and Charlotte Mason; criss-crossing cross-country correspondence; a play with three different names and two different copyrights; police misconduct, a jail visit, and threats of legal action; numerous attempts at reconciliation; and a final scene of such drama it could be the basis of a play fully the equal of the one its protagonists had written. If *The Mule-Bone* was Zora and Langston's child, the fight over its fate was their epic custody battle.

But there's also a truly simple version of this terribly complex tale. It appears in Zora's folklore collection, *Mules and Men*, published three years later. Imagine Langston as a dog whose bark sounds like "ours," Zora as a cat whose meow sounds like "my ham," and *The Mule-Bone* as the leg of a pig . . .

De dog and de cat used to live next door to one 'nother and both of 'em loved ham. Every time they git a chance they'd buy a slice of ham.

One time both of 'em got holt of a li'l extry change so de dog said to de cat, "Sis Cat, we both got a li'l money, and it would be fine if bofe of us could buy a ham apiece. But neither one of us ain't got enough money to buy a whole ham by ourselves. Why don't we put our money together and buy us a ham together?"

"Aw right, Brer Dawg. T'morrer bein' Sat'day, le's we go to town and git ourselves a ham."

So de next day they went to town and bought de ham. They didn't have no convenience so they had to walk and tote it. De dawg toted it first and he said as he walked up de road wid de ham over his shoulder, "Ours! Ours! Ours! Our ham!"

After a while it was the cat's time to tote de meat. She said, "My ham, my ham, my ham." Dawg heard her but he didn't say nothin'.

When de dawg took it agin he says, "Ours, ours, our ham!" Cat toted it and says, "My ham, my ham."

Dawg says, "Sis Cat, how come you keep on sayin' 'My ham' when you totes our meat. Ah always say, 'Our ham.'"

De Cat didn't turn him no answer, but every time she toted de ham she'd say "My ham" and ever time de dawg toted it he'd say "Ours."

When they was almost home, de cat was carryin' de ham and all of a sudden she sprung up a tree and set up there eatin' up de ham. De dawg did all he could to stop her, but he couldn't clim' and so he couldn't do nothin' but bark. But he tole de cat, "You up dat tree eatin' all de ham, and Ah can't git to you. But when you come down ahm gointer make you take dis Indian River for uh dusty road."

Perhaps, like the dog and the cat, Langston and Zora were never meant to be friends, being of fundamentally different species . . .

▼▼▼

In early January 1931, Langston attended a performance of a play put on by his old friends Rowena and Russell Jelliffe, a white couple who ran the Karamu Theatre in Cleveland and directed an amateur black theatrical troupe called the Gilpin Players. Langston had known them from his high-school days; the Jelliffes had taken him in for a period when his mother had left town, and he had shared his first poems with them. After the performance at their Little Theatre, Mrs. Jelliffe told Langston that the Players were considering a new play called *The Mule-Bone* written by a New York woman. Mrs. Jelliffe had not yet seen the script, but the Samuel French agency had offered it to the Players for the annual downtown production.

Back in October 1930, not long after the Hedgerow Players incident, and perhaps inspired by it, Zora had copyrighted the play under the title *De Turkey and de Law* in her name alone. (This version would not see print until 2008, when it was included in Zora's *Collected Plays*.) Even after copyrighting it, Zora continued to work on it, excising, as best she could, whatever she considered Langston's contributions.

De Turkey and de Law was Zora's first full-length dramatic work; she had written a large number of short plays and sketches and one musical comedy (*Meet the Momma*, an immature effort).

It is a fully fledged, well-rounded, and effective drama, by far her most mature theatrical opus thus far. The story is simple: Jim and Dave, long-time friends, are competing for the attention of Daisy, and each promises to shoot her a turkey; Dave kills it but Jim knocks him on the head with a bone of old man Brazzle's dead mule, the orneriest animal in local history; Jim takes the turkey, and tells Daisy that he shot it; a trial follows, in which Jim is sentenced to be run out of town; and finally the two friends are reconciled. The first act, digressive and casual, takes place on Joe Clarke's store porch in Eatonville; it consists of a series of games: first a children's game, chick mah chick mah craney crow, a Southern variation of the widespread hawk-and-chickens counting game; then checkers; a card game resembling whist; the game-like pursuit of buying treats for women; and, through it all, variations on what Zora always called "lying," or telling tall tales. Even its climactic moment—Dave's return from his turkey hunt without a turkey but with a head wound—is underplayed, Zora eschewing the melodrama in which she had indulged in *Color Struck*, *Spears*, and her dramatization of the story of Ham, *The First One*. The second act is a showcase for the dozens: most of it consists of squabbling between the town's Baptists and Methodists. Set outside of and then inside the Baptist church, which doubles as the courthouse, the act is dominated by the women on opposing sides challenging each other to fight. The trial finally gets moving, but is repeatedly interrupted by more insults; at its crux, as it turns out, is the technical question of whether a mule bone is a weapon or not. Reverend Simms, the Methodist, claims it isn't, but Reverend Singletary, the Baptist, proves it is from the fact that Samson killed three thousand people with the jawbone of an ass. Jim is convicted of using a deadly weapon on Dave and sentenced to exile. In the third act, Jim meets Daisy as he's leaving town and Daisy tells him she'll go with him if he'll find himself a job, Dave appears as well, both agree that they'd rather live without her than work for white folks like she does, and they go back to town together. In comparison with the first two acts, the third is somewhat tame because only three people are on stage rather than the whole town. Yet there's not a dull line in the entire play, and it is, in my opinion, despite the stereotypes and stock characters, the closest Zora ever came to writing a dramatic masterpiece, outshining not only her earlier efforts but her later plays *Spunk* and *Polk County*. It's a shame that Zora's copyrighted version has never been staged, and that her subsequent revisions to it have been lost.

Zora had rewritten this October version before giving it to Mason and Van Vechten for their opinion in November. Zora wrote Van Vechten, "Langston and I started out together on the idea of the story I used to tell you about in Eatonville, but being so much apart from rush of business, I started all over again while in Mobile and this is the result of my work alone." Van Vechten, believing her, and liking the play, had given it to Lawrence Langner, head of the Theatre Guild in New York, without telling her. The Guild turned it down, but an official there, Barrett Clark, who was an employee of Samuel French, a theatrical rights and publication company, had then sent it, on his own initiative and without consulting Van Vechten or Zora, to the Gilpin Players. It was no longer called *De Turkey and de Law*, though. Either Zora or someone else had changed the title back to *The Mule-Bone*.

Langston was astonished to hear of the play. Before the script actually arrived in Cleveland, he wrote to Zora, but didn't send the letter. Then, after seeing the script on January 16, he wrote to Van Vechten, asking his advice. "Is there something about the very word theatre that turns people into thieves?" he asked him.

The next day, completely coincidentally, Louise Thompson arrived in Cleveland, having been employed by the American Interracial Seminar to improve relations between the races. The reason for her visit had nothing to do with Langston, but she visited him anyway. She then met with the Jelliffes, with whom she was already friendly, and backed up Langston's assertion of authorship. The same day, the Gilpin Players received the play, and Langston saw it. It was apparently Zora's version of all three acts (the first act had two different endings to choose from), along with an earlier version of the third act. Langston thought Zora's improvements to the first act were ill-considered, and called her version, in a letter to Van Vechten, "messed-up . . . a grand tangle . . . an amusing comedy spoiled."

The following day, January 18, Langston talked to Zora on the phone. She told Langston truthfully that she had no idea the manuscript had ever left Van Vechten's hands, did not know how it had arrived in Cleveland, and was not at all enthusiastic about the Gilpin Players putting it on, since they were an amateur troupe. But she wouldn't talk about the authorship question on the phone. Instead she wrote him a long letter that day, in which she explained why she had broken with him:

Now Langston, let us have a heart to heart chat about this play business. Please believe that what I am saying is absolutely sincere. I mean every word, so that you can bank on it.

In the beginning, Langston, I was very eager to do the play with you. ANYthing you said would go over big with me. But scarcely had we gotten under way before you made three propositions that shook me to the foundation of myself. First: That three-way split with Louise. No Langston, nobody has in the history of the world given a typist an interest in a work for typing it. . . . I do object to having my work hi-jacked. There is no other word for it. I don't see how, even if in your magnificent gallantry you had offered it, she could have accepted it. . . .

Then your argument that if we paid her money, that it ought to be something fancy. I still don't follow your reasoning. First you give *me* no credit for intelligence at all. Knowing the current prices for typists, you must despise my mental processes to have broached the subject at all. You know what you said, so I don't need to go into that.

Then when these had failed you come forward with the Louise-for-business-manager plan. . . .

Now about the play itself. It was my story from beginning to end. It is my dialogue; my situations. But I am not concerned about that. Langston, with God as my judge, I don't care anything about the money it might make nor the glory. I'd be willing to give it all to you off hand. But the idea of *you,* LANGSTON HUGHES, trying to use the tremendous influence that you knew you had with me that some one else might exploit me cut me to the quick. . . .

I told Godmother that I had done my play all by myself, and so I did, and for the reasons stated before. . . . [But] I realized that I could expect you to be promising many things that wouldn't do me a bit of good [perhaps a reference to Louise, or perhaps to the Hedgerow offer]. That and that only is my reason for going it alone. I haven't gone happily. Just felt obliged to. I didn't intend to be evasive. With anyone else but you I could have said a plenty. Would have done so long ago but I have been thinking of you as my best friend for so long, and as I am not in love with anyone, that naturally made you the nearest person to me on earth, and the things I had in mind seemed too awful to say to you, I just couldn't say them. I tried for a long time to bring the subject up with you, but I just couldn't. I just kept trying to make a joke of it to myself, but somehow the sentences in my mind wouldn't laugh themselves off. So now, it is all said.

Zora divulged that she had recently rewritten the first act (again), and asked for some time to think things over. In a postscript, she added, regarding the version she had given Van Vechten, "I don't think that you can point out any situations or dialogue that are yours. You made some suggestions, but they are not incorporated in the play."

Langston sent his letter to Zora on the same day and they crossed each other. Only the end of it survives: "I'd also immensely like to know your attitude about our collaboration on the play. You were so strange and evasive the last time I saw you that I didn't know what you were about. Would you mind explaining it all to me?" Then, on the 19th, without consulting his coauthor, and before receiving her letter, Langston copied his versions of acts one and three and Zora's version of act two and sent it to the US Copyright office to be copyrighted in his name, although he acknowledged Zora's coauthorship on the title page, which read, "THE MULE-BONE / A COMEDY OF NEGRO LIFE IN / THREE ACTS / BY / LANGSTON HUGHES and ZORA HURSTON." He received a copyright, despite the fact that the entire play had already been copyrighted by Zora alone, perhaps because the different titles of the two versions gave the registrar no indication that the work had been copyrighted earlier. At some point over the next few days, Langston prepared an edition for the Gilpin Players that lightly revised his version of the play but excised the street scene that opened act two, and this is the version that would, in 1991, be published and produced as *Mule Bone*.

Mule Bone's second and third acts are quite similar to those of *De Turkey and de Law*. Zora had changed the first act to conform more closely to her 1925 short story "The Bone of Contention," reintroducing the turkey, which had been absent from the original first act, having the fight take place offstage rather than in front of Joe Clarke's store, and more richly characterizing the female characters. In attempting to excise Langston's contributions, Zora had transformed it from a somewhat aimless cacophony into a tightly structured presentation. But Langston went back to what must have been the original version, with no turkey in sight, and scrubbed all mention of the turkey from the second and third acts. It seems that Zora had not yet gotten around to changing her version of the third act from the original very much when she filed for copyright the previous October, but by the time she sent the play to Van Vechten in November, the third act was quite different (according to both Langston and Zora)—and is now lost. At any rate, the second and third acts of *Mule Bone* were lightly rewritten—by either Zora, Langston, or both—*after* the October version (*De Turkey and de Law*), since the few differences between them appear to be polishing rather than revision.

Why was Langston so eager to protect his authorship of a play that he probably had little to do with, that he hadn't worked on in months, and that conflicted in a fundamental manner with his present political and social concerns? While he may have felt that the play was an unparalleled theatrical introduction to black folklore, his overriding motive seems to have been his intense devotion to theatrical performance—and its potential financial rewards. Langston had not yet had any success in the theatrical world, but ever since he was little he had constantly dreamed of it, and would remain devoted to the theater for the rest of his life. His longtime friends the Jelliffes were planning to produce a play he had had a hand in, which would be his first produced play. He was not going to give up that chance without a fight. Moreover, he had worked on it for months, and the play would probably not have been written without his efforts. He must have felt proud of it, despite his turn away from this sort of subject matter.

The same day he applied for his copyright, January 19, he made an attempt to patch things up with Zora. He argued that the production wouldn't be some no-name amateur production but instead would garner significant publicity, appropriate to "the first Negro folk-comedy ever written." (Langston likely wasn't aware of *You Mus' Be Bo'n Ag'in*, though he would shortly learn all about it.) He argued that the Gilpin Players were a well-established and highly regarded troupe whose performances were attended by "New York scouts and agents." "Let's not be niggers about the thing, and fall out before we've even gotten started," he wrote to Zora. (Zora wrote back jestingly, "How dare you use the word 'nigger' to me. You know I don't use such a nasty word. I'm a refined lady and such a word simply upsets my conglomeration." The sarcasm is clear—she used the word frequently, even in a letter she wrote to Mason the same day as her reply to Langston.)

Langston also wrote to Van Vechten that day, outlining the situation as he saw it, and adding, "This morning I got some legal advice on the matter and with all the proof I have: a file of notes in my own handwriting, pages of constructions and situations, carbons of the first draft, and the testimony of the stenographer who worked with us for three or four weeks, Zora can certainly do nothing with MULE-BONE without my permission. Why she should have set out to do so is beyond me." (It seems not to have occurred to Langston that he had done the same thing in showing the play to Jasper Deeter the previous September, nor that he had just copyrighted the work without asking his coauthor.) He begged Van Vechten to see Zora and to talk with the Guild, explaining that time was of the essence as the Gilpin Players had a two-week season of performances beginning February 15 and wanted to put on some version of the play on that date. (To be specific, the Players planned to open the play under the auspices of the Cleveland newspaper *The Plain Dealer* at a downtown theater for two performances and then move to the Karamu Theatre on Central Avenue for five nights; there would be other performances for special groups like librarians or art museum patrons; and then there would possibly have been a week at the prestigious Ohio Theatre downtown.)

Van Vechten meanwhile wrote to Langston that he was not surprised by Zora's behavior. "Even if she has entirely rewritten the play in a version of her own," he argued, "she had no moral right to do so without getting your permission." The next day (January 20), Zora came for a visit, where, as he wrote Langston, she "cried and carried on no end about how fond she was of you, and how she wouldn't have had this misunderstanding for the world." (Van Vechten may have exaggerated Zora's contrition in order to help heal a rift he saw himself as having helped cause; twelve years later he remembered Zora's display of emotion quite differently—"She had a tantrum in my library," he wrote Langston, "and threw herself on the floor and screamed and yelled! Bit the dust in fact.") Carl communicated Zora's reservations about having the play produced in Cleveland and strongly advised Langston not to do so: "A stock production will be very dangerous and might kill the chances of the play completely. . . .

I have an excellent opportunity to get this play into the hands of [Herman] Shumlin, the producer of Grand Hotel [a successful Broadway play of 1930]. . . . [He] would be furious about a stock production unless he had authorized it."

▼▼▼

Back on January 15, Godmother had given Zora a dressing down. According to Mason's notes, first she grilled Zora—"Have you heard from Langston at all[?] Were you satisfied with Alain about your work[?] . . . Did you have a Christmas party at your own place[?]" They then had an argument about money, which concluded with Godmother telling her, "This is the reason the whole white world says[,] '[Y]ou can't do anything with Negroes. They are unreliable[.]' " It's hard to imagine any words more insulting.

Zora had gotten used to being demeaned by Godmother. But being demeaned by Langston was something else. On the evening of January 20, Zora phoned Godmother and told her everything. According to Mason's notes, Zora said that Langston and Louise had been having an affair. In addition, Langston had taken her ideas in the past and sold them to Caroline Dudley Reagan for *La Révue Negre*, the vaudeville show of nine theatrical sketches that introduced Josephine Baker to Paris; he had met with Theresa Helburn of the Theatre Guild and offered her the play; Louise had demanded a third of the play's royalties for the typing she'd done; and Langston had been smoking and drinking and spending nights at Louise's. No evidence exists for any of these complaints; Zora was making things up.

After Langston had fallen out with Mason, Zora, who was utterly dependent on Godmother, may have had no choice but to insist that Langston had nothing to do with the latest version of the play. But Zora's suggestion of an affair between Louise and

Langston, who would remain friends for decades, seems truly improbable, even if Zora believed it. As Louise later said, "If Langston had approached me in another way, I might have been receptive, but he never did. I accepted Langston on that plane, that we were the best of friends and comrades."

Mason advised Zora to wire Cleveland that the play was in the hands of her literary agent. Zora promised to write God-mother a letter.

Then Langston's apologetic letter arrived, and suddenly everything changed.

Zora had directed the Samuel French agency to wire the Jelliffes that she had denied them permission to stage *The Mule-Bone*, and the agency did so that day. But that evening Zora wired her own approval of the performance to the Jelliffes three times, just to be sure. Once they'd received the wires, the Gilpin Players went into production mode.

She also sat down and wrote Langston two letters. "I am in fault in the end and you were in fault in the beginning. I shall freely acknowledge my share at anytime and place. Somehow I don't mind re-versing myself, especially when it moves me towards pleasanter relationships." She promised to "write God-mother a letter leaving you in a white light. Not that you have been slandered, but she dotes so on our rock-bottom sincerity that she would be upset to know of a spat, however trivial it might turn out for us." Of course, she didn't tell Langston that she had already "slandered" Langston to Mason and told her about the "spat," and that Godmother was indeed "upset." Zora also promised to go to Cleveland in a few days, a course of action which the Samuel French editor Barrett Clark had advised her to take, explaining that the play was "so exotic" that a non-New York production was essential to see how well it would work.

"Now get this straight, Langston," she wrote him in the second letter that evening. "You are still dear to me. I don't care whom you love nor whom you marry, nor whom you bestow your worldly goods upon. I will never have any feeling about that part. I have always felt that if you had married anyone at all it would make no difference in our relationship. I *know* that no man on earth could change me towards you." She then explained why she had left Westfield in June:

> Langston, please believe me when I say that my thoughts were too painful to me for me to talk to you. I couldn't hear myself saying certain unpleasant phrases to you. So I just went off to myself and tried to resolve to have no more friendships. Tears unceasing have poured down inside me.
>
> So I just went off to work the play out alone—carefully not using what was yours. Please believe me when I say the money doesn't matter. You can have anything I have at any time.

This may be the most loving—and saddest—letter Zora ever wrote to Langston.

But the very same evening, enclosing a copy of this sweet letter, Zora wrote to Mason, "Langston is weak. Weak as water. When he has a vile wretch [Louise] to push him, he gets vile." She did concede that Langston had come around. "When he is under noble influences like yours, you know how fine he can be. Personally, I think that he has so much in him, that it is worth my swallowing and forgetting if by extending a friendly hand I can bring him back into the fold. I think we are in a spot now to make a grand slam. . . . I don't want to be unjust to anyone ever. Especially Langston." She acknowledged Langston's apology, and said, "Godmother, I am so happy that Langston has taken an honorable view of the thing, that I would give him part."

Carl Van Vechten was also trying to placate Langston. He wrote him that same day, "What you say about the stenographer . . . is very amusing and I am convinced that this whole situation arises out of some feeling on Zora's part of which you are wholly unconscious."

As for Langston, having received Zora's letter of the 18th, he now (on January 20) replied to her accusations about Louise. He insisted that "Louise has been paid for her work and . . . has, of course, no other interest in the play," and that he had early on cancelled the idea of Louise having anything to do with the handling of it. "Don't be absurd about Louise—because you know better than that," he admonished Zora. He once again offered "to do what I can to get the play in shape for presentation out here, and to work with you at any time or anywhere in the future that will be to the benefit of the play *Mule-Bone*. I think it would be a great shame for the first Negro comedy to go to pieces on account of selfish or foolish disagreement among us." He then threatened legal action if Zora should proceed without him. "The play is *ours*, neither yours nor mine, and I feel it is too good to be lost. . . . You're an awfully amusing person, Zora."

The next day, not yet having received Zora's conciliatory letter, still upset by her accusations about Louise, and acting upon a suggestion from Van Vechten, Langston drafted an eleven-page letter to his lawyer, Arthur Spingarn, offering a compromise: two-thirds of the royalties would go to Zora and one-third to himself. In it he told his version of the complete history of the collaboration between them, and attempted to decisively prove that Zora's version could not have been entirely her own. ("Maybe she has lost her mind," he suggested.) Most significantly, he outlined his contributions to the basic plot of the play. In doing so, he lied, claiming that it was he who made Jim a Baptist and Dave a Methodist and that it was he who had the idea of making the entire town split into two camps along religious lines. Those elements were in Zora's original 1925 story. He asked Spingarn to collect all the evidence, to get in touch with Zora, and to ask her to accept his royalty offer.

But then, when Langston received Zora's conciliatory letter, he was delighted, and told her so. He couldn't wait to see her in Cleveland.

Meanwhile, Mason received a packet from Zora containing Zora's "tears unceasing" letter to Langston, her accompanying letter to Mason, a registered letter from Cleveland saying that the Theatre Guild would be interested in a production of the play there as a tryout for a New York production, and Langston's apologetic letter that, according to Godmother, "gave away his fear of Godmother's psychic discernment if their storys [*sic*] about the progress of the play did not agree." Godmother called Zora in the afternoon to ask if this letter had come after her phone conversation with Zora the previous evening. Zora told her that it had, and added, according to Mason, that Langston had now "threaten[ed] to have the law on" Zora.

This was indeed the case: Langston's January 20 letter to Zora, the one which called her "an awfully amusing person," had included the warning, "if you make any further attempts to dispose of any script based on the play which we did together and now called *Mule-Bone*, it will be a matter for my lawyers and The Author's Guild, to both of whom I have written full details." Zora's receipt of this threat soured everything.

To top it all, the same evening that Mason received Zora's package, January 21, Langston and a couple of friends were arrested on false pretenses (a cab driver accused them of denting his car) and spent the night in a "bitter cold" jail cell with steel walls and nothing to sleep on or cover themselves with. It was no secret at that time that the Cleveland police had been hassling and arresting African Americans and making them pay fines for no reason.

The following day, Langston wrote to Zora, calling her "my darling," and opening, "Brazzle's mule is one ungodly beast. He's done a mean piece of kicking lately, but I trust once more that the ghost of his dead carcass is ready to repose in piece [*sic*]! We're all sorry! Last night in jail with my back turned to the wall, I thought deeply on the subject." He outlined the royalty arrangement he had suggested to Spingarn and asked her to call him, then concluded, "It'll be great to see you. Maybe you'll like this big old dirty town. I hope so. There's a low-down night club that almost equals the Sugar Cane" (a Harlem joint famous for its narrow, underground entrance and great entertainment).

On January 24, Zora had a meeting with Spingarn. As previously noted, Spingarn had been an NAACP official since 1911; he had defended falsely accused African Americans, expanded voting rights, and worked closely with W. E. B. Du Bois. He showed her the eleven-page letter Langston had written him. She was newly infuriated, and quite rightly so. Spingarn wrote Hughes in her presence, telling him that Zora insisted that he had "grossly exaggerated" his role in the collaboration and that "virtually all" of the play had been her work. Spingarn reminded Langston that Zora had shown Langston the same script as the one that came to Cleveland the previous fall, with her name on it as the sole author, "and that you made no comment on it at the time, except to say, couldn't there be two versions." The implication was clear: Langston had already admitted that Zora's version was hers alone. Zora also told Spingarn forthrightly that Langston's threat of a lawsuit had "aroused her ire."

In reply, Langston suggested to Spingarn that he get in touch with Louise to ascertain the facts of the play's composition. Spingarn then wrote to Langston, "I am sure that [Zora] is at bottom very friendly disposed toward you and that she really has been more hurt by what she thinks is an ungenerous attitude on your part than by anything else." Louise Thompson, however, had a very different view of the matter, and wrote to Langston, "The only thing I can say is that Zora is crazy, but unfortunately maliciously so."

One thing that especially hurt Langston was that, according to Spingarn, Alain Locke was now taking Zora's side, even though he knew nothing whatsoever about the matter—he visited Spingarn on the evening of the 25th and expatiated at length on his belief that Zora was in the right and Langston in the wrong. He also suggested to Mason that Langston was trying to "blackmail" Zora. Locke had been running hot and cold about Langston ever since their dalliance in Italy; most recently, he had visited Langston at Lincoln in April 1929 and had come away full of praise for the way Langston had been handling his controversial senior project on the students' apathy about the all-white faculty. So Locke's interference in the matter was quite a surprise, especially because Langston was unaware that Locke even knew that he and Zora had worked on a play together. He wired the professor as soon as he received Spingarn's letter: "PLEASE PUT ME STRAIGHT ON ZORAS ATTITUDE AND YOUR KNOWLEDGE OF MATTER BY RETURN WIRE COLLECT I AM AFRAID I DON'T UNDERSTAND" and Locke wired back, "CONGRATULATIONS ON THE HARMON AWARD BUT WHAT MORE DO YOU WANT." (Langston had just received the Federated Council of Churches' Harmon Gold

Award for Literature for *Not Without Laughter*, which came with a check for four hundred dollars; Locke had nominated him for it.) Langston never forgave him.

On January 26, Langston attended the Gilpin Players' reading of the first act of *The Mule-Bone*, and was favorably impressed. "They are mostly working people," he would write to Zora, "and not many high-hats, as their theatre is located in the heart of the low-down colored district right on Central Avenue." With the play about to be produced, Langston was getting desperate to patch things up. He wrote two letters to Zora on the 27th. In one, he begged, "Zo darling, whatever your personal feeling toward me may be, let's not break up what promises to be a good play." Alluding to Zora's anger over Louise, he told her that there were plenty of typists in Cleveland, including some male ones (among them likely those who had worked for Langston preparing *The Mule-Bone* for the Library of Congress and for the Gilpin Players). "I'm not mad. Are you? I'm perfectly willing to be friends again, and awfully sorry about anything I might have done to make you angry."

On January 29, Rowena Jelliffe received a letter from one of the Gilpin Players, Paul Banks, who was in New York and had called on Zora. Apparently Zora told Banks that Langston had lied about the play, that she had convinced Spingarn of this, that he would no longer represent Langston, that she had Locke on her side, and that she was coming soon to Cleveland but would under no circumstances give Langston any credit for the play. The letter upset Mrs. Jelliffe, who tried to call both Zora and Spingarn, but failed to reach either one. The next day, Jelliffe wrote Spingarn a long letter telling him about the evidence that the play had been cowritten: Louise Thompson's account of the play's composition and the work notes for the play in Langston's handwriting. She told him straight out that she would not produce the play under Zora's name alone, and emphasized her strong belief in Louise's integrity. In the meantime, the *Plain Dealer* announced the forthcoming production of a Negro comedy by Zora Neale Hurston and Langston Hughes.

Also on January 29, Charlotte Mason wrote a full account of the *Mule-Bone* contretemps in her journal, almost entirely dependent on the account Zora had given her. As a precis of Zora's point of view, it's unmatched. It reveals that Zora had gotten Langston to tell Mason and Cornelia Chapin the plot of the play, but Zora insisted that Langston's only real contribution to it was the idea of setting the last act on a railroad track. The actual writing of the play, Zora told Godmother, "consisted in her [Zora] staying at her place and doing the work while L. and Louise T. went off to his rooms. When they'd come back L. would say [']lets see how much you got done then—that's fine *we're* getting along splendidly.'" This contradicts Louise's account, and is unlikely to be accurate. "This went on for a few days and then Z and L. phoned Godmother and she told them not to go on with the play[,] to put it aside as it would conflict with Zora's completing the real work she was doing[,] that her book must get ahead. The play was then dropped." Or so Godmother thought at the time. She went on to describe the rest of the events: Langston's visit to the Theatre Guild and the Hedgerow Players, his supposed affair with the still-married Louise Thompson, the contretemps in Cleveland, and Langston's continual "contrivings and plottings."

▼▼▼

Zora arrived in Cleveland on the evening of February 1, Langston's twenty-ninth birthday (or so he thought). She brought a letter of introduction that Alain Locke had written to Rowena

Jelliffe expressing his absolute confidence in Zora and his trust that Jelliffe would share it once she had heard Zora's story. Locke, who was sure that Louise had been sleeping with Langston and doubtless shared Zora's jealousy, had promised Mason he would take Zora's side in any dispute with Langston, and he backed her fully in his letter.

That same evening, the Gilpin Players decided not to perform *The Mule-Bone*, having heard nothing further from Zora on the matter, and Zora having failed to sign an agreement regarding credit and royalty terms. (In its place, they would shortly stage another of those too-rare beasts—a full-length African American–authored nonmusical comedy—Andrew Burris's *You Mus' Be Bo'n Ag'in*, giving it its final performance.) But they were open to reconsidering their decision.

Langston and Zora met the following day, February 2, at Karamu House. Langston described the meeting to Spingarn the next day.

> Miss Hurston's main grievance seemed to be Miss Thompson. She seemed to feel that by taking the play alone and go[ing] off with it she was thus protecting me and herself from what she chose to call "a gold digger." I asked her why she did not tell me of her ill feeling in the fall when I tried to resume work with her, and she said she could not bear to tell me. As to the play itself, Miss Hurston agreed that I had some part in its making, and she said she would sign an agreement to work together again jointly with me. . . . [But] Miss Hurston insisted that the play which had been sent to Cleveland under her name had been a "new" play, anyhow, and that "there wasn't an idea of mine left in it." . . . Miss Hurston was very nice at this first conference, though,

and we agreed that it was all over and settled and that we would sign together for a Gilpin production, should they re-decide to do it.

The Jelliffes then set up a meeting for the following day. But that meeting ended up taking place at Langston's mother's house, since Langston was now under his doctor's orders to remain in bed there, ill with what was diagnosed as influenza and tonsillitis.

Meanwhile, Zora had discovered that Louise had been in Cleveland before her (on January 17), that she had spoken to the Jelliffes, and that she knew them personally. The only full accounts we have of Zora's wild reaction to this news are Langston's, and the harsh light they shine on Zora may well be distorting—or not. At any rate, in his letters to Spingarn and Van Vechten, Langston told his version of what transpired on February 3.

Early in the morning, Zora phoned Rowena Jelliffe and accused her of conspiring with Langston before contacting her. Jelliffe pointed out that this wasn't going to get settled over a phone call and suggested that they all get together again. So at five in the afternoon, in Langston's room, Zora, the Jelliffes, Paul Banks, and Langston all gathered.

"She made such a scene as you cannot possibly imagine," Langston wrote to Van Vechten after the meeting.

> It was mostly about Miss Thompson. Zora laid her out. Also laid out the Jelliffe's [sic]. Also me. She pushed her hat back, bucked her eyes, ground her teeth, and shook manuscripts in my face, particularly the third act which she claims she wrote alone by herself while Miss Thompson and I were off doing Spanish together. (And the way she

said *Spanish* meant something else). [Most likely, Langston had been teaching Spanish to Louise, since he was fluent and she wasn't.] She admitted that we had worked jointly, and that certain characterizations were mine, but she dared and defied me to put my finger on a line that was my own. One line at the end of the 1st act had been mine, but she took that out, she said. Anyway, she had written a "new" play by herself; she hadn't come to Cleveland to be made a fool of, nor to submit to any sly tricks such as she felt Mrs. Jelliffe had pulled by having the nerve to put my name with hers on the play. Her agent had said the Jelliffes were honorable people—but now—why she couldn't even bear the sight of their Settlement House, it was so muddy and dirty in the yard, etc! etc! in an absolutely crazy vein, until Mr. Jelliffe asked his wife to no longer remain to be further insulted—whereupon they all left, Zora in a rage without even saying Goodbye to me or mother. I haven't told you the half of it. . . . But nine-tenths of Zora's talk here was not about the play at all, but Madame Thurman [Louise was still married to Wallace Thurman]—the very thought of whom seemed to infuriate Zora. The play was a mere side-issue. . . . And in all cases the stenographer was a hussy! . . . Do you think she is crazy, Carlo?

Carrie Clark, Langston's mother, followed Zora into the hallway to give her a piece of her mind, and Langston had to get out of bed to restrain his mother. Zora was undeterred. She sent a telegram to Mason that evening: "DARLING GODMOTHER ARRIVED SAFELY HAVE PUT THE PERSON [Langston] ON THE RUN PLAY STOPPED LOUISE THOMPSON HAD BEEN SENT FOR TO BOLSTER CASE I SMASHED THEM ALL BE HOME BY WEEKEND ALL MY LOVE ZORA."

Two nights later, Zora went to a dance in Langston's honor at the prestigious Omega Psi Phi Fraternity in Cleveland while he remained in bed because of his throat. In a letter to Louise, Langston wrote,

> There Zora, I understand, told everyone that I was stealing her work, as well as saying some very unpleasant things about you. She has started a great swirl of malicious gossip here about all of us, the Jelliffes as well. The Gilpins have split up into groups some for the Jelliffes, some against, and the whole thing has developed into the most amazing mess I ever heard of. . . . Certainly none of us expected such a performance from the lady! It seems that now Zora chooses to be not only contrary and untruthful, but malicious and hurtful as well. (I have received the most insulting note I have ever heard tell of from 399 [Godmother's Park Avenue address]. How she thinks of such ungodly things to say I don't know.) . . .
>
> We all feel that you must be warned against her in New York. . . .
>
> Find yourself a mule-bone because the free-for-all is on.

Langston also sent a telegram to Locke, asking for his "SLANT ON THINGS." Locke did not reply.

In his autobiography, Langston claimed that after this he "never heard from Miss Hurston again." But he certainly did, a number of times, and he even might have met with her years later. In fact, shortly after arriving back in New York, Zora wrote Langston a brief letter announcing her return and dealing with a few practical matters, including the fact that she was returning to Rowena Jelliffe a check she had sent Zora to cover half of her travel expenses to

Cleveland. But her tone was cold. The sign-off that had been, in 1929, "Love and everything deep and fine, Honey / Lovingly, / Zora" had now turned into "Lots of luck. / Sincerely, / ZORA NEALE HURSTON."

When Langston appealed to Mason, she rebuffed him in a short letter written on February 12.

> Dear Langston,
>
> What a sorrowful, misguided way to have come!
>
> Has not the year spent in tarnishing the wings proved that "keeping accounts" had nothing to do with your failure to do creative writing. The great tragedy is, Langston, we cannot run away from Ourselves.
>
> Child, why build a labyrinth about yourself that causes you to wander in a miasma of untruth?
>
> Langston, you know by past experience I never judge anyone on hearsay or by their surface actions. I hope I have lived a true enough existence to prove that eternally.
>
> Face yourself, Langston. Go forward and the Gods in space sustain you. May these three hundred dollars carry you over while you find the outdoor work you feel is necessary now for your health.
>
> > Faithfully,
> > "Godmother."

Back in May, Langston had maintained that his failure to write anything of value since completing *Not Without Laughter* had been caused by his financial relationship with Godmother: that being paid to produce was inimical to the freedom he felt necessary to write from his heart. In fact, being freed from Mason's surveillance had resulted in some of the best poems of his career. But if Mason was aware of this work, she certainly didn't recognize it as such. Her assessment of his "failure to do creative writing"—combined with her certainty that he was lying to her and her condescending admonishment to "face yourself"—couldn't have been more cruel.

On March 5, Zora went to see Spingarn. She told him she wanted to rewrite the play so that nothing of which Langston had claimed was his would appear in it, and asked for a release of Langston's rights. Spingarn, of course, pleaded that he had to ask his client and couldn't answer immediately. The next day, Langston replied, "I think it would be just as well to let Miss Hurston have the play, don't you? Or at least her part of it." He then asked Spingarn how they should handle the copyright issue.

Meanwhile, Alain Locke had been butting in again. In a late-January letter to Godmother he accused Langston of "false egotism" and in March he ridiculed Langston's hopes to go to the Caribbean as "shameful—or rather shameless. Well—he'll have a long rope—but eventually it will pull taut." Locke seemed to be in a paroxysm of vindictiveness, writing Mason of Van Vechten, who was still friendly with both Langston and Zora and had just recovered from an episode of blood poisoning, "Why can't he die! Nothing seems to kill him." It was not for nothing that Zora would later describe Locke to James Weldon Johnson as a "malicious, spiteful litt[l]e snot."

For her part, Zora was flattering Mason to the hilt, presumably worried that she would be the next person Godmother would abandon. And, indeed, in March Mason ended Zora's employment and reduced her monthly stipend to $100. That month, Zora nevertheless called Mason "the Guard-mother who sits in the Twelfth Heaven and shapes the destinies of the primitives"; she would later compare her to the holy grail and Mahatma

Gandhi; and she even signed one letter (which included a verse hymn to Mason's godlike grace) "Devotedly, your pickaninny." (She had already used this word to describe herself in correspondence with a previous white benefactor, Annie Nathan Meyer.) Her apparent dependence on and worship of Mason was, no doubt, rendered more satisfactory by the fact that Hughes had definitively fallen from Godmother's graces.

In mid-March Langston sent Zora a clipping about another literary quarrel, comparing it to theirs and offering some sort of help (both the letter and clipping are lost). Zora responded perfunctorily, but not without irony, drawing an implicit comparison to her behavior in Cleveland: "I am calm again and went to a party and had a nice time."

On March 25, Spingarn wrote Langston, who was back in Westfield, that he had phoned Zora that morning, and that she had "repeated that you had practically nothing to do with the play and that rather than give you an interest, she would tear it up." Spingarn had told Zora that the manuscript showed that Langston had done a considerable amount of work on it. Zora replied that if Langston wanted to meet her at Spingarn's office to go over the manuscript, and that if he could show her that he had done this work, she would then enter into an arrangement. But then, after speaking to her agent, Raymond Crossett, who worked in Elizabeth Marbury's agency, she phoned Spingarn again and said she thought it was best not to have such a meeting after all. Zora wrote Godmother that day, "I find that Langston is in town, and that he copied whole hunks out of my play in Cleveland and NOW tries to say that while he didn't write the thing in the beginning, he made all those 'emendations' on the play last Fall. I can't conceive of such lying and falsehood. . . .

[But] I have even learned to live above Langston's vileness." She added a postscript: "I'd love for Langston to face me in your presence." She wrote to Spingarn at the same time, and enclosed a copy of that letter with her letter to Mason: "I think it would be lovely for your client to be a play-wright but I'm afraid that I am too tight to make him one at my expense. You have written plays, why not do him one yourself? Or perhaps a nice box of apples and a well chosen corner. But never no play of mine. / Most emphatically yours." And on April 18, Zora wrote Mason, "I know that Langston says he was going to Cuba, but I suspect he is really gone to hunt up Eatonville to pretend that he knew about it all along."

When Langston returned to New York City in early August, he made no attempt to contact Zora, Mason, or Locke. Until, that is, he learned that the Marbury agency had hired Wallace Thurman to revise *De Turkey and de Law*, and that Langston's name was nowhere on the script. (Thurman had done no work on it and, not wanting to be involved in the controversy, never would.) Langston went to the agency, accompanied by a close family friend, Ethel Harper. Zora and Langston wrote quite different accounts of what happened next, but it appears that Crossett asked Harper to keep her mouth shut or get out of his office, called Langston a liar, and told him he had no rights at all in the play and was free to hire any lawyer he chose. "I just love fights," Crossett said. Langston tried to be nice, saying he was collaborating with Wallace Thurman on a play and wanted the Marbury office to handle it, but Crossett replied that although he handled Thurman's affairs he would refuse to touch anything to do with Langston, since he had shown himself to be "a person of no honor." When Langston tried to explain that Zora was just jealous of Louise, Crossett replied that he was only interested in the authorship of the play and that "his place was an office and not a clearing house for Harlem gossip." When Langston complained of Zora's "violent disposition" and the way she had called him and the Jelliffes liars and crooks, Crossett replied that if Langston's tactics in Cleveland had been the same as those he was employing now, in his office, Zora was more than justified in her accusations. "It no longer even annoys me," Zora wrote to Mason. "Give a calf enough rope—"

Hughes wrote a long complaint to the Dramatists Guild. Thurman, who claimed to still love his wife Louise, said he didn't know whom to believe. The play was, for now, abandoned.

And for the rest of his long life, Langston had almost no contact with the two women who had meant the most to him in that decade in which he was at the height of his career and the toast of the town.

10

1932–1960

The Aftermath

Langston dated "the end of the Harlem Renaissance" to the "literary quarrel" he'd had with Zora in the spring of 1931. "We were no longer in vogue.... Colored actors began to go hungry, publishers politely rejected new manuscripts, and patrons found other uses for their money." Many of the participants dispersed. Charles Johnson and James Weldon Johnson had taken positions at Fisk University in Nashville; Jessie Fauset had left *The Crisis*; and in August A'Lelia Walker died.

The rest of the story is aftermath: thirty years of acrimony between Langston and Zora, broken only by occasional moments of regret.

▼▼▼

"You know there comes a time when you have to sort of take sides," said Bruce Nugent years later. "Sometimes between people that you love very much. And I didn't realize how important Zora was to me until that upsetting thing of Langston's. And I thought,

Oh, I hope that Langston isn't going to be hurt if I go over to Zora. So I ran over to Zora. . . . She was so pleased to see me run away from Langston and come up to her, because Zora was one of the few people that knew how close Langston and I were."

In January 1932, Langston visited Jacksonville, Florida, on a book tour, and Zora's brother John "entertained him magnificently," or so Zora wrote to Godmother. It's unlikely that John and Langston had previously been in contact, but, as Langston and Zora had found on their 1927 road trip, African Americans in the South were happy to welcome African American visitors from the North. Langston thanked her in a letter. She probably did not respond. He also visited Eatonville, the home of *Mule Bone*.

That March, Langston once again had a tiff with a collaborator—this time with a playwright named Kaj Gynt, with whom he had written a musical called *Cock o' the World*. Gynt, who knew Zora, told her that Langston had been rather harsh to her on the phone, so Zora called him to intervene on her behalf. Langston was "polite and rather cordial" about the whole thing, and asked Zora to send Mason his regards.

In May, Zora moved back to Eatonville, which proved to be a more conducive place to finish *Mules and Men* than New York City. Langston wrote her there to renounce his claim upon *The Mule-Bone*; Zora subsequently learned that he wanted "some material" from her, but it's unclear exactly what. Rather than receiving Langston's offer graciously, Zora wrote to Mason,

> It is one of the most unworthy things he ever did. His manner of doing so. What moved him to do so, I dont know, but it is certain he hopes to gain something from me or from some one connected with me. . . . I have been wondering if you had brought pressure to bear upon him. . . . I can see

by Langston's letter that he thinks it expedient to placate me. On the back of the envelope he wrote a conciliatory phrase, but in the letter he "regrets that I dont choose to tell the truth about the matter." Honest Godmother it requires all my self-restraint to keep from tearing the gin-hound to pieces. If I followed my emotions I'd take a weapon and go around the ham-bone looking for meat.... He has nothing, *nothing* there except the suggestion "Zora, let's write a play." If that is the way to become co-author I shall write to [George Bernard] Shaw, [Eugene] O'Neil [*sic*] and [J. M.] Barry [*sic*] at once and horn in on all that they do.

▼▼▼

In February 1932, Wallace Thurman published his caustic roman à clef about the Harlem Renaissance, *Infants of the Spring.* While practically all the Niggerati came in for a drubbing, few were attacked as mercilessly as Zora, who appeared as Sweetie May Carr:

Sweetie May was a short story writer, more noted for her ribald wit and personal effervescence than for any actual literary work. She was a great favorite among those whites who went in for Negro prodigies. Mainly because she lived up to their conception of what a typical Negro should be.... Her repertoire of tales was earthy, vulgar and funny. Her darkies always smiled through their tears, sang spirituals on the slightest provocation, and performed buck dances when they should have been working. Sweetie May was a master of southern dialect, and an able raconteur, but she was too indifferent to literary creation to transfer to paper that which she told so well. The intricacies of writing bored her, and her written work was for the most part turgid and unpolished. But Sweetie May knew her white folks.

"It's like this," she had told Raymond [a character based on Thurman himself]. "I have to eat. I also wish to finish my education. Being a Negro writer these days is a racket and I'm going to make the most of it while it lasts. . . . And the only way I can live easily until I have the requisite training [to be an anthropologist] is to pose as a writer of potential ability. *Voila!* I get my tuition paid at Columbia. I rent an apartment and have all the furniture contributed by kind-hearted o'fays [white people]. . . . About twice a year I manage to sell a story. It is acclaimed. I am a genius in the making. . . ."

Zora had never before received such an assault in print. But it set the tone for future critiques by black male writers, especially the one that Langston would pen eight years later.

▼▼▼

In June 1932, Langston, together with a group of twenty other African Americans under the leadership of Louise Thompson, boarded the SS *Europa* in New York City to journey to Moscow, where they'd been promised contracts to make *Black and White*, a Communist Party–backed movie about black life in the United States set in Birmingham, Alabama. Coincidentally, Alain Locke was on the boat too, en route to a European spa, boarding with a young political scientist he was in love with named Ralph Bunche, who would win the Nobel Peace Prize just eight years later. Locke did his best to avoid Langston and Louise, though he didn't fail to disparage them in letters to Godmother: Langston had "coarsened and aged considerably" and was completely under the thumb of Louise, who "was bloated with drink." Zora, hearing of all this, also got a few digs in. As for Langston, he pointedly refused to shake Locke's hand when they met.

The farce that ensued in Moscow and Odessa could be the basis for a terrific Coen Brothers movie, featuring a scheming US colonel, an incompetent Soviet screenwriter, rebellious black New Yorkers frolicking nude on a Black Sea beach, and perhaps the involvement of Stalin himself. In all, the episode was a complete fiasco; the troupe ended up turning on Langston, calling him a "Communist Uncle Tom." And indeed, Langston was writing poem after poem of Communist propaganda. Charlotte Mason was moved to comment sarcastically to Locke, "I only hope L—— was not weaving some of Zora's play that she took to Cleveland into this Negro film from Russia."

When he finally returned to the United States after spending time in Turkestan, Uzbekistan, China, and Japan (from where the government expelled him as an "undesirable"), Langston, ensconced in a cottage in Carmel, California, finished a spate of bitter short stories that he would publish as *The Ways of White Folks*; in them, he took revenge upon Godmother. The protagonist of "The Blues I'm Playing" was a black pianist named Oceola Jones, who appears to have been modeled somewhat on Zora— she even marries a medical student. Her wealthy white patron, the demanding and condescending Dora Ellsworth, is very clearly based on Charlotte Mason. Another story, "Rejuvenation Through Joy," parodies Mason's teachings in its tale of a charlatan who starts a health colony for the wealthy using primitivist philosophy and Harlem jazz. The stories are cutting. "The Blues I'm Playing" was published in *Scribner's Magazine*; it wouldn't be surprising if Mason read it. One passage seems drawn directly from life: "Mrs. Ellsworth . . . never made uncomplimentary remarks about Negroes, but frequently did about Jews. Of little [Yehudi] Menuhin she would say, for instance, 'He's a *genius*— not a Jew,' hating to admit his ancestry."

As for Louise, she would continue to be very close to Langston, founding with him the Harlem Suitcase Theater in 1938, while continuing her political activism. Having been widowed in 1934, she married, in 1940, William L. Patterson, head of the International Labor Defense and a leading Communist.

▼▼▼

Zora had been writing furiously. In 1931 she finished *Barracoon*, wrote sketches for two theatrical reviews, published the long essay "Hoodoo in America" in the *Journal of American Folklore*, and wrote and organized a folk concert called *The Great Day*. In 1933 she wrote her first novel, *Jonah's Gourd Vine*, and revised *Mules and Men*; the former came out in 1934 and the latter in 1935 with a foreword by Franz Boas. Both were published by Lippincott, a major publisher, and were very well received in the mainstream press. In December 1933, Zora decided to rewrite *Mule Bone*, as she now called it, and spent about six weeks doing so. She wrote Carl Van Vechten that it was "much improved." Tragically, the revision, which she sent to Van Vechten's niece Elizabeth Hull, has not come to light. Then, in 1936, she wrote her masterpiece, *Their Eyes Were Watching God*, in the space of seven weeks.

Langston, by contrast, was writing comparatively little. His play *Mulatto* was enjoying a huge success on Broadway—it would be the most-performed African American–authored play until Lorraine Hansberry's *A Raisin in the Sun* eclipsed its record over twenty years later. But it had been completed in 1930, and the version presented on Broadway had been heavily rewritten by its producer—so much so that Langston felt ashamed of it. Besides

The Ways of White Folks (1934), Langston would hardly write anything of real consequence until 1940, when he finished his autobiography. He appeared to many to have lost his way and become a minor figure.

▼▼▼

In February or March 1934, Carl Van Vechten wrote to Langston, who was now living in Carmel, California, about how good Zora's novel *Jonah's Gourd Vine* was and suggested that he and Zora "kiss and make up." Langston replied, "Awfully glad about her novel! Is she still mad at me?" Van Vechten responded evasively: "I don't see how Zora or anybody else can be mad with you." And there the matter rested.

Zora, however, still felt as though she were in competition with Langston. In April 1934 she told Eslanda Robeson (Paul Robeson's wife and manager, and an anthropology student in London at the time), "One night, Alan [*sic*] Locke, Langston Hughes and Louise Thompson wrassled with me nearly all night long that folk sources were no[t] important, nobody was interested, waste of time, it wasnt art or even necessary thereto, ought to be suppressed, etc. etc., but I stuck to my guns." This appears to be a rather curious fiction—Langston and Locke certainly held no such beliefs during the time they knew Zora well, and encouraged Zora's research. Perhaps she was trying to ingratiate herself with the Robesons at Langston and Locke's expense.

Then, in July, Zora wrote a strange letter to Walter White, accusing him of spreading word that Langston had written a play with her. White denied doing so, and there is no evidence of it. In an October letter to Locke, Zora wrote, "I am very busy earning a living. But I am earning it, not chiseling as our friend Langston is doing." Zora might have been referring to the fact that the

San Francisco arts patron Noël Sullivan was paying a stipend to Langston, much as Mason had done, while Mason had stopped paying Zora in 1932. "They tell a lurid tale of his brazen antics at Fisk," she continued. Langston did not visit Fisk, and it's not clear what were the "brazen antics" Zora referred to. But evidently Langston was still very much on her mind.

Also in October, the Little Theatre in New York asked to read *Mule Bone* for a possible production. Nothing came of it.

The rebellious British heiress Nancy Cunard's *Negro: An Anthology* was published in London that year. The 854-page folio-size volume opened with Langston's "I, Too"; it included seven pieces by Zora and six poems and a short article by Langston. In "Characteristics of Negro Expression," Zora spoke well of Langston's work, but it is possible that she had written the essay in 1930 or earlier, prior to their breakup, and given it to Cunard in 1931 without revising it.

Then, in December 1934, both Rudolph Fisher and Wallace Thurman died. The only bright lights of the Niggerati still active and publishing were now Zora and Langston.

Zora had remained in close contact with Charlotte Mason, writing a song for her seventy-seventh birthday: "I have taken form from the breath of your mouth / From the vapor of your soul am I made to be." But she eventually loosened her ties to Mason—she began to refer to her as "the Park Avenue dragon" as early as 1933. She never resented her, though; Hemenway attests that "when Godmother fell ill, Zora would light hoodoo candles and commune with Mrs. Mason's spirit, successfully praying her back to health."

In 1937, though, Zora finally turned on Alain Locke. In response to a review in *Opportunity* that slammed *Their Eyes Were Watching God* for not being concerned enough with racism and class struggle, she wrote, "Up to now, Dr. Locke has not produced one single idea, or suggestion of an idea that he can call his own. . . . Dr. Locke is abstifically [*sic*] a fraud, both as a leader and as a critic. He knows less about Negro life than anyone in America. And if what he did in *The New Negro* is a sample, he does not know anything about editing and criticism either." Fortunately for her, *Opportunity* magazine refused to publish her response. And a few years later, Zora was just as friendly with Locke as she had ever been, if not more so.

Zora mostly remained in the South, with sojourns in the Caribbean, though she occasionally came back to Harlem. Both she and Langston attended the June 1938 funeral of James Weldon Johnson there; his car had been hit by a train. There is no record of whether they acknowledged each other.

A year later, Langston published "Poet to Patron," a cutting poem about his relationship with Godmother. The bitterness had not diminished.

▾▾▾

In November 1939, Arna Bontemps visited North Carolina College for Negroes in Durham, where Zora was now on the faculty. According to Bontemps, Zora prevailed on him to write a letter to Langston to "try to patch up their quarrel," and told him what she wanted him to say. Bontemps wrote Langston,

> Zora is really a changed woman, still her old humorous self, but more level and poised. She told me that the cross of her life is the fact that there has been a gulf between you and her. She said she wakes up at night crying about it even yet. I told her not to be ridiculous, that you have never ceased to insist that she is wonderful. After that she could

not do too much for me. When I told her that I was going to tell you what she said, she even promised to try to get me a job in the South someplace. So, in order that she won't change her mind, I hope you'll write her a sweet letter, or at least send a nice Christmas card. She also said another thing that sounds reasonable to me. She said her hysterics, etc. were not provoked by you at all, and I believe it. She said, or intimated, that the whole thing could be traced to old-fashioned female jealousy between her and Louise, jealousy over the matter of influence over you. When you look at it this way, it is hard to blame poor Zora. She can't help it if she's a woman. Anyhow, she's sure she's never been so well despite her sins of the past, and if I had a bigger sheet of paper, I could give a lot of reasons why it would be grand if you'll recognize her flag of truce.

This letter clearly flatters Langston. It paints Zora and Louise as his acolytes, struggling over his favor. Perhaps this is indeed what Zora wanted Langston to believe at this point, but it seems uncharacteristic of her, to say the least. Bontemps would soon share the attitude of most male black writers towards Zora: a few years later he would call her, in another letter to Langston, "the muse of black-face comedy" and her books "the products of reactionary thinking."

Langston did not respond to Bontemps's plea. Bontemps was puzzled as to why. Zora "was probably waiting for a response, having more than nudged me in exacting this promise from me that I would write it," he later recounted. Instead, a couple of weeks later, Langston made a joke about Zora's recent marriage to—and forthcoming divorce from—a young man named Albert Price in a letter to Van Vechten.

▾▾▾

Langston devoted half a dozen pages of his 1940 autobiography, *The Big Sea*, to his friendship with Zora; his portrayal of
her dripped with condescension. "Of this 'niggerati,'" Langston
wrote, "Zora Neale Hurston was certainly the most amusing.
Only to reach a wider audience, need she ever write books"—
this was written *after* Zora had published three novels and two
collections of folklore—"because she is a perfect book of entertainment in herself. In her youth she was always getting schol-
arships and things from wealthy white people, some of whom
simply paid her just to sit around and represent the Negro race
for them, she did it in such a racy fashion." This, of course, is
nonsense.

"She was full of side-splitting anecdotes, humorous tales, and
tragicomic stories, remembered out of her life in the South as a
daughter of a travelling minister of God. She could make you
laugh one minute and cry the next." Langston here echoes Richard Wright's damning 1937 review of *Their Eyes Were Watching God*:
"Her characters eat and laugh and cry and work and kill; they
swing like a pendulum eternally in that safe and narrow orbit
in which America likes to see the Negro live: between laughter
and tears."

Langston continued: "To many of her white friends, no doubt,
she was a perfect 'darkie,' in the nice meaning they give the
term—that is a naïve, childlike, sweet, humorous, and highly
colored Negro." He could have added that, until his adoption of
Communism in the 1930s, most whites regarded him as the same,
except for the "highly colored" part.

Even in praising Zora's anthropological gifts, Langston made
her look silly. "But Miss Hurston was clever, too," he wrote,

praising her as "a fine folk-lore collector," then describing her ability to "stop the average Harlemite on Lenox Avenue and measure his head with a strange-looking, anthropological device and not get bawled out for the attempt." Rather than engaging in some antiquated phrenological experiment, as Langston here implied, Zora was, under the direction of her teacher and advisor Franz Boas, attempting to *disprove* phrenological theories of racial inequality. Langston emphasized her frivolousness—the only things in her West 66th Street apartment he mentions are her "decorative silver birds, perched atop the linen cabinet" and a footstool; he tells how she once served "a *hand*-chicken dinner, since she [had no] forks." But as Zora pointed out in an initial draft of her autobiography, "'hand chicken' [is] jointed fried chicken to be eaten with the hand"—it has nothing to do with not having cutlery. Finally, Langston related a tale Zora apparently told him of how she once "borrowed" a nickel from a poor blind beggar's cup. And it is with this vile anecdote that Langston closed his humorous but malicious portrait.

Fifty pages later Langston detailed, with less condescension, his Southern road trip with Zora. But then, when he described their falling out over *The Mule-Bone*, he cruelly distorted the facts so as to take credit for its creation and to blame Zora for acting as if it were her own work on the pretext of foolish jealousy. He inaccurately claimed to have based the play on Zora's story, while she had only "authenticated and flavored the dialogue and added highly humorous details"; he had done the typing (no mention is made of Louise's involvement); Zora had *left the play with him* to polish off. Zora then sent the play, *unrevised*, to her agent, claiming it as her own, and explaining to Langston that if she had included his name on it he would have simply spent any money he earned from it "on a girl she didn't like" (who was apparently *not* Louise, since Langston had discussed her by name earlier in the book). This agent then, presumably under Zora's direction, sent the play to the Jelliffes. Langston belittled Zora again here, remarking, "Girls are funny creatures!"

Zora read *The Big Sea.* When halfway through it, before she got to the part about herself, she called it "very good" in a letter to Fannie Hurst, and said she hoped to write a review of it. And when Langston gave a talk publicizing the book in September 1940 at the 135th Street Branch Library, Zora attended. Bruce Nugent did too: "As soon as I came into the library I knew Zora was there. Of course, there was a crush of people, and this was Zora's doing. . . . Langston was very elated that she had come to it." Langston may have been unconscious of how much he had belittled Zora in his book. There's no record of whether they exchanged greetings.

Upon finishing the book, Zora changed her mind about reviewing it. At the time, she was writing her own autobiography, albeit reluctantly, at the request of her publisher. As if it were the opposite of Langston's *The Big Sea,* she titled it *Dust Tracks on a Road,* and in it, she mentioned Langston only once, in passing, in a passage about Mason.

Zora wrote a chapter for *Dust Tracks* on friendship, which was later cut from the book; in it, she named a host of her friends, past and present—forty in all. She started with Charlotte Mason, then moved to Carl Van Vechten and Fannie Hurst; Langston was conspicuously absent.

A problematic book, *Dust Tracks* has been called "one of the most un-self-revealing autobiographies ever written." Alice Walker says it "rings false"; she calls it "the most unfortunate thing Zora ever wrote." This is a sharp contrast to the opinions of white reviewers of its time, several of whom called it the *best* thing she'd yet written. Whatever its merits (which are considerable), at least Zora abstained from putting down Langston in it. In this aspect, it was quite unlike the book that had inspired it.

▾▾▾

Shortly after *The Big Sea*, in which Langston carefully omitted any mention of his communist poems or the Communists he knew so well, was published, the *Saturday Evening Post* reprinted, without permission, Hughes's 1932 poem "Goodbye Christ," a poem he had written in the Soviet Union which proposed replacing Jesus with "A real guy named / Marx Communist Lenin Peasant Stalin Worker ME." The storm of negative publicity that followed may have enticed Zora, who was in California at the time, to attack Langston. He laughed it off, remarking to the composer William Grant Still, "They tell me Zora laid me low in Pasadena."

Despite having gotten nowhere with *Mule Bone* so often, Zora had not given up on it. In 1945, she repurposed some of its material for a novel set in Eatonville. The plot centered around a "village youth" expelled from town, as Jim had been in *Mule Bone*. In the novel he travels around, having adventures, visits heaven and hell, and after seven years returns as the town hero. Rejected by her publisher because it seemed both sloppy and strained, it has since been lost. Zora confessed to Van Vechten that her dream project was to write a history of Herod the Great. In the end, that was the project to which she would devote most of her remaining energy.

The next year, Charlotte Mason died at the age of ninety-two, having spent her last thirteen years in New York Hospital. She had broken her hip in 1933, fell in love with the view from her hospital room, adored being waited on hand and foot, and—mostly deaf, partially blind, arthritic, and unable to walk—refused to go home. Of all her acolytes, Alain Locke was the only one who kept faithfully in touch; Langston and Zora had not seen her since her accident, and by the end she had even alienated Cornelia and Katherine Chapin, who nonetheless received the bulk of her million-dollar estate. Doubtless because of her desire to remain anonymous, no obituary announced her death, and none of her former beneficiaries made any public comment on it.

In 1948, Zora was arrested, charged with abusing a ten-year-old boy in Harlem. The black world was scandalized; Zora's name was on the front page of practically every black newspaper. The charges were patently false—Zora had not even been in the United States during the period the abuse was supposed to have taken place—but that did not prevent the scandal from humiliating her, paining her more than any other event of her life. Many of her old friends offered support, but Langston sniggered about the scandal in a letter to Bontemps. Zora's attorneys, however, subpoenaed Langston, asking him to testify about her good character; he agreed to do so. The case was mercifully dropped, and Langston did not have to see his former collaborator in court. Zora moved to Florida.

In 1950, Langston transformed his successful play *Mulatto*, which he had written in the months after Zora had absconded with *Mule Bone*, into an opera entitled *The Barrier*, with music composed by Jan Meyerowitz. Before it opened on Broadway (for an extremely short run), it was given a two-week tryout at a seedy theater in Washington, D.C., the New Gayety. According to a letter Zora wrote four years later, she attended a performance (though she was living in Florida at the time), and Langston asked her, along with some other African American theatergoers, to help explain to him why it was "getting such a poor reception." Zora, who was puzzled by Langston wanting her advice after what they'd been through, told him the main fault was in the character of the protagonist: "There was nothing about the hero to inspire admiration and induce sorrow at his lynching. In fact, one might be tempted to go forth and help do the job." Zora's frankness was appreciated neither by Langston nor by the others at the meeting, all of them "upper-class," as Zora categorized them. The entire story seems somewhat apocryphal, however.

Zora had become increasingly conservative over the years. Estranged from the African American community by the attacks on her and her writing in the black press and from black intellectuals, she had few black friends and lived mostly among Southern whites. Langston, meanwhile, was under continual fire for his former association with Communism, being put under surveillance by the FBI, denounced in the US Senate, and forced to testify before Joseph McCarthy's subcommittee on investigations about his radical past. His career, however—as a poet, Broadway lyricist, newspaper columnist, translator, librettist, and anthologist—was at its peak.

Perhaps it was inevitable, then, that Zora would join in attacking Langston for his politics. In 1951, she published a rabidly anticommunist article in the *American Legion Magazine* in which she mentioned Langston and Louise's 1932 trip to Russia. One of the illustrations was a box whose heading read "NO DISCUSSION OF COMMUNISM AND THE NEGRO IS COMPLETE WITHOUT MENTION OF THESE CHARACTERS," and one of the six pictured was Langston, "Author of 'Goodbye Christ.'" Three years later Zora wrote, in an unpublished letter to the *Saturday Evening Post*, that she had learned all about Communism from Langston. "I had known him since I came to New York in 1925," she explained. "I thought him very innocent-like and full of simplicity and virtues. I was to discover later that his shy-looking mein [*sic*] covered a sly opportunism that was utterly revolting."

▼▼▼

When I was in Savannah, retracing Zora's and Langston's 1927 road trip, I had a long conversation with the storyteller Imani Mtendaji, who lives and practices there. As soon as I told her about my project, she brought up *The Book of Negro Folklore*. That book is practically her Bible, the primary source of her tales.

Langston Hughes and Arna Bontemps had assembled it in 1958. A 624-page collection of folktales, songs, and other material, it could very well have fulfilled Zora's contractual obligation to Charlotte Mason (to compile "the music, poetry, folk-lore, literature, hoodoo, conjure, manifestations of art and kindred subjects relating to and existing among the North American negroes"), but it also met her own definition of folklore: "the boiled-down juice of human living."

It was not the first anthology that Hughes and Bontemps had put together: they had published *The Poetry of the Negro* in 1949. But *The Book of Negro Folklore* was more ambitious. The final manuscript, as Langston commented to Van Vechten, was nearly a foot and a half tall and weighed ten pounds; it was the first comprehensive anthology of its kind. In it, Zora was more heavily represented than any other single author, with twenty-six tales and sermons, mostly from *Mules and Men*, but also from *Jonah's Gourd Vine* and *Dust Tracks on a Road*. *The Book of Negro Folklore* was modeled largely after folklorist Benjamin Botkin's monumental 1944 volume *A Treasury of American Folklore*, which had included twenty-one of Zora's tales.

All of Zora's books, by this time, were out of print. Zora didn't fit into the now prescribed role of a black writer: to speak truth to power. The rise of writers like Richard Wright, Ralph Ellison, and James Baldwin had changed what African Americans were expected to write. For them, Zora Neale Hurston, who had, in 1955, written a widely distributed letter condemning court-ordered desegregation, was as passé as a minstrel show.

But now, finally, twenty-seven years after the *Mule Bone* controversy, a Langston-Zora collaboration of sorts had been published—this time *without* Zora's name on the cover. It's a shame that Langston didn't ask Zora to participate in the project—she would probably have made some significant improvements.

Regardless, *The Book of Negro Folklore* was—with the exception of an uninspiring introduction by Bontemps, a condescending essay on street cries by a white Southern newspaper writer, and an atrociously clueless painting on the jacket by pulp artist Everett Kinstler—a triumphal representation of everything both Zora and Langston had stood for. For it was not, despite its title, limited to material gathered from the folk. It included plenty of literary interpretations of folk material, by authors ranging from Langston and Zora to Ralph Ellison, Richard Wright, Gwendolyn Brooks, and Margaret Walker. Much of it was solidly in the vein of *Fine Clothes to the Jew, Mules and Men,* and *Mule Bone.* It represented African American culture in much the same way Zora, Langston, and Godmother had envisioned it in the 1920s— free from politics, free from white folks, free from pretentiousness or middle-class values. Zora had written Langston back in 1928, "I am getting inside of Negro art and lore. I am beginning to *see* really and when you join me I shall point things out and see if you see them as I do." That same year she had written Locke, "I am using the vacuum method, grabbing everything I see. Langston is responsible for that to a great extent." In other words, Zora's and Langston's vision coincided: both to get *inside* the folkways of the African American community and to encompass them in all their variety. With this volume, the ideals the two writers had aspired to back when their friendship was strong were largely fulfilled.

All that was missing was the popular success that both craved. Although the book was well received and went through several printings, it never made the kind of splash that the two of them had envisioned for *Mule Bone*, and it has long been out of print.

Zora died penniless two years later, on January 28, 1960, at the age of sixty-nine. She had been living in a segregated nursing home in Fort Pierce, Florida, after suffering a stroke the previous October; a second stroke killed her. She most likely never saw *The Book of Negro Folklore*. Laudatory obituaries ran in all the major papers and magazines. Carl Van Vechten remembered her fondly, and wired money to help pay for her funeral. There is no record of Langston mentioning her death.

However, four years later, Langston sent the draft of *Mule Bone* that he had prepared for the Gilpin Players to the magazine *Drama Critique*. They published act three of the play under both his name and Zora's. A portion of the legendary collaboration between Zora and Langston had finally seen the light.

The Legacy

Many writers have characterized Langston as a naïf. Zora is usually either a madwoman (as Louise Thompson and a number of African American men saw her) or a stereotypical strong black woman (as many contemporary women portray her). These represent the extremes of their characters. At the time of their final falling out, Zora represented Langston as a cunning liar, Locke concurred, and Mason was convinced. Almost everyone else who wrote about him said he was scrupulously honest. But nobody was scrupulously honest in this affair. Langston lied to his own lawyer about *Mule Bone*'s composition, Zora exaggerated Langston's actions to Mason, and both of their autobiographies are studded with falsehoods and omissions.

Langston's pattern of sudden and almost violent breaks with close friends (Locke, Cullen, Mason, Zora) is notable, for few of them ever got over their resentment of him, regardless of who instigated the rupture. Did each of these men and women fall in love with him in some way or another, only to find their affection unreturned? That is the impression one gets from Arnold Rampersad's biography, and it makes perfect sense given Langston's tendency to shy away from emotional attachments. Zora had another explanation for these breaks: that "his shy-looking mein covered a sly opportunism that was utterly revolting." But that seems far too harsh a judgment.

Given the fact that Langston never let anyone get too close to him, I would venture that his defense against the threat of excessive intimacy that his best friends posed consisted in varying degrees of evasiveness, condescension, and turning his charm onto others. Although we have no evidence of it, it's possible that while working with Zora, Langston felt threatened by how close she felt to him, and as a defense exaggerated his feelings for Louise in Zora's presence.

As for Zora, she was passionate, jealous, headstrong, and never shrank from saying what was on her mind, regardless of the consequences. Wildly inconsistent; prone to sycophancy, flights of fancy, and dangerous rages; unscrupulous and backstabbing; and unshakeable in her belief in her own powers, she was a force to be reckoned with. She was by no means a madwoman, but neither was she a woman of integrity and backbone.

Langston was not the only naïf. They *both* believed in Charlotte Mason, each other, their common goal of a real Negro folk drama, and the basic generosity of human beings. In the end, all their beliefs came to naught.

Zora never again found a friend as close, constant, and true as Langston had been. Langston did—his friendships with Arna Bontemps and Carl Van Vechten were at least as intimate and productive as that with Zora. Yet he had to have missed Zora's passion, joie de vivre, and insouciance. It would have been hard not to miss such an extraordinary presence in his life.

▼▼▼

In "The Inside Light—Being a Salute to Friendship," a chapter Zora's publisher convinced her to exclude from her autobiography, Zora gave a curious metaphor for friendship. She described "lonesome-looking old red hills . . . lying there looking useless." But in the twilight, a "herd of friendly shadows" gambols happily at the foot of those hills, and one can see "the departing sun, all colored-up with its feelings, saying a sweet good night to those lonesome hills, and making them a promise that he will never forget them. . . . 'I will visit you with my love,' says the sun." It is a strikingly one-sided relationship.

"I have never been as good a friend as I meant to be," she continued. "I keep seeing new heights and depths of possibilities which ought to be reached, only to be frustrated by the press of life which is no friend to grace." She thanks her friends who "have flown into that awful place west and south of old original Hell and, with great compassion, lifted me off of the blistering coals and showed me trees and flowers." There is no hint of reciprocity from her here. Of course, the chapter functions as a kind of acknowledgment, but as the only thing she wrote on the subject of friendship, it's striking how lonely it feels.

In keeping with this metaphor, Zora's letters to Langston are full of what he did for her and what he meant to her. But what did she do for him, and what did she mean to him? Was their friendship only a one-way street, with Langston smiling upon Zora, giving her his encouragement, and getting nothing in return?

I doubt it. Perhaps Zora forgot what she had done for Langston; perhaps she never knew. Most of Langston's letters to Zora are lost, so it can appear that Langston never admitted how valuable their friendship had been for him. Perhaps, even without

her, he might have still coedited *Fire!!*, written "The Negro Artist and the Racial Mountain," and put together *The Book of Negro
Folklore*. Perhaps for Langston, having a friend like Zora didn't
really matter in the long run. But I find that impossible to believe
from the joy he expressed during their road trip, the fact that he
continually encouraged her writing, his sage advice regarding
Locke and Godmother, and his passion for what she had done in
Mule Bone.

On the other hand, by pointedly excluding him from "The
Inside Light," Zora certainly tried to pretend that *Langston* had
never mattered to *her*.

"I loved my friend," begins and ends one of Langston's best-
known poems, first published in May 1925, the month he met
Zora. The equivalence of love and friendship is at the heart of
not just this poem, but of Langston's entire mode of existence.
His letters to Charlotte Mason are full of this equation, as was
his relationship with Louise Thompson.

And this equivalence applies to his feeling for Zora. Theirs
wasn't the friendship of the lonely red hill and the sun, or, in
Marcel Proust's simile, "a madman who believes the furniture is
alive and talks to it." Theirs was the friendship of those who, as
Langston wrote in his 1926 poem "Harlem Night Song," "roam
the night together / Singing. / I love you."

▼▼▼

Langston would continue to enjoy success as a writer, and
remained more or less at the center of Harlem literature and
culture until his death in 1967. But he realized quite soon after
his breakup with Zora and Mason that he had to base his writing
on something other than Negro folk traditions. He found that
something in a passion for social and racial justice. His com-

passionate portrayals of the problematic relationships between black and white people would energize his best fiction, poetry, and plays from this time on. He emerged from the darkness and torment of 1930 and 1931 a fundamentally changed man. He even went so far as to implicitly repudiate "The Negro Artist and the Racial Mountain," saying, in 1950, "The most heartening thing for me is to see Negroes writing works in the general American field, rather than dwelling on Negro themes solely."

Zora, on the other hand, continued for a time to believe in the singular traditions of African Americans. She produced plays and fictions of all sorts and, in 1936, wrote perhaps the greatest American novel of the twentieth century. And underlying all her best work was her firm faith in the singularity of her people. They were, she felt, fundamentally different from white folks— a belief Langston too continued to share. Her writing, however, would quickly be condemned in no uncertain terms by the majority of the black literati—all men, of course—including Richard Wright, Alain Locke, Sterling Brown, and Ralph Ellison. They all said that she paid too little attention to the myriad injustices inflicted upon black people; that she glorified the aspects of black life that whites ridiculed; that she was playing to the white folks' visions, and "making the white folks laugh," in Wright's words.

Soon, refusing to compromise and thus abandoned by practically all of her black friends, she lost her faith in black culture and went adrift. The concluding chapter of an early draft of her autobiography, written in 1941, was called "Seeing the World as It Is," and in it she made the case that "Negroes are just like anybody else. . . . I wash myself of race pride and repudiate race solidarity [and] by the same token I turn my back upon the past." It is wholly incompatible with the beliefs she had espoused for years. And from then on, success eluded her. By the time of her death in 1960, despite having published more books than any African American woman in history, all of them had fallen out of print, and she was buried in an unmarked grave.

Alice Walker helped resuscitate Zora's reputation in a 1975 article for *Ms.* magazine entitled "In Search of Zora Neale Hurston." She later wrote of "the quality I feel is most characteristic of Zora's work: racial health—a sense of black people as complete, complex, *undiminished* human beings, a sense that is lacking in so much black writing and literature." I believe that Langston shared that sense, especially in his work of the 1920s. As a college student, Walker had been befriended and supported by none other than Langston Hughes. Just a few months before his death in 1967, he published *The Best Short Stories by Negro Writers.* It was a synthesis of sorts: it included his own "Thank You, M'am," Zora's "The Gilded Six-Bits," and the first story published by Walker, who was only twenty-one years old, "To Hell with Dying." Alice Walker is indeed, in a sense, the last living link between these two writers. Unfortunately, however, as Walker informed me, Langston never spoke to her about Zora, and she never asked him about her either. Exactly how Langston felt about Zora at the end of his life can only be guessed.

Nevertheless, the debt that contemporary black fiction, drama, and poetry owe to the innovations of Langston and Zora is immense. For in their wake, and partially because of their writings, African American literature has followed a largely different path than white American literature. For earlier writers like James Weldon Johnson, art in America *had* to be, in scholar Ann Douglas's words, "a miscegenated affair, whatever the denials and demurrals on either side." Langston and Zora were the first great American writers who implicitly claimed that their work was purely black.

As a result of their pioneering work, most of the trends that dominated white American fiction, poetry, and drama through the remainder of the twentieth century found few parallels in African American work. Similarly, the trends that shaped that work, from the social protest novels of the 1940s to the Black Arts movement of the late '60s and the Afrofuturism, street lit, and slam poetry that followed, found few parallels in mainstream white literature either. Although there was distinctive African American literature long before Zora and Langston, they helped to keep the most vital strands of it separate by insisting that its value was distinct from that of white literature, and by writing lasting works that proved the point.

Would they have accomplished this even if they had not been such good friends? Certainly their idiosyncratic writing styles were firmly in place by the time they met. Yet their most important statements about black art—Langston's "The Negro Artist and the Racial Mountain" and Zora's "How It Feels to Be Colored Me" and "Characteristics of Negro Expression"—were written only after they had gotten to know each other, and reflected their conversations. Charlotte Mason's ideas, however abhorrent they may seem today, influenced them both, and helped them forge their path. The three of them shared an uncommon—for the time—reverence for the traditions, behavior, and character of the black lower and working classes, and this reverence would shine through their work from beginning to end. This reverence helped maintain the singularity of African American literature, and made it come alive as a distinct and unique body of work. Zora and Langston's friendship played a vital role in establishing the identity of African American literature in its time—and throughout its future.

ACKNOWLEDGMENTS

In writing these words of thanks, I am probably leaving out more people who helped me than I'm including. My memory is somewhat faulty, this book has been so long in the making, and I have a tendency to be excessively concise.

The idea for this book came out of research I did for *Darkest America*, a book I wrote with Jake Austen; he instilled in me a certain way of thought that I try to not lose sight of. My agent, William Clark, and editor, Amy Cherry, were supportive from the start and helped me develop the project organically; Amy made hundreds of valuable suggestions, brought many of its scenes to life, and steered me to the right course whenever I went too deep into the woods or was unfair to one of its protagonists. Nancy Green expertly copyedited the book, tightening many of its nuts and bolts.

The staff at the libraries of the University of Kansas, Yale University, Emory University, and Howard University were all extremely helpful, going out of their way to make my research pleasant and easy; I'd especially like to thank Randall K. Burkett at Emory for discussing the Louise Thompson Patterson papers with me. Carla Kaplan helpfully answered my questions about her astonishingly deep research into Hurston and Mason's lives and writings. For granting me permission to use written material, I'm grateful to Craig Tenney and Alex Smithline at Harold Ober Associates, MaryLouise Patterson, Leah Hattermer Hemenway, Peter London at HarperCollins, and Adam Reed at the Joy Harris Literary Agency.

Talking with Imani Mtendaji illuminated Southern history, made real to me aspects of Zora and Langston's Southern road trip, and helped me understand how their connections to folklore remain alive. My conversations with my fellow Chicago writers, including Jacqueline Stewart, Julian Dibbell, Ethan Michaeli, and Ben Austen, gave me much insight and courage. I worked with several editors at the *Oxford American* on an article I wrote for them about my attempt to retrace Zora and Langston's 1927 Southern road trip; Jay Jennings was exceptionally helpful, making hundreds of suggestions that improved the article immeasurably, and Maxwell George and Eliza Borne were masterful in their edits. Andrew Szanton read the first draft and alerted me to details I never would have thought of without him.

My children Thalia and Jacky have provided excellent aperçus over the years and have kept my spirits light and even.

Most importantly, from the beginning, I have discussed practically everything in the book with my wife, Karen Duys; she has been my sounding board, traveling companion, unofficial editor, and constant support, making thousands of valuable suggestions, and investing untold hours of her time in bringing this work to fruition. This book would have been impossible without her brilliance, dedication, and love.

NOTES

EPIGRAPH

viii   Alice Walker, "Turning Into Love: Some Thoughts on Meeting and Surviving Langston Hughes," *Callaloo*, no. 41 (Autumn 1989), 664–65.

INTRODUCTION: LOVINGLY YOURS

3   *a perfect 'darkie'*   Langston Hughes, *The Big Sea: An Autobiography* (New York: Alfred A. Knopf, 1940), 239.

3   *best friend ... nearest person*   Hurston to Hughes, January 18, 1931, in Carla Kaplan, ed., *Zora Neale Hurston: A Life in Letters* (New York: Doubleday, 2002), 203.

4   *the most prolific*   Charles H. Nichols, ed., *Arna Bontemps–Langston Hughes Letters 1925–1967* (New York: Dodd, Mead, 1980), 8.

5   *the cross of her life*   Bontemps to Hughes, November 24, 1939, in Nichols, *Bontemps–Hughes Letters*, 44.

I. OPPORTUNITY

8 *banquets, after-lodge suppers* Advertisement, *The Nation* 115, no. 2995 (November 29, 1922), 592.

8 *if you had a pocket flask* Bruce Nugent, interview by Robert E. Hemenway, n.d., Robert E. Hemenway Personal Papers, PP487, Kenneth Spencer Research Library, University of Kansas Libraries.

9 *something was always arranged* Nugent, interview.

9 *the root of the so-called* Zora Neale Hurston, *Dust Tracks on a Road*, in *Folklore, Memoirs, & Other Writings*, ed. Cheryl A. Wall (New York: Library of America, 1995), 682.

9 *did more to encourage* Langston Hughes, *The Big Sea: An Autobiography* (New York: Alfred A. Knopf, 1940), 218.

10 *the greatest gathering* Arnold Rampersad, *The Life of Langston Hughes*, Vol. 1, *1902–1941, I, Too, Sing America*, 2nd ed. (New York: Oxford University Press, 2002), 107.

13 *highly polished stuff* David Levering Lewis, *When Harlem Was in Vogue* (New York: Penguin, 1997), 95.

14 *The women ate heartily* Zora Neale Hurston, "Spunk," in *The Complete Stories* (New York: HarperCollins, 1995), 32.

15 *You are America* Langston Hughes, "America," in *The Collected Poems of Langston Hughes*, ed. Arnold Rampersad (New York: Alfred A. Knopf, 1994), 52.

16 *all Africa awoke* Zora Neale Hurston, "Black Death," in *Complete Stories*, 206.

17 *Zora was patronizingly fond* Nugent, interview.

17 *peasant mind and imagination* Alain Locke, "The Negro Spirituals," in *The New Negro*, 1st Touchstone ed. (New York: Simon & Schuster, 1997), 204.

17 *primitive in the American Negro* Alain Locke, "The Legacy of the Ancestral Arts," in *The New Negro*, 254.

18 *a sort of 'Dean'* Johnson to Locke, March 7, 1924, Alain Locke Papers, Moorland-Spingarn Research Center, Howard University.

19 *stuffed with a pedantry* Quoted in Leonard Harris and Charles Molesworth, *Alain L. Locke: Biography of a Philosopher* (Chicago: University of Chicago Press, 2008), 271.

21 *bright, rangy, intelligent* Carl Van Vechten, *The Splendid Drunken Twen-*

ties: Selections from the Daybooks, 1922–30, ed. Bruce Kellner (Urbana: University of Illinois Press, 2003), 86.

22 *lots of bangles* Robert E. Hemenway, *Zora Neale Hurston: A Literary Biography* (Urbana: University of Illinois, 1977), 61.

22 *but she had an ease* Arna Bontemps, interview by Robert E. Hemenway, November 18, 1970, Hemenway Papers.

22 *the gift of walking* Fannie Hurst, "Zora Hurston: A Personality Sketch," *Yale University Library Gazette* 35, no. 1 (July 1960), 19.

22 *Zora is picturesque* Carl Van Vechten, "Some 'Literary Ladies' I Have Known," *Yale University Gazette* 26, no. 3 (January 1952), 113.

23 *He had done everything* Richard Bruce Nugent, "Lighting *FIRE!!,*" insert in reprint of *Fire!!* 1, no. 1 (1982).

24 *is a clever girl* Hughes to Van Vechten, June 4, 1925, in *The Selected Letters of Langston Hughes*, ed. Arnold Rampersad and David Roessel with Christa Fratantoro (New York: Alfred A. Knopf, 2015), 46.

2. I LAUGH, AND GROW STRONG

25 *city of five lakes* Zora Neale Hurston, *Mules and Men*, in *Folklore, Memoirs, & Other Writings*, ed. Cheryl A. Wall (New York: Library of America, 1995), 12.

25 *a Negro town* Zora Neale Hurston, *Dust Tracks on a Road*, in *Folklore, Memoirs*, 561, 565.

26 *a center of wealth* Ibid., 563.

26 *extra strong* Ibid., 585.

26 *the one girl who could take* Ibid.

26 *was the heart and spring* Ibid., 599–601.

27 *Like clearcut stereopticon slides* Ibid., 596–98.

28 *certain instructions* Ibid., 617.

28 *Papa held me tight* Ibid., 617–18.

29 *She called me a sassy* Ibid., 625–627.

30 *to finish the job* Ibid., 627.

30 *I was hungry* Fannie Hurst, "Zora Hurston: A Personality Sketch," *Yale University Library Gazette* 35, no. 1 (1960), 17.

31 *I had been in school* Hurston, *Dust Tracks*, 662.

32 *He could stomp* Ibid., 744.

32 *At the time I was going* Herbert Sheen, interview by Robert E. Hemenway, n.d., Robert E. Hemenway Personal Papers, PP487, Kenneth Spencer Research Library, University of Kansas Libraries.

33 *greatest ambition is* Quoted in Valerie Boyd, *Wrapped in Rainbows: The Life of Zora Neale Hurston* (New York: Scribner, 2003), 87.

34 *making the white folks laugh* Richard Wright, "Between Laughter and Tears," *New Masses* 25 (October 5, 1937), 22.

34 *I am not black* Langston Hughes, *The Big Sea: An Autobiography* (New York: Alfred A. Knopf, 1940), 11.

35 *My grandmother never* Ibid., 303.

36 *Then it was that books* Ibid., 16–17.

37 *the people will live on* Carl Sandburg, *The People, Yes* (New York: Harcourt Brace, 1936), 284.

37 *Carl Sandburg's poems* Hughes, *Big Sea*, 29.

38 *My father hated Negroes* Ibid., 40–41.

39 *I was in love with Harlem* Langston Hughes, "My Early Days in Harlem," *Freedomways* 3 (1963), 312, in *The Collected Works of Langston Hughes*, Vol. 9: *Essays on Art, Race, Politics, and World Affairs* (Columbia: University of Missouri Press, 2002), 395–96.

39 *At last!* Hughes, *Big Sea*, 80.

39 *Manhattan takes me* Langston Hughes, "The Fascination of Cities," *Crisis* 31, no. 3 (January 1926), 138–40, in *Collected Works 9*, 30.

40 *The octoroon choruses* Quoted in Carla Kaplan, *Miss Anne in Harlem: The White Women of the Black Renaissance* (New York: HarperCollins, 2013), 113.

40 *Everybody seemed to make me* Hughes, "My Early Days," 396.

41 *learned people* Hughes, *Big Sea*, 93.

42 *Melodramatic, maybe* Ibid., 3.

42 *ur-trope* Henry Louis Gates Jr., *The Signifying Monkey: A Theory of African-American Literary Criticism* (New York: Oxford University Press, 1989), 143.

43 *All my childhood* Hughes to Mason, February 23, 1929, Langston Hughes Papers, Beinecke Rare Book and Manuscript Library, New Haven.

44 *that poetry should be* Arnold Rampersad, *The Life of Langston Hughes*, Vol. 1: *1902–1941, I, Too, Sing America*, 2nd ed. (New York: Oxford University Press, 2002), 146.

44 *I, too, sing America* Langston Hughes, "I, Too," in *The Collected Poems of Langston Hughes*, ed. Arnold Rampersad (New York: Alfred A. Knopf, 1994), 46.

45 *Write to him* Cullen to Locke, January 20, 1923, quoted in Jeffrey C. Stewart, *The New Negro: The Life of Alain Locke* (New York: Oxford University Press, 2018), 342.

46 *looking like a virile* Quoted in Leonard Harris and Charles Molesworth, *Alain L. Locke: Biography of a Philosopher* (Chicago: University of Chicago Press, 2008), 160.

46 *infatuation with Greek ideals* Locke to Hughes, February 10, 1923, quoted in Rampersad, *Life*, 68.

46 *how wonderful it would be* Hughes to Locke, undated, Alain Locke Papers, Moorland-Spingarn Research Center, Howard University.

46 *afraid of learned people* Hughes, *Big Sea*, 93.

46 MAY I COME NOW PLEASE Hughes to Locke, telegram, February 2, 1924, Alain Locke Papers.

46 *I had been reading* Hughes to Locke, February 4, 1924, Alain Locke Papers.

46 *I do not recognize myself* Locke to Hughes, February 5, [1924], Alain Locke Papers.

47 *We've been having a jolly* Hughes to Jackman, August 1, 1924, in *The Selected Letters of Langston Hughes*, ed. Arnold Rampersad and David Roessel with Christa Fratantoro (New York: Alfred A. Knopf, 2015), 37.

47 *See Paris and die* Locke to Cullen, July 26, 1924, quoted in Rampersad, *Life*, 92.

47 *every breath has the soothe* Locke to Hughes, August 10, 1924, quoted in Stewart, *New Negro*, 440.

48 *galvanized* Arna Bontemps, *The Harlem Renaissance Remembered: Essays, Edited with a Memoir* (New York: Dodd, Mead, 1972), 19.

48 *lose my boyish faith* Langston Hughes, "L'histoire de ma vie" (unpublished, 1925), quoted in Rampersad, *Life*, 98.

49 *Never before had I seen* Langston Hughes, "Our Wonderful Society: Washington," *Opportunity* 5 no. 8 (August 1927), 226–27, in *Collected Works* 9, 42.

3. THE NIGGERATI

52 *first publicity break* Langston Hughes, *The Big Sea: An Autobiography* (New York: Alfred A. Knopf, 1940), 212.

53 *furniture party* Quoted in Valerie Boyd, *Wrapped in Rainbows: The Life of Zora Neale Hurston* (New York: Scribner, 2003), 120.

53 *violently interested in Negroes*   Carl Van Vechten, "The Reminiscences of Carl Van Vechten: A Rudimentary Narration," Oral History Research Office, Columbia University, 193.

53 *the Livingstone of this*   Richard Bruce Nugent, *Gentleman Jigger: A Novel*, ed. Thomas H. Wirth (Philadelphia: Da Capo Press, 2008), 57–58.

53 *Photographs from around 1924*   Emily Bernard, ed., *Remember Me to Harlem: The Letters of Langston Hughes and Carl Van Vechten* (New York: Knopf, 2001), xiii–xiv.

54 *Jazz, the blues*   Van Vechten to Mencken, May 29, 1925, quoted in David Levering Lewis, *When Harlem Was in Vogue* (New York: Penguin, 1997), 98.

54 *personal nourishment*   Lewis, *When Harlem Was in Vogue*, 99.

55 *You just did what you wanted*   Quoted in Jeff Kisseloff, *You Must Remember This: An Oral History of Manhattan from the 1890s to World War II* (New York: Harcourt, Brace, Jovanovich, 1989), 289.

55 *There were men and women*   Mabel Hampton, interview by Joan Nestle, Lesbian Herstory Archives, quoted in Boyd, *Wrapped in Rainbows*, 129.

55 *seemed to thrive without*   Arnold Rampersad, *The Life of Langston Hughes*, Vol. 1: *1902–1941, I, Too, Sing America*, 2nd ed. (New York: Oxford University Press, 2002), 133.

56 *obscured and shielded*   Ann Douglas, *Terrible Honesty: Mongrel Manhattan in the 1920s* (New York: Farrar Straus & Giroux, 1995), 97.

56 *Silence is as good*   Hughes, *Big Sea*, 200.

56 *smiling and self-effacing*   Wallace Thurman, *Infants of the Spring* (New York: Macaulay Co., 1932), 143.

57 *Behind the warm smile*   Arthur Koestler, *The Invisible Writing* (New York: Macmillan, 1954), 111.

57 *Once, dressed for a party*   Robert E. Hemenway, *Zora Neale Hurston: A Literary Biography* (Urbana: University of Illinois, 1977), 30.

58 *the arts of the people*   Zora Neale Hurston, "Folklore and Music," in *Folklore, Memoirs, & Other Writings*, ed. Cheryl A. Wall (New York: Library of America, 1995), 876.

58 *From the earliest rocking*   Zora Neale Hurston, *Mules and Men*, in *Folklore, Memoirs*, 9.

58 *the greatest anthropologist*   Zora Neale Hurston, *Dust Tracks on a Road*, in *Folklore, Memoirs*, 683, 687.

59 *Oh, if you knew*   Hurston to Meyer, [January 1926], in Carla Kaplan, ed., *Zora Neale Hurston: A Life in Letters* (New York: Doubleday, 2002), 77.

60 *a person of the most contradictory*   Zora Neale Hurston, "Fannie Hurst," *Saturday Review of Literature* (October 9, 1937), 15.

60 *shorthand was short*   Fannie Hurst, "Zora Hurston: A Personality Sketch," *Yale University Library Gazette* 35, no. 1 (1960), 17.

61 *all in greased curls*   Hurst to Van Vechten, April 1926, quoted in Boyd, *Wrapped in Rainbows*, 121.

61 *She drove with a sure*   Hurst, "Zora Hurston," 17.

61 *with my foot in the gas*   Hurston, "Fannie Hurst," 16.

62 *a period of solitary wandering*   Hughes to Mason, February 23, 1929, Langston Hughes Papers, Beinecke Rare Book and Manuscript Library, New Haven.

62 *Hughes ought to stop*   Hurston to Cullen, March 11, [1926], in Kaplan, *Letters*, 84.

63 *the Aframerican is merely*   George Schuyler, "The Negro-Art Hokum," *Nation* 122 (June 16, 1926), 662–63.

63 *urge within the race*   Langston Hughes, "The Negro Artist and the Racial Mountain," *Nation* 122 (June 23, 1926), 692–94, in *The Collected Works of Langston Hughes*, Vol. 9: *Essays on Art, Race, Politics, and World Affairs* (Columbia: University of Missouri Press, 2002), 32.

63 *Negroes should be concerned*   Countee Cullen, "The Dark Tower," *Opportunity* 6, no. 3 (March 1928), 90.

63 *I would like to be white*   Hughes, "Negro Artist," 31.

63 *the Negro middle class*   Ibid.

63 *Nordicized Negro intelligentsia*   Ibid.

64 *I am not tragically colored*   Zora Neale Hurston, "How It Feels to Be Colored Me," *The World Tomorrow* 11 (May 1928), 215–16, in *Folklore, Memoirs*, 827.

64 *All art is propaganda*   W. E. B. Du Bois, "Criteria of Negro Art," *The Crisis* 32 (October 1926), 290–97, quoted in Leonard Harris and Charles Molesworth, *Alain L. Locke: Biography of a Philosopher* (Chicago: University of Chicago Press, 2008), 214.

65 *the folk temperament*   Alain Locke, "Beauty Instead of Ashes," *The Nation* 126, no. 3276 (April 18, 1928), 434.

65 *genius and talent*   Alain Locke, "Art or Propaganda?," *Harlem* 1, no. 1 (November 1928), 12.

65 *We do* not *hate white people*   Zora Neale Hurston, "Why the Negro Won't Buy Communism," *American Legion Magazine,* June 1951, 59.

65 *It was, Zora knew*   Boyd, *Wrapped in Rainbows,* 145–46.

65 *Only now am I*   Hughes to Mason, February 23, 1929, in *The Selected Letters of Langston Hughes,* ed. Arnold Rampersad and David Roessel with Christa Fratantoro (New York: Alfred A. Knopf, 2015), 84.

66 *Yo quisiera ser Negro*   Nicolás Guillén, "Conversación con Langston Hughes," *El Diario de la Marina,* March 2, 1930, in *Prosa de Prisa (1929–1985)* (Havana: Ediciones Unión, 2002), 19.

66 *a song to the morning*   Hurston, "Art and Such," in *Folklore, Memoirs,* 908.

66 *This is the way it is*   Hurst, "Zora Hurston," 20.

67 *Sometimes, I feel discriminated*   Hurston, "How It Feels," 829.

68 *lacking in bitterness*   Hurston, *Mules and Men,* 230.

68 *naive, quaint, complaisant*   Sterling A. Brown, "Old Time Tales," *New Masses* 18, no. 9 (February 25, 1936), 25.

68 *there are no bitter*   Hurston, "High John de Conquer," in *Folklore, Memoirs,* 927.

68 *the blues are not*   Ralph Ellison, *Shadow and Act* (New York: Random House, 1964), 257.

68 *Bitterness . . . is the graceless*   Hurston, *Dust Tracks,* 765.

69 *Why dont I put*   Hurston to Cullen, March 5, 1943, in Kaplan, *Letters,* 481–482.

70 *The game of keeping*   Hurston, "How It Feels," 828.

70 *accepted the notion*   Arnold Rampersad, Introduction, *The New Negro,* ed. Alain Locke (New York: Simon & Schuster, 1992), xvi.

70 *the poor Negro*   Hurston to Charlotte Osgood Mason, October 15, 1931, in Kaplan, *Letters,* 234.

71 *there is no fundamental*   Franz Boas, *The Mind of Primitive Man,* rev. ed. (New York: Macmillan, 1938), v.

72 *Primitivism* was *the avant-garde*   Emily Bernard, *Carl Van Vechten and the Harlem Renaissance: A Portrait in Black and White* (New Haven: Yale University Press, 2012), 70–71.

72 *This orchestra grows rambunctious*   Hurston, "How It Feels," 828.

73 *All the tom-toms*   Langston Hughes, "Poem," in *The Collected Poems of Langston Hughes,* ed. Arnold Rampersad (New York: Alfred A. Knopf, 1994), 32.

73   *the eternal tom-tom*   Hughes, "Negro Artist," 35.

73   *a sanctified church*   Carl Van Vechten, *The Splendid Drunken Twenties: Selections from the Daybooks, 1922–30*, ed. Bruce Kellner (Urbana: University of Illinois Press, 2003), 120.

74   *'The Crisis' is the house*   Hurston to Locke, October 11, 1927, in Kaplan, *Letters*, 109.

74   *Always guiding unobtrusively*   Richard Bruce Nugent, "Lighting *FIRE!!*," insert in reprint of *Fire!!* 1, no. 1 (1982).

74   *sweltering summer evenings*   Hughes, *Big Sea*, 236.

75   *colored people can't help*   Hughes to Locke, August 12, 1926, Alain Locke Papers, Moorland-Spingarn Research Center, Howard University.

75   *our people to a 'T'*   Carrie Hughes to Langston Hughes, November 3, 1926, in Carmaletta M. Williams and John Edgar Tidwell, eds., *My Dear Boy: Carrie Hughes's Letters to Langston Hughes, 1926–1938* (Athens: University of Georgia Press, 2013), 28.

75   *Life to [Van Vechten]*   W. E. B. Du Bois, "Books," *Crisis* (December 1926), 81–82, quoted in Edward White, *The Tastemaker: Carl Van Vechten and the Birth of Modern America* (New York: Farrar, Straus & Giroux, 2014), 212.

75   *As many black people*   White, *Tastemaker*, 210.

76   *unmistakable message*   Lewis, *When Harlem*, 188.

76   *Negroes aren't any worse*   Carl Van Vechten, *Nigger Heaven* (New York: Alfred A. Knopf, 1927), 235.

76   *blacks must hold on*   Bernard, *Carl Van Vechten*, 72.

76   *a birthright that all*   Van Vechten, *Nigger Heaven*, 89.

77   *a Negro quarterly of the arts*   Langston Hughes, "The Twenties: Harlem and Its Negritude," *African Forum* I (1966), 11–20, in *Collected Works 9*, 473.

77   *Strangely brilliant*   Hughes, *Big Sea*, 234.

77   *Over collards and black-eyed peas*   Bruce Nugent, interview by Robert E. Hemenway, n.d., Robert E. Hemenway Personal Papers, PP487, Kenneth Spencer Research Library, University of Kansas Libraries.

78   *We got carried away with ourselves*   Hughes, "The Twenties," 473.

79   *FIRE . . . weaving vivid*   "Foreword," *Fire!!*, 1, no. 1 (November, 1926), i.

79   *It celebrated jazz*   Steven Watson, *The Harlem Renaissance: Hub of African-American Culture, 1920–1930* (New York: Pantheon, 1995), 91.

80   *Wally and I*   Nugent, interview.

80   *had done more for*   Bernard, *Carl Van Vechten*, 176.

81 *a beautiful piece of printing* "The Looking Glass," *The Crisis* 33 (January 1927), 158, quoted in Lewis, *When Harlem*, 197.

81 *hurt his feelings* Fred Bair to Countee Cullen, n.d., quoted in Eleonor Van Notten, *Wallace Thurman's Harlem Renaissance* (Amsterdam: Rodopi, 1994), 151.

81 *roasted it* Hughes, *Big Sea*, 237.

81 *Writer Brands 'Fire'* Rean Graves, "Writer Brands 'Fire' as Effeminate Tommyrot," *Baltimore Afro-American*, December 25, 1926, quoted in Bernard, *Carl Van Vechten*, 178; Kaplan, *Letters*, 793; and Hughes, *Big Sea*, 237.

81 *A good deal of it* Alain Locke, untitled book review, *The Survey*, August 15–September 15, 1927, 563; quoted in Faith Berry, *Langston Hughes: Before and Beyond Harlem*, 2nd ed. (New York: Citadel, 1992), 82.

81 *very drunk & abusive* Van Vechten, *Splendid Drunken*, 123.

81 *a phenomenally good cook* Nugent, *Gentleman Jigger*, 25.

4. ENTER GODMOTHER

83 *My Mother-God* Hurston to Mason, October 15, 1931, in Carla Kaplan, ed. *Zora Neale Hurston: A Life in Letters* (New York: Doubleday, 2002), 231.

83 *true conceptual Mother* Hurston to Mason, May 10, 1931, in Kaplan, *Letters*, 218.

83 *You renew your promise* Hurston to Mason, May 18, 1930, in Kaplan, *Letters*, 187–89.

84 *The little figure* Blanche Coates Matthias, "Unknown Great Ones," *The Woman Athletic* (June 1923), 13.

85 *never forgetting a minutiae* Carla Kaplan, *Miss Anne in Harlem: The White Women of the Black Renaissance* (New York: HarperCollins, 2013), 221.

85 *younger races unspoiled* Unsourced quotation in Aberjhani and Sandra L. West, eds., *Encyclopedia of the Harlem Renaissance* (New York: Facts on File, 2003), 211.

85 *used to secretly listen* Louise Thompson Patterson, autobiography, Louise Thompson Patterson papers, 1909–1999, Stuart A. Rose Manuscript, Archives, and Rare Book Library, Emory University.

86 *Let us recognize* Natalie Curtis, *The Indians' Book* (New York: Harper & Brothers, 1907), 574.

86 *all things financial* Ibid., 410.

86 *She* craved *people* Kaplan, *Miss Anne*, 250.

87 *She hated to be separated* Ibid., 212.

87 *unusual personal powers* Ibid., 409–10.

87 *That is the reward* Matthias, "Unknown Great Ones," 13.

88 *rigid, controlled, disciplined* Alain Locke, "The Legacy of the Ancestral Arts," in *The New Negro*, 1st Touchstone ed. (New York: Simon & Schuster, 1997), 254, 266.

88 *tremendous rapport* Mrs. R. O. Mason, notebooks, Alain Locke Papers, Moorland-Spingarn Research Center, Howard University, quoted in Arnold Rampersad, *The Life of Langston Hughes*, Vol. 1: *1902–1941, I, Too, Sing America*, 2nd ed. (New York: Oxford University Press, 2002), 147.

89 *flowing spirit... miraculous power* Mason to Locke, August 1 and 16, 1927, Alain Locke Papers, quoted in David Levering Lewis, *When Harlem Was in Vogue* (New York: Penguin, 1997), 152.

89 *I am eternally black* Mason to Locke, December 10, 1927, Alain Locke Papers, quoted in Kaplan, *Miss Anne*, 193.

89 *slough off this weight* Quoted in Leonard Harris and Charles Molesworth, *Alain L. Locke: Biography of a Philosopher* (Chicago: University of Chicago Press, 2008), 242.

90 *almost arbitrary way* Bruce Nugent, interview by Robert E. Hemenway, n.d., Robert E. Hemenway Personal Papers, PP487, Kenneth Spencer Research Library, University of Kansas Libraries.

90 *A Gripping Story* Zora Neale Hurston, "The Back Room," *Pittsburgh Courier* (February 19, 1927), section 2, 1, quoted in Glenda R. Carpio and Werner Sollers, "Part One: 'The Book of Harlem,' 'Monkey Junk,' and 'The Back Room,'" *Amerikastudien 55*, no. 4 (2010), 564.

90 *born Lillie Barker* Hurston, "The Back Room," reprinted in *Amerikastudien 55* no. 4 (2010), 577–81.

91 *Thank you, thank you* Hurston to Hughes, n.d. [December 1926], Langston Hughes Papers, Beinecke Rare Book and Manuscript Library, New Haven.

91 *cast a dark shadow* Hurston to Sheen, January 7, 1955, in Kaplan, *Letters*, 725–26.

91 *Who had cancelled* Zora Neale Hurston, *Dust Tracks on a Road*, in *Folklore, Memoirs, & Other Writings*, ed. Cheryl A. Wall (New York: Library of America, 1995), 744.

93　*was Hughes's poorest*　Arnold Rampersad, Introduction, *The Collected Works of Langston Hughes*, Vol. 1: *The Poems, 1921–1940* (Columbia: University of Missouri Press, 2001), 9.

93　LANGSTON HUGHES—THE SEWER DWELLER　William M. Kelley, "Langston Hughes: The Sewer Dweller," *New York Amsterdam News* (February 9, 1927), 22.

93　*unsanitary, insipid*　*Chicago Whip* (February 26, 1927), quoted in Rampersad, *Life*, 140.

93　*a study in the perversions*　*Philadelphia Tribune* (February 12, 1927), quoted in Rampersad, *Life*, 140.

93　*positively sick*　J. A. Rogers, untitled review of *Fine Clothes to the Jew*, *Pittsburgh Courier* (February 12, 1927), section 2, 4.

93　*It would have been just*　Benjamin Brawley, *The Negro Genius: A New Appraisal of the Achievement of the American Negro in Literature and the Arts* (New York: Mead & Co., 1937), 248.

93　*the outstanding book*　"What to Read," *The Crisis* (March 1927), quoted in Faith Berry, *Langston Hughes: Before and Beyond Harlem*, 2nd ed. (New York: Citadel, 1992), 84.

94　*humble people*　Langston Hughes, "These Bad New Negroes: A Critique on Critics," in *The Collected Works of Langston Hughes*, Vol. 9: *Essays on Art, Race, Politics, and World Affairs* (Columbia: University of Missouri Press, 2002), 38.

94　*the masses of our people*　Langston Hughes, *The Big Sea: An Autobiography* (New York: Alfred A. Knopf, 1940), 267.

94　*with attendants in livery*　Ibid., 312.

94　*a mystical vision*　Mason, notebooks, quoted in Rampersad, *Life*, 147–48.

95　*every piece was rare*　Hughes, *Big Sea*, 312–13.

95　*Who is this woman?*　Jeffrey C. Stewart, *The New Negro: The Life of Alain Locke* (New York: Oxford University Press, 2018), 548.

95　*Mask in one pocket*　Stewart, *New Negro*, 557.

95　*about my plans*　Hughes, *Big Sea*, 313.

95　*our first real hours*　Mason to Hughes [n.d.], Hughes Papers.

95　*my winged poet Child*　Mason to Hughes, June 5, 1927, Hughes Papers.

96　*My precious Boy*　Mason to Hughes [n.d.], Hughes Papers.

96　*If Locke was her*　Kaplan, *Miss Anne*, 222.

96　*The Gods be praised*　Mason to Hughes, June 29, 1928, Hughes Papers.

96 *You know your 'Godmother'* Mason to Hughes, July 22, 1928, Hughes Papers.

97 *I greet thee Morning Star* Mason to Hughes, September 23, 1928, Hughes Papers.

5. THE COMPANY OF GOOD THINGS

98 *No sooner had I* Langston Hughes, *The Big Sea: An Autobiography* (New York: Alfred A. Knopf, 1940), 296.

99 *I knew where the material was* Zora Neale Hurston, *Dust Tracks on a Road*, in *Folklore, Memoirs, & Other Writings*, ed. Cheryl A. Wall (New York: Library of America, 1995), 687.

99 *stopping on the way* Hughes, *Big Sea*, 296.

101 *through grandiose promises* "South Now Trying to Stop Migration by Legislation," *Chicago Defender*, June 25, 1927, 1.

102 *Do what they would* Zora Neale Hurston, *Jonah's Gourd Vine*, in *Novels & Stories*, ed. Cheryl A. Wall (New York: Library of America, 1995), 128.

103 *The palm trees* Langston Hughes, notebooks, Langston Hughes Papers, Beinecke Rare Book and Manuscript Library, New Haven.

103 *we went to eat* Hughes, *Big Sea*, 296.

103 *Once, at a ritzy* Valerie Boyd, *Wrapped in Rainbows: The Life of Zora Neale Hurston* (New York: Scribner, 2003), 277.

104 *a talented pianist and poet* Hughes, *Big Sea*, 296.

104 *Mobile, July 23* Hughes, notebooks, Hughes Papers.

105 *We're still burying* Karen Savage, "In Alabama, Community Founded by Former Slaves Now Under Siege by Tar Sands," *Bridge the Gulf* (August 20, 2013), http://bridgethegulfproject.org/blog/2013/alabama-community-founded-former-slaves-now-under-siege-tar-sands.

107 *Distance from station* Hughes, notebooks, Hughes Papers.

108 *my own brown goddess* Hughes to Harold Jackman, quoted in Jeffrey C. Stewart, *The New Negro: The Life of Alain Locke* (New York: Oxford University Press, 2018), 434.

109 *pilgrimage through the South* Mason to Hughes, July 26, 1927, Hughes Papers.

109 *I am having the time* Gwendolyn Bennett, "The Ebony Flute," *Opportunity* (September 1927), 276.

111 *How wide open*   Mason to Hughes, August 3, 1927, Hughes Papers.

112 *Out of death and darkness*   Hughes, notebooks, Hughes Papers.

112 *There is no weakness here*   Ibid.

112 *rather mixed audience*   Mayme V. Holmes, "Hughes Reads Poems to Summer Students," *The Tuskegee Messenger* 3, no. 17 (September 10, 1927), 3.

113 *Dear Langston—Finished*   Hurston to Hughes [n.d.], Hughes Papers.

114 *Saw man driving*   Hughes, notebooks, Hughes Papers.

114 *to show that good feeling*   "Barbecue in Georgia," *Chicago Defender*, August 20, 1927, A2.

115 *Passed a town last night*   Hughes to Van Vechten, August 15, 1927, in Emily Bernard, ed., *Remember Me to Harlem: The Letters of Langston Hughes and Carl Van Vechten* (New York: Knopf, 2001), 59.

115 *advancing . . . the vanguard*   Frank Horne, "Henry A. Hunt, Sixteenth Spingarn Medallist," *The Crisis* 37, no. 8 (August 1930), 261.

116 *marvelous*   Hughes to Van Vechten, August 15, 1927, in Bernard, *Remember Me*, 58.

116 *backwoods church entertainment*   Ibid., 58–59.

117 *a marvelous patchwork*   Hughes, *Big Sea*, 299.

117 *Homestead now occupied*   Hughes, notebooks, Hughes Papers.

118 *We are charging home*   Hughes and Hurston to Van Vechten, August 17, 1927, Hughes Papers, quoted in Boyd, *Wrapped in Rainbows*, 152.

118 *famous conjur-man*   Hughes, *Big Sea*, 297.

119 *a tall, red-skinned*   Ibid.

119 *but we had to have a victim*   Hurston to Van Vechten, August 26, 1927, in Kaplan, *Letters*, 106.

119 *Zora and Langston* had *to conjure*   Imani Mtendaji, discussion with author, Savannah, Georgia, July 2015.

119 *huge apocryphal Bible*   Hughes, *Big Sea*, 298.

119 *if the devil or an evil spirit*   Tobit 6:5–7.

119 *darkened the room*   Hughes, *Big Sea*, 298.

119 *Palm of Gilead*   Hughes, notebooks, Hughes Papers.

119 *mumbled an incantation*   Hughes, *Big Sea*, 298.

119 *Burning of hell fire*   Hughes, notebooks, Hughes Papers.

119 *After the stones*   Hughes, *Big Sea*, 298.

120 *was a poor one*   Ibid.

120 *A black woman so evil*   Hughes, notebooks, Hughes Papers.

121 *Don't let nobody tell you*   Steven Watson, *The Harlem Renaissance: Hub of African-American Culture, 1920–1930* (New York: Pantheon, 1995), 101.

121 *Get the fuck away*   Edward White, *The Tastemaker: Carl Van Vechten and the Birth of Modern America* (New York: Farrar, Straus & Giroux, 2014), 180.

121 *You didn't have to go*   Hughes, *Big Sea*, 296.

121 *The trouble with white folks*   Ibid.

122 *Hubbard drove in*   Hughes, notebooks, Hughes Papers.

123 *talented tenth*   W. E. Burghardt Du Bois, "The Talented Tenth," *The Negro Problem: A Series of Articles by Representative American Negroes of To-Day* (New York: James Pott & Co., 1903), 33.

123 *Southern railroad shops*   Hughes, notebooks, Hughes Papers.

123 *Nobody wants me*   Ibid.

124 *met a little woman*   Ibid.

125 *Somehow all the back*   Hurston to Van Vechten, August 26, 1927, in Kaplan, *Letters*, 105–6.

126 *Most of the Negroes*   Hughes to Locke, October 8, 1927, Alain Locke Papers, Moorland-Spingarn Research Center, Howard University.

126 *worn [her] down*   Hurston to Annie Nathan Meyer, October 7, 1927, in Kaplan, *Letters*, 108.

6. A DEEP WELL OF THE SPIRIT

127 *Can you guess*   Mason to Hughes [n.d.], Langston Hughes Papers, Beinecke Rare Book and Manuscript Library, New Haven.

128 *I would come to*   Zora Neale Hurston, *Dust Tracks on a Road*, in *Folklore, Memoirs, & Other Writings*, ed. Cheryl A. Wall (New York: Library of America, 1995), 597.

128 *got on famously*   Hurston to Hughes, September 21, 1927, Hughes Papers.

128 *It was decreed*   Hurston, *Dust Tracks*, 797.

129 *We must do it with*   Hurston to Hughes, September 21, 1927, Hughes Papers.

129 *My relations with Godmother*   Hurston, *Dust Tracks*, 688.

130 *hem me up*   Ibid.

130 *That is nothing!*   Ibid., 689.

130 *There she was sitting*   Ibid.

131 *seven hours that went*   Langston Hughes, diary, October 22, 1927, Hughes Papers.

131 *a golden star*   Mason to Hughes, September 9, 1928, Hughes Papers.

131 *I loved her*   Langston Hughes, *The Big Sea: An Autobiography* (New York: Alfred A. Knopf, 1940), 315–16.

131 *Concerning Negroes*   Ibid., 316.

132 *collect all information*   Agreement between Charlotte L. Mason and Zora Hurston, December 1, 1927, Alain Locke Papers, Moorland-Spingarn Research Center, Howard University.

133 *new suits of dinner clothes*   Hughes, *Big Sea*, 316–17.

7. THIS IS GOING TO BE BIG

135 *intellectually dishonest*   Hurston to Hughes, n.d., Langston Hughes Papers, Beinecke Rare Book and Manuscript Library, New Haven.

135 *Why can't our triangle*   Hurston to Locke, October 11, 1927, in Carla Kaplan, ed., *Zora Neale Hurston: A Life in Letters* (New York: Doubleday, 2002), 109.

135 *I am truly dedicated*   Hurston to Hughes, March 8, 1928, Hughes Papers.

136 *all of the songs*   Hurston to Hughes [n.d.], Hughes Papers.

136 *Langston, Langston*   Hurston to Hughes, March 8, 1928, Hughes Papers.

136 *Are you planning to join*   Hurston to Hughes, April 12, 1928, Hughes Papers.

136 *To create a Negro culture*   Langston Hughes, diary, August 1, 1929, Hughes Papers.

137 *I began to hate*   Hughes to McKay, September 13, 1928, in *The Selected Letters of Langston Hughes*, ed. Arnold Rampersad and David Roessel with Christa Fratantoro (New York: Alfred A. Knopf, 2015), 77–81.

137 *I've never felt*   Hughes to McKay, June 27, 1929, in *Selected Letters*, 88.

137 *It is almost useless*   Zora Neale Hurston, application for Rosenwald Foundation Fellowship, December 14, 1934, quoted in Robert E. Hemenway, *Zora Neale Hurston: A Literary Biography* (Urbana: University of Illinois, 1977), 207.

138 *Of course, you know*   Hurston to Hughes, May 1, 1928, Hughes Papers.

138 *Without flattery*   Hurston to Hughes, July 10, 1928, Hughes Papers.

138 *She was very anxious* Hurston to Locke, December 16, 1927, in Kaplan, *Letters*, 134.

138 *I accepted the money* Hurston to Boas, December 27, 1928, in Kaplan, *Letters*, 135.

139 *I'm heartbroken over* Hurston to West, December 5, 1928, in Kaplan, *Letters*, 134.

139 They got the point *and enjoyed it* Hurston to Hughes, March 8, 1928, Hughes Papers.

139 *Two men came over* Hurston to Hughes, July 10, 1928, Hughes Papers.

139 *How gloriously primitive!* Mason to Hughes, July 28, 1928, Hughes Papers.

139 *Oh, honey . . . you ought* Hurston to Hughes, November 22, 1928, Hughes Papers.

139 *My they liked it* Hurston to Hughes, April 3, 1929, Hughes Papers.

139 *could admire his ability* Bruce Nugent, interview by Robert E. Hemenway, n.d., Robert E. Hemenway Personal Papers, PP487, Kenneth Spencer Research Library, University of Kansas Libraries.

140 *I discover therein* Hughes to Locke, February 27, 1928, in *Selected Letters*, 73.

140 *That sounded reasonable* Zora Neale Hurston, *Mules and Men*, in *Folklore, Memoirs, & Other Writings*, ed. Cheryl A. Wall (New York: Library of America, 1995), 63.

142 *I had five psychic* Ibid., 190.

142 *On the third night* Zora Neale Hurston, *Dust Tracks on a Road*, in *Folklore, Memoirs*, 699.

142 *transform[ed] her from* Hemenway, *Zora Neale Hurston*, 123.

142 *make plenty of suggestions* Hurston to Hughes, May 31, 1929, Hughes Papers.

143 *precious Brown Boy* Leonard Harris and Charles Molesworth, *Alain L. Locke: Biography of a Philosopher* (Chicago: University of Chicago Press, 2008), 240.

143 *I'll be even more* Hurston to Hughes [n.d.], Hughes Papers.

143 *Such a pity* Mason to Locke, May 21, 1930, quoted in Jeffrey C. Stewart, *The New Negro: The Life of Alain Locke* (New York: Oxford University Press, 2018), 621.

144 *a neat little colony* Hurston to Hughes, May 31, 1929, Hughes Papers.

144   *Langston, really,* MULATTO   Hurston to Hughes [n.d.], Hughes Papers.

145   *Gee, I felt forlorn*   Hurston to Hughes [October 15, 1919], Hughes Papers.

145   *Your last letter*   Hurston to Hughes, December 10, 1929, Hughes Papers.

145   *Dearest Godmother, All the week*   Hughes to Mason, draft, February 23, 1929, Hughes Papers.

146   *Because I love you*   Hughes to Mason, additional draft, February 23, 1929, Hughes Papers.

146   *better Negro*   Mason to McKay, draft, October 19, 1929, Alain Locke Papers, Moorland-Spingarn Research Center, Howard University, quoted in Carla Kaplan, *Miss Anne in Harlem: The White Women of the Black Renaissance* (New York: HarperCollins, 2013), 230.

147   *I am a Black God*   Mason to Locke, draft, April 1, 1928, Locke papers, quoted in Kaplan, *Miss Anne,* 230.

147   *simply exploded*   Hurston to Hughes [n.d.], Hughes Papers.

147   *that white people could not be trusted*   Hurston to Locke, June 14, 1928, in Kaplan, *Letters,* 121.

148   *destroys my self-respect*   Hurston to Hughes [n.d.], Hughes Papers.

148   *that a certain influential*   Hurston, *Mules and Men,* 212.

148   *stating that she would*   Ibid.

150   *Suddenly, just like manna*   Louise Thompson Patterson, autobiography, Louise Thompson Patterson papers, 1909–1999, Stuart A. Rose Manuscript, Archives, and Rare Book Library, Emory University.

151   *She has walked with God*   Ibid.

151   *There is a spontaneity*   Ibid.

152   *When she talked about*   Ibid.

152   *dropped a spoon or something*   Ibid.

152   *This is a lovely table*   Ibid.

153   *The quiet informal way*   Locke to Mason, April 16, 1929, Locke Papers.

153   *In the primitive world*   Langston Hughes, *The Big Sea: An Autobiography* (New York: Alfred A. Knopf, 1940), 311.

154   *awfully bad*   Hughes to McKay, June 27, 1929, in *Selected Letters,* 88.

155   *broken hearted—not even*   Hughes to Thurman, July 29, 1929, in *Selected Letters,* 89.

155   *who must have done*   Hughes, *Big Sea,* 305.

155   *probably due to overwork*   M. E. Stites, [medical report], Life Extension Institute, November 7, 1929, Hughes Papers.

156 *Everyone... wanted to be introduced* Arnold Rampersad, *The Life of Langston Hughes,* Vol. 1: *1902–1941, I, Too, Sing America,* 2nd ed. (New York: Oxford University Press, 2002), 178.

8: THE BONE OF CONTENTION

158 *She used to talk about Zora* Louise Thompson Patterson, autobiography, Louise Thompson Patterson papers, 1909–1999, Stuart A. Rose Manuscript, Archives, and Rare Book Library, Emory University.

158 *How do you like that one?* Louise Thompson Patterson, interview by Robert E. Hemenway, June 22, 1976, Robert E. Hemenway Personal Papers, PP487, Kenneth Spencer Research Library, University of Kansas Libraries.

159 *I am her friend* Zora Neale Hurston, *Dust Tracks on a Road,* in *Folklore, Memoirs, & Other Writings,* ed. Cheryl A. Wall (New York: The Library of America, 1995), 739–40.

159 *fell in love with* Ibid., 798.

160 *folk material, stacks* Langston Hughes, *The Big Sea: An Autobiography* (New York: Alfred A. Knopf, 1940), 320.

160 *This breath from the spiritual* Zora Neale Hurston, *Mules and Men* (draft), Langston Hughes Papers, Beinecke Rare Book and Manuscript Library, New Haven.

160 *Dear Boy, What is* Mason to Hughes, March 24, 1928, Hughes Papers.

160 *It was immensely cheering* Hughes to Mason, draft [n.d.], Hughes Papers.

161 *thinks it would be a mistake* Locke to Hurston, April 28, 1930, Alain Locke Papers, Moorland-Spingarn Research Center, Howard University, quoted in Valerie Boyd, *Wrapped in Rainbows: The Life of Zora Neale Hurston* (New York: Scribner, 2003), 194.

162 *it was the regular thing* Charlotte Mason, diary, January 29, 1931, Locke Papers.

164 *I would do the construction* Hughes to Spingarn, January 21, 1931, in Zora Neale Hurston and Langston Hughes, *Mule Bone: A Comedy of Negro Life,* ed. George Houston Bass and Henry Louis Gates Jr. (New York: HarperCollins, 1991), 230.

165 *I plotted out and typed* Hughes, *Big Sea,* 320.

165   *Zora, a very gay*   Ibid.

166   *Some of my friends*   Hurston to Lawrence Jordan, May 31, 1930, in Carla Kaplan, ed., *Zora Neale Hurston: A Life in Letters* (New York: Doubleday, 2002), 190.

166   *Pay me, Langston!*   Hurston to Hughes, January 18, 1931, in Kaplan, *Letters*, 202.

167   *That struck me as merely*   Ibid.

167   *not to go on with*   Charlotte Mason, diary, January 29, 1931, Locke Papers.

167   *I knew that my friend*   Hughes, *Big Sea*, 325.

168   *The way she talked to Langston*   Arnold Rampersad, *The Life of Langston Hughes*, Vol. 1: *1902–1941, I, Too, Sing America*, 2nd ed. (New York: Oxford University Press, 2002), 185.

168   *That beautiful room*   Hughes, *Big Sea*, 325–26.

169   *There were other guests*   Ibid., 326.

169   *cried like a baby*   Louise Thompson Patterson, autobiography, Louise Thompson Patterson papers, 1909–1999, Stuart A. Rose Manuscript, Archives, and Rare Book Library, Emory University.

169   *My voice seemed far away*   Hughes, *Big Sea*, 327.

170   *Dine with some of the men*   Langston Hughes, "Advertisement for the Waldorf Astoria," in *The Collected Poems of Langston Hughes*, ed. Arnold Rampersad (New York: Alfred A. Knopf, 1994), 144.

170   *the cause was an escalating*   Carla Kaplan, *Miss Anne in Harlem: The White Women of the Black Renaissance* (New York: HarperCollins, 2013), 234.

171   *disenchanted with [Mason's] 'vision'*   Ibid., 230, 231, 235.

171   *did not want Hurston distracted*   Ibid., 235.

172   *kind and sincere talks*   Hughes to Mason [draft], June 6, 1930, Hughes Papers.

172   *You have been more beautiful*   Hughes to Mason [draft], May 28, 1930, Hughes Papers.

172   *Washington is lovely*   Hughes to Mason [draft, n.d.], Hughes Papers.

173   *top vegetables*   Mason to Hughes, June 3, 1930, Hughes Papers.

173   *Your letter stating your desires*   Mason to Hughes, June 6, 1930, Hughes Papers.

174   *In all my life I have never*   Hughes to Mason [draft], June 6, 1930, Hughes Papers.

175 *done her in*   Patterson, autobiography.

175 *Louise, you're so fond*   Ibid.

175 *Zora Neale Hurston's here*   Ibid.

175 *Arna Bontemps always believed*   Ibid.

176 *the nearest person on earth*   Hurston to Hughes, January 18, 1931, in Kaplan, *Letters*, 203.

177 *Langston was not one*   Patterson, autobiography.

178 *I felt that I was among*   Hurston to Hughes, January 18, 1931, in Kaplan, *Letters*, 202.

178 *I love you, Godmother.*   Hughes to Mason [draft], June 15, 1930, Hughes Papers.

179 UNDER PRESENT CONDITIONS   Mason to Hughes, telegram, June 17, 1930, Hughes Papers.

179 *For the beauty of your eyes*   Hughes to Mason [draft, n.d.], Hughes Papers.

179 *As the sun sets*   Mason to Hughes, July 10, 1930, Hughes Papers.

180 *Since Toomer*   David Levering Lewis, *When Harlem Was in Vogue* (New York: Penguin, 1997), 251.

180 *I had wanted*   Hughes, *Big Sea*, 306.

180 *the novel both Hughes*   Angela Flournoy, "How Langston Hughes Brought His Radical Vision to the Novel," *New York Times*, January 2, 2018.

181 *I ask you to help the gods*   Hughes to Mason [draft], August 15, 1930, Hughes Papers.

182 *Subdued and time-lost*   Langston Hughes, "Afro-American Fragment," in *Collected Poems*, 129.

182 *The Communists are*   Nancy Cunard, *Negro Anthology* (London, Wishart & Co., 1934), 146.

183 *I send my greetings*   Langston Hughes, "Greetings to Soviet Workers," *New Masses* 6, no. 7 (December, 1930), 23.

183 *Dreamed last night*   Hurston to Hughes [postcard, n.d., postmarked August 11, 1930], Hughes Papers.

184 *seemed to think*   Hughes to Van Vechten, January 16, 1931, Hughes Papers.

185 *see what a certain person*   Hurston to Mason, November 25, 1930, in Kaplan, *Letters*, 194.

185 *When I came back*   Hughes to Spingarn, January 21, 1931, in Hurston, *Mule Bone*, 231–32.

187 *curt note*   Patterson, autobiography.

187 *short but excruciating*   Thompson to Hughes, October 4, 1930, in Evelyn Louise Crawford and MaryLouise Patterson, eds., *Letters from Langston: From the Harlem Renaissance to the Red Scare and Beyond* (Oakland, University of California Press, 2016), 32.

187 *Well, what do you want*   Patterson, autobiography.

187 *I had never had such*   Ibid.

188 *especially about the acceptance*   Locke to Mason, January 12, 1930 [1931], Locke Papers.

188 *indulging her fantasies*   Patterson, autobiography.

188 *I am helping myself*   Mason to Locke, August 8, 1930, quoted in Rampersad, *Life*, 193.

188 *I am beginning to feel*   Hurston to Mason, November 11, 1930, in Kaplan, *Letters*, 192.

188 *first serious whack*   Hurston to Van Vechten, November 14, 1930, Hughes Papers.

188 *the play has great wit*   Charlotte Mason, diary, November 8, 1930, Alain Locke Papers.

189 *It was my hope*   Mason to Hughes, January 10, 1931, Hughes Papers.

9: A MIASMA OF UNTRUTH

190 *the most notorious literary*   Henry Louis Gates Jr., "A Tragedy of Negro Life," in Zora Neale Hurston and Langston Hughes, *Mule Bone: A Comedy of Negro Life*, ed. George Houston Bass and Henry Louis Gates Jr. (New York: HarperCollins, 1991), 5.

191 *De dog and de cat*   Zora Neale Hurston, *Mules and Men*, in *Folklore, Memoirs, & Other Writings*, ed. Cheryl A. Wall (New York: Library of America, 1995), 154–55.

194 *Langston and I started*   Hurston to Van Vechten, November 14, 1930, in Carla Kaplan, ed. *Zora Neale Hurston: A Life in Letters* (New York: Doubleday, 2002), 193.

194 *Is there something about*   Hughes to Van Vechten, January 16, 1931, Langston Hughes Papers, Beinecke Rare Book and Manuscript Library, New Haven.

195 *messed-up*   Hughes to Van Vechten, January 18, 1931, Hughes Papers.

195 *Now Langston, let us*   Hurston to Hughes, January 18, 1931, in Kaplan, *Letters*, 202–4.

197 *I'd also immensely like*   Hughes to Hurston, January 18, 1931, in Hurston, *Mule Bone*, 210.

199 *the first Negro folk-comedy*   Hughes to Hurston, January 19, 1931, in Hurston, *Mule Bone*, 214–215.

199 *How dare you use*   Hurston to Hughes, January 20, 1931, in Kaplan, *Letters*, 205.

199 *This morning I got*   Hughes to Van Vechten, January 19, 1931, Hughes Papers.

200 *Even if she has entirely*   Van Vechten to Hughes [n.d., January 19, 1931], in Hurston, *Mule Bone*, 216.

200 *cried and carried on*   Van Vechten to Hughes [n.d., January 20, 1931], in Hurston, *Mule Bone*, 223.

200 *She had a tantrum*   Van Vechten to Hughes, August 17, 1942, in Emily Bernard, ed., *Remember Me to Harlem: The Letters of Langston Hughes and Carl Van Vechten* (New York: Knopf, 2001), 209.

200 *A stock production will be*   Van Vechten to Hughes, January 20, 1931, in Bernard, *Remember Me*, 77.

201 *Have you heard from*   Charlotte Mason, diary, January 15, 1931, Alain Locke Papers, Moorland-Spingarn Research Center, Howard University.

202 *If Langston had approached*   Arnold Rampersad, *The Life of Langston Hughes*, Vol. 1: *1902–1941, I, Too, Sing America*, 2nd ed. (New York: Oxford U. Press, 2002), 196.

202 *I am in fault in the end*   Hurston to Hughes, January 20, 1931, in Kaplan, *Letters*, 204–5.

202 *so exotic*   Hurston to Mason, January 20, 1931, in Kaplan, *Letters*, 209.

203 *Now get this straight*   Hurston to Hughes, January 20, 1931, quoted in Robert E. Hemenway, *Zora Neale Hurston: A Literary Biography* (Urbana: University of Illinois, 1977), 143, and Faith Berry, *Langston Hughes: Before and Beyond Harlem*, 2nd ed. (New York: Citadel, 1992), 112.

203 *Langston is weak.*   Hurston to Mason, January 20, 1931, in Kaplan, *Letters*, 208–9.

204 *What you say about*   Van Vechten to Hughes, January 20, 1931, in Bernard, *Remember Me*, 77.

204 *Louise has been paid*   Hughes to Hurston, January 20, 1931, in Hurston, *Mule Bone*, 221–22.

204 *Maybe she has lost*   Hughes to Spingarn, January 21, 1931, in Hurston, *Mule Bone*, 233.

205 *gave away his fear*   Charlotte Mason, diary, January 29, 1931, Locke Papers.

205 *threaten[ed] to have the law*   Ibid.

205 *if you make any further*   Hughes to Hurston, January 20, 1931, in Hurston, *Mule Bone*, 221.

206 *bitter cold*   Hughes to Van Vechten, January 22, 1931, Hughes Papers.

206 *Brazzle's mule*   Hughes to Hurston, January 22, 1931, in Hurston, *Mule Bone*, 240–41.

206 *grossly exaggerated*   Spingarn to Hughes, January 24, 1931, in Hurston, *Mule Bone*, 244–45.

207 *I am sure that*   Spingarn to Hughes, January 27, 1931, in Hurston, *Mule Bone*, 250.

207 *The only thing I can say*   Thompson to Hughes, January 28, 1931, in Hurston, *Mule Bone*, 253.

207 PLEASE PUT ME STRAIGHT   Hughes to Locke, January 28, 1931, Locke Papers.

207 CONGRATULATIONS ON THE HARMON AWARD   Locke to Hughes, telegram [January 1931], quoted in Hughes to Spingarn, January 30, 1931, in *The Selected Letters of Langston Hughes*, ed. Arnold Rampersad and David Roessel with Christa Fratantoro (New York: Alfred A. Knopf, 2015), 107.

208 *They are mostly working people*   Hughes to Hurston, January 27, 1931, in Hurston, *Mule Bone*, 248.

208 *Zo darling, whatever*   Hughes to Hurston, January 27, 1931, Locke Papers, quoted in Valerie Boyd, *Wrapped in Rainbows: The Life of Zora Neale Hurston* (New York: Scribner, 2003), 213.

209 *consisted in her*   Charlotte Mason, diary, January 29, 1931, Locke Papers.

210 *Miss Hurston's main grievance*   Hughes to Spingarn, February 3, 1931, in Hurston, *Mule Bone*, 259–60.

211 *She made such a scene*   Hughes to Van Vechten, February 4, 1931, Hughes Papers.

212 DARLING GODMOTHER ARRIVED   Hurston to Mason, telegram, February 3, 1931, in Kaplan, *Letters*, 209.

213 *There Zora, I understand* Hughes to Thompson, February 7, 1931, in *Selected Letters*, 106–7.

213 SLANT ON THINGS Hughes to Locke, telegram [February 1930], quoted in Locke to Mason, February 10, 1931, Locke Papers.

213 *never heard from Miss Hurston* Langston Hughes, *The Big Sea: An Autobiography* (New York: Alfred A. Knopf, 1940), 334.

214 *Love and everything deep* Hurston to Hughes, December 10, 1929, Hughes Papers.

214 *Lots of luck* Hurston to Hughes, February 14, 1931, in Kaplan, *Letters*, 211.

214 *Dear Langston, What a sorrowful* Mason to Hughes, February 12, 1931, Hughes Papers.

215 *I think it would be just* Hughes to Spingarn, March 6, 1931, in Hurston, *Mule Bone*, 268.

215 *false egotism* Locke to Mason, January 29, 1931, Locke Papers.

215 *shameful—or rather* Locke to Mason, March 20, 1931, Locke Papers.

215 *Why can't he die!* Locke to Mason, March 29, 1931, Locke Papers.

215 *malicious, spiteful* Hurston to James Weldon Johnson, February 1938, in Kaplan, *Letters*, 413.

215 *the Guard-mother who sits* Hurston to Mason, March 10, 1931, in Kaplan, *Letters*, 212.

216 *Devotedly, your pickaninny* Hurston to Mason, July 23, 1931, in Kaplan, *Letters*, 223.

216 *I am calm again* Hurston to Hughes, March 18, 1931, in Kaplan, *Letters*, 213.

216 *repeated that you had* Spingarn to Hughes, March 25, 1931, Hughes Papers.

216 *I find that Langston* Hurston to Mason, March 25, 1931, in Kaplan, *Letters*, 214.

217 *I think it would be lovely* Hurston to Spingarn, March 25, 1931, Hughes Papers.

217 *I know that Langston says* Hurston to Mason, April 18, 1931, in Kaplan, *Letters*, 218.

217 *I just love fights* Hughes to Spingarn, August 14, 1931, in Hurston, *Mule Bone*, 274.

217 *a person of no honor* Hurston to Mason, August 14, 1931, in Kaplan, *Letters*, 224–25.

218 *his place was an office*   Ibid.

218 *violent disposition*   Ibid.

218 *It no longer even*   Ibid.

10: THE AFTERMATH

219 *the end of the Harlem Renaissance*   Langston Hughes, *The Big Sea: An Auto-biography* (New York: Alfred A. Knopf, 1940), 331, 334.

219 *You know there comes a time*   Bruce Nugent, interview by Robert E. Hemenway, n.d., Robert E. Hemenway Personal Papers, PP487, Kenneth Spencer Research Library, University of Kansas Libraries.

220 *entertained him magnificently*   Hurston to Mason, January 21, 1932, in Carla Kaplan, ed. *Zora Neale Hurston: A Life in Letters* (New York: Doubleday, 2002), 242.

220 *polite and rather cordial*   Hurston to Mason, March 27, 1932, in Kaplan, *Letters*, 247.

220 *It is one of the most unworthy*   Hurston to Mason, May 17, 1932, in Kaplan, *Letters*, 255–56.

221 *Sweetie Mae was*   Wallace Thurman, *Infants of the Spring* (New York: Macaulay, 1932), 142.

222 *coarsened and aged considerably*   Quoted in Leonard Harris and Charles Molesworth, *Alain L. Locke: Biography of a Philosopher* (Chicago: University of Chicago Press, 2008), 269.

223 *I only hope L——*   Quoted in Harris, *Alain L. Locke*, 270.

223 *Mrs. Ellsworth*   Langston Hughes, *The Ways of White Folks* (New York: Alfred A. Knopf, 1933), 113.

224 *much improved*   Hurston to Van Vechten, January 22, 1934, in Kaplan, *Letters*, 288.

225 *kiss and make up*   Van Vechten to Hughes [n.d.], in Emily Bernard, ed., *Remember Me to Harlem: The Letters of Langston Hughes and Carl Van Vechten* (New York: Knopf, 2001), 119.

225 *Awfully glad about*   Hughes to Van Vechten, March 5, 1934, in Bernard, *Remember Me*, 121.

225 *I don't see how*   Van Vechten to Hughes, March 20, 1934, in Bernard, *Remember Me*, 121.

225 *One night, Alan*   Hurston to Robeson, April 18, 1934, in Kaplan, *Letters*, 299.

225 *I am very busy*   Hurston to Locke, October 8, 1934, in Kaplan, *Letters*, 312.

226 *I have taken form* Hurston to Mason, May 10, 1931, in Kaplan, *Letters*, 219.

226 *the Park Avenue dragon* Hurston to Ruth Benedict, December 4, 1933, in Kaplan, *Letters*, 284.

226 *when Godmother fell ill* Robert E. Hemenway, *Zora Neale Hurston: A Literary Biography* (Urbana: University of Illinois, 1977), 108.

227 *Up to now, Dr. Locke* Zora Neale Hurston, "The Chick with One Hen," Zora Neale Hurston Collection, Beinecke Rare Book and Manuscript Library, New Haven.

227 *try to patch up* Arna Bontemps, interview by Robert E. Hemenway, November 18, 1970, Hemenway Papers.

227 *Zora is really a changed* Bontemps to Hughes, November 24, 1939, in Charles H. Nichols, ed., *Arna Bontemps–Langston Hughes Letters 1925–1967* (New York: Dodd, Mead, 1980), 44.

228 *the muse of black-face* Bontemps to Hughes [n.d., 1943], in Nichols, *Bontemps*, 128.

228 *was probably waiting* Bontemps, interview.

229 *Of this 'niggerati'* Hughes, *Big Sea*, 238–39.

229 *Her characters eat and laugh* Richard Wright, "Between Laughter and Tears," *New Masses* 25 (October 5, 1937), 22.

229 *To many of her white friends* Hughes, *Big Sea*, 239.

230 *'hand-chicken'* Zora Neale Hurston, *Dust Tracks on a Road*, in *Folklore, Memoirs, & Other Writings*, ed. Cheryl A. Wall (New York: Library of America, 1995), 799.

230 *authenticated and flavored* Hughes, *Big Sea*, 320, 332.

231 *very good* Hurston to Hurst, August 4, 1940, in Kaplan, *Letters*, 461.

231 *As soon as I came* Nugent, interview.

231 *one of the most un-self-revealing* Kaplan, *Letters*, 436.

231 *rings false* Alice Walker, Foreword, Hemenway, *Zora Neale Hurston*, xvii.

232 *A real guy named* Langston Hughes, "Goodbye Christ," in *The Collected Poems of Langston Hughes*, ed. Arnold Rampersad (New York: Alfred A. Knopf, 1994), 166.

232 *They tell me Zora* Hughes to Still, May 27, 1941, quoted in Arnold Rampersad, *The Life of Langston Hughes*, Vol. 2: *1941–1967, I Dream a World*, 2nd ed. (New York: Oxford University Press, 2002), 9.

232 *village youth* Hurston to Van Vechten, September 12, 1945, in Kaplan, *Letters*, 529.

233 *getting such a poor*   Hurston to William Bradford Huie, September 6, 1954, in Kaplan, *Letters*, 720.

234 NO DISCUSSION OF COMMUNISM   Zora Neale Hurston, "Why the Negro Won't Buy Communism," *American Legion Magazine,* June 1951, 14.

234 *I had known him since*   Hurston to *Saturday Evening Post*, September 2, 1954, in Kaplan, *Letters*, 718.

235 *the music, poetry, folk-lore*   Agreement between Charlotte L. Mason and Zora Hurston, December 1, 1927, Alain Locke Papers, Moorland-Spingarn Research Center, Howard University.

235 *the boiled-down juice*   Zora Neale Hurston, "Folklore and Music," in *Folklore, Memoirs*, 875.

236 *I am getting inside*   Hurston to Hughes, March 8, 1928, Hughes Papers.

236 *I am using the vacuum*   Hurston to Locke, October 15, 1928, in Kaplan, *Letters*, 129.

CONCLUSION: THE LEGACY

240 *lonesome-looking old red*   Zora Neale Hurston, *Dust Tracks on a Road*, in *Folklore, Memoirs, & Other Writings*, ed. Cheryl A. Wall (New York: The Library of America, 1995), 785–87.

241 *I loved my friend*   Langston Hughes, "Poem," in *The Collected Poems of Langston Hughes*, ed. Arnold Rampersad (New York: Alfred A. Knopf, 1994), 52.

241 *a madman who believes*   Marcel Proust, *In Search of Lost Time: Finding Time Again* (New York: Penguin, 2003), 184.

241 *roam the night together*   Langston Hughes, "Harlem Night Song," in *Collected Poems*, 94–95.

242 *The most heartening thing*   Langston Hughes, "Some Practical Observations: A Colloquy," *Phylon* 11 (Winter, 1950), 307–11, in *The Collected Works of Langston Hughes*, Vol. 9: *Essays on Art, Race, Politics, and World Affairs* (Columbia: University of Missouri Press, 2002), 310.

242 *Negroes are just like*   Hurston, *Dust Tracks*, 785–87.

243 *the quality I feel*   Alice Walker, Foreword, Robert E. Hemenway, *Zora Neale Hurston: A Literary Biography* (Urbana: University of Illinois, 1977), xii.

243 *a miscegenated affair*   Ann Douglas, *Terrible Honesty: Mongrel Manhattan in the 1920s* (New York: Noonday Press, 1996), 340.

READINGS

PRIMARY SOURCES

Most of Zora Neale Hurston's fiction can be found in *Novels & Stories*, ed. Cheryl A. Wall (New York: Library of America, 1995) and *The Complete Stories* (New York: HarperCollins, 1995). The latter is not actually complete: four additional stories set in Harlem, including "The Back Room," can be found in *Amerikastudien 55*, no. 4 (2010), and another one, "Under the Bridge," in *American Visions* (December/January 1997). Zora's unfinished novel about Herod the Great remains unpublished, and a number of her other novels have been lost.

Most of Hurston's nonfiction can be found in *Folklore, Memoirs, & Other Writings*, ed. Cheryl A. Wall (New York: The Library of America, 1995), which also includes the previously unpublished portions of her autobiography, *Dust Tracks on a Road*. This volume does not, however, include a large number of her essays. Two of these were especially important to my work: "The Chick with One Hen" (her unpublished attack on Alain Locke), Zora Neale Hurston Collection, Beinecke Rare Book and Manuscript Library, New Haven; and "Fannie Hurst," *Saturday Review of Literature* (October 9,

1937). It also does not include her book on Cudjo Lewis, *Barracoon: The Story of the Last Slave* (New York: HarperCollins, 2018). In addition, some of her work of the 1940s that is not in *Folklore, Memoirs* can be found in *Go Gator and Muddy the Waters: Writings by Zora Neale Hurston from the Federal Writers Project*, Pamela Bordelon, ed. (New York: W. W. Norton, 1999).

All but one of Hurston's surviving plays can be found in *Collected Plays*, ed. Jean Lee Cole and Charles Mitchell (New Brunswick, NJ: Rutgers U. Press, 2008). (The sole omission is a brief one-act set in Harlem entitled "The Funeral of Harlem's Sheik" or "The Death of Sugarfoot," Langston Hughes Papers, Beinecke Rare Book and Manuscript Library, New Haven.) Most significantly, this volume includes *De Turkey and de Law*, Hurston's copyrighted version of *Mule Bone*. Zora subsequently made extensive revisions to *Mule Bone*; she sent the rewritten play to Elizabeth Shaffer Hull, Carl Van Vechten's niece, in 1934, but I have not been able to trace its present whereabouts, if it still exists.

Practically all of Hurston's surviving correspondence has been collected in Carla Kaplan, ed. *Zora Neale Hurston: A Life in Letters* (New York: Doubleday, 2002). Unfortunately, one of the most important of Hurston's letters to Langston Hughes, dated January 20, 1931 (one of two written that day), appears to have been lost; it is quoted extensively in Robert E. Hemenway, *Zora Neale Hurston: A Literary Biography* (Urbana: University of Illinois, 1977), 143, and in Faith Berry, *Langston Hughes: Before and Beyond Harlem*, 2nd ed. (New York: Citadel, 1992), 112.

Almost all of Langston Hughes's important works have been published in eighteen volumes in *The Collected Works of Langston Hughes* (Columbia: University of Missouri Press, 2001–2004). The first volume includes Hughes's first books of poetry organized as he meant them to be, whereas in *The Collected Poems of Langston Hughes*, ed. Arnold Rampersad (New York: Alfred A. Knopf, 1994), the poems are arranged in order of first publication. The fourth volume consists of *Not Without Laughter*. The fifth volume includes *Mulatto, Mule Bone*, and other plays. The ninth volume includes Hughes's most important essays. The thirteenth volume comprises his first autobiography, *The Big Sea*. And the fifteenth includes *The Ways of White Folks* and other short stories.

Langston Hughes and Arna Bontemps, *The Book of Negro Folklore* (New

York: Dodd, Mead, 1958) is one of many anthologies they published, but it represents, in many ways, a fulfillment of the wishes of Mason, Hurston, and Hughes during the period when their relationship was closest.

A small portion of Langston's voluminous correspondence has been collected in the following books, among others: Charles H. Nichols, ed., *Arna Bontemps–Langston Hughes Letters 1925–1967* (New York: Dodd, Mead, 1980); Emily Bernard, ed., *Remember Me to Harlem: The Letters of Langston Hughes and Carl Van Vechten* (New York: Alfred A. Knopf, 2001); and Arnold Rampersad and David Roessel with Christa Fratantoro, eds., *The Selected Letters of Langston Hughes* (New York: Alfred A. Knopf, 2015).

Hughes's diaries, unfortunately, have not yet been published; they are a wonderful read, though, and are housed in the Langston Hughes Papers, Beinecke Rare Book and Manuscript Library, New Haven.

Zora Neale Hurston and Langston Hughes, *Mule Bone: A Comedy of Negro Life*, ed. George Houston Bass and Henry Louis Gates Jr. (New York: HarperCollins, 1991) includes most of the correspondence having to do with the play from all parties involved.

Charlotte Osgood Mason's correspondence and diaries, Alain L. Locke's voluminous correspondence, and Louise Thompson Patterson's unfinished autobiography all remain unpublished. Mason's and Locke's work is in the Alain Locke Papers, Moorland Spingarn Research Center, Howard University; Patterson's is in the Louise Thompson Patterson Papers, 1909–1999, Stuart A. Rose Manuscript, Archives, and Rare Book Library, Emory University.

The best firsthand accounts of the Niggerati can be found in two novels: Wallace Thurman, *Infants of the Spring* (New York: Macaulay, 1932) and Richard Bruce Nugent, *Gentleman Jigger: A Novel*, ed. Thomas H. Wirth (Philadelphia: Da Capo Press, 2008). And the group's full fruition is in *Fire!!* 1, no. 1 (reprint, 1982).

Carl Van Vechten, *The Splendid Drunken Twenties: Selections from the Daybooks, 1922–30*, ed. Bruce Kellner (Urbana: University of Illinois Press, 2003) is essentially a celebrity-filled list of parties, nightspots, and hangovers. It's a wonderful resource, as is that landmark publication of the Harlem Renaissance, Alain L. Locke, *The New Negro*, 1st Touchstone ed. (New York: Simon & Schuster, 1997).

The best general book on the era is Ann Douglas, *Terrible Honesty: Mongrel Manhattan in the 1920s* (New York: Farrar, Straus & Giroux, 1995). My admiration for this volume knows no bounds.

Of the many books about the Harlem Renaissance, four are worth special mention: David Levering Lewis, *When Harlem Was in Vogue* (New York: Penguin, 1997); Steven Watson, *The Harlem Renaissance: Hub of African-American Culture, 1920–1930* (New York: Pantheon, 1995); George Hutchinson, *The Harlem Renaissance in Black and White* (Cambridge, MA: Belknap Press of Harvard University Press, 1997); and Cary D. Wintz and Paul Finkelman, *Encyclopedia of the Harlem Renaissance* (New York: Routledge, 2004). While Lewis's and Watson's books are my favorites, all four are essential for a full understanding of the movement.

Zora Neale Hurston, Langston Hughes, Carl Van Vechten, and Alain Locke are the subjects of two full biographies each. Robert E. Hemenway, *Zora Neale Hurston: A Literary Biography* (Urbana: University of Illinois, 1977) is a pioneering study and benefits from a number of interviews with people who knew Hurston well. Valerie Boyd, *Wrapped in Rainbows: The Life of Zora Neale Hurston* (New York: Scribner, 2003) is definitive and beautifully written. Faith Berry, *Langston Hughes: Before and Beyond Harlem* [2nd ed.] (New York: Citadel, 1992) suffers from limited information and occasional sloppiness, but remains the best one-volume account of Hughes's life. Arnold Rampersad, *The Life of Langston Hughes*, Vol. 1: *1902–1941, I, Too, Sing America*, 2nd ed. (New York: Oxford U. Press, 2002) and Vol. 2: *1941–1967, I Dream a World*, 2nd ed. (New York: Oxford U. Press, 2002) is a monumental and practically perfect achievement. Emily Bernard, *Carl Van Vechten and the Harlem Renaissance: A Portrait in Black and White* (New Haven: Yale University Press, 2012) is a particularly brilliant book, but Edward White, *The Tastemaker: Carl Van Vechten and the Birth of Modern America* (New York: Farrar, Straus & Giroux, 2014) is more comprehensive. Leonard Harris and Charles Molesworth, *Alain L. Locke: Biography of a Philosopher* (Chicago: University of Chicago Press, 2008) has, I dare say, been supplanted by Jeffrey C. Stewart, *The New Negro: The Life of Alain Locke* (New York: Oxford University Press, 2018), though it does include some information that the latter omits.

Louise Thompson has been the subject of only one biography, but it's succinct and invaluable: Keith Gilyard, *Louise Thompson Patterson: A Struggle for Justice* (Durham, NC: Duke University Press, 2017). There has been no full-length biography of Charlotte Mason, but Carla Kaplan, *Miss Anne in Harlem: The White Women of the Black Renaissance* (New York: HarperCollins, 2013) includes a superlative brief one.

I also found Genevieve West, *Zora Neale Hurston & American Literary Culture* (Gainesville: University of Florida Press, 2005) helpful in contextualizing Hurston's work, and Rachel A. Rosenberg, "Looking for Zora's *Mule Bone*: The Battle for Artistic Authority in the Hurston-Hughes Collaboration," *Modernism/Modernity* 6, no. 2 (April 1999), 79–105, important for its close reading of the *Mule Bone* revisions.

I consulted a large number of other primary and secondary sources, but these are the ones I found most valuable, and the ones I would recommend the most highly to readers of this book.

CREDITS

INDEX